WOMEN AND DUALISM

A Sociology of
Knowledge Analysis

LYNDA M. GLENNON

Douglass College

Rutgers—The State University of New Jersey

LONGMAN
New York and London

WOMEN AND DUALISM
A Sociology of Knowledge Analysis

Longman Inc., New York
Associated companies, branches, and representatives
throughout the world.

Developmental Editor: Nicole Benevento
Editorial and Design Supervisor: Linda Salmonson
Interior Design: Pencils Portfolio, Inc.
Cover Design: Edgar Blakeney
Manufacturing and Production Supervisor: Louis Gaber
Composition: Fuller Typesetting of Lancaster
Printing and Binding: Fairfield Graphics

Library of Congress Cataloging in Publication Data

Glennon, Lynda M.
    Women and dualism.

    Bibliography: p.
    Includes index.
    1. Feminism.   I. Title.
HQ1154.G52   301.41'2   78–11036
ISBN 0–582–28076–1 pbk.

Manufactured in the United States of America

CONTENTS

Acknowledgments   iv
Introduction   1

1   Women and Dualism   16

2   Instrumentalism   46

3   Expressivism   69

4   Synthesism   97

5   Polarism   119

6   Social Location of the Women's Liberation
     Movement   147

7   The Feminist Struggle with Modernity   169

8   A Concluding Note on the Limits of
     One-Dimensionality   199

Appendix: Theoretical Background   206
Bibliography   236
Index   248

ACKNOWLEDGMENTS

I wish to thank Peter L. Berger for his encouragement and support of my work and the invaluable friendship that has endured through our various philosophical and political differences. I also wish to thank the members of my dissertation committee—Harry C. Bredemeier, Chris Downing, and Rhoda Goldstein—for their continuing support.

Many friends shared their concern and criticism over the years in which I was undertaking this work. I wish to name specifically Robert Bresemann, Flo Chadwick, Carol Clark, Barbara Cullen, Anna Falco, Chuck Harbaugh, Laura Jacknick, Dale Johnson, Marian Jude, John Leggett, Shirley Mallory, Hector Mishkin, Dan O'Neill, Thomas Ridley, Paul Rowan, Brian Ruonavaara, Karl-Ludwig Schiebel, Trent Schroyer, Juan Skimbie, Werner Stark, Marcia Storch, Minda Tessler, Joe Tougas, Bill Weidner, and Carole Wilbourn. A special word of thanks is due to Richard Butsch, whose encouragement and criticism have been most important in my work.

A number of friends and colleagues read parts of the manuscript and gave me the benefit of their insights: Judy Balfe, Nancy Topping Bazin, Larry Baron, Sarane Boocock, Nathan Church, Rose Coser, Paul Creelan, Laurie Cummings, Anne Foner, Susan Friedman, Terri Glatz, Cathy Greenblatt, Marilyn Johnson, Sandra Joshel, Robert Kelly, Judith Lorber, Ann Parelius, and Don Redfoot.

I also wish to acknowledge my gratitude to my students, undergraduate and graduate, who have indeed taught me, as well as to my friends in the women's movement whose lives have served as models of struggle for personal and intellectual growth.

Finally I wish to thank my mother and father for all they made possible for me. To them I dedicate this work.

Excerpts from "Alix at Ms." by Anonymous. Excerpted from *Ms.* Magazine. Copyright © 1975 Ms. Magazine Corp. All rights reserved.

Excerpts from *Community and Society* by Ferdinand Torries. Translated by Charles P. Loomis. Reprinted by permission of Michigan State University Press. Copyright © 1957 by Michigan State University Press. All rights reserved.

Excerpts from "Confessing: Forum" by Elinor Langer. Copyright © 1974 Elinor Langer. All rights reserved.

Excerpts from "The Controversy Over Androgyny" by Irene Reville and Magaret Blanchard. Copyright © 1974 Women, a Journal of Liberation. All rights reserved.

Excerpts from *Crisis of Psychoanalysis* by Erich Fromm. Copyright © 1970 Fawcett World. All rights reserved.

Excerpts from "Cultural Contradictions and Sex Roles" by Mirra Komarovsky. From *Selected Studies in Marriage and the Family,* edited by Robert F. Winch, Robert McGinnis, and Herbert H. Berrington. Copyright © 1962 Holt, Rinehart and Winston.

Excerpts from *Family Socialization and Interaction Process* by Talcott Parsons and Robert F. Boles. Copyright © 1955 The Free Press. All rights reserved.

Excerpt from *Fear of Flying* by Erica Jong. From *Fear of Flying* by Erica Jong. Copyright © 1973 by Erica Mann Jong. Reprinted by permission of Holt, Rinehart and Winston.

Excerpts from *The First Sex* by Elizabeth Gould Davis. Reprinted by permission of G. P. Putnam's Sons and Joan Daves from *The First Sex* by Elizabeth Gould Davis. Copyright © 1971 by Elizabeth Gould Davis.

Excerpts from *Male and Female* by Margaret Mead. Excerpted from pp. 166–68, 345–46, 358–59 (Dell edition) in *Male and Female* by Margaret Mead. Copyright © 1949 by Margaret Mead. By permission of William Morrow & Company.

Excerpt from "Man on Woman" by Benjamin Barber. Copyright © 1973 World View Publishers. All rights reserved.

Excerpt from "Marriage and the Construction of Reality" by Peter L. Berger and Hansfried Kellner. From *Recent Sociology Number Two,* edited by Hans Peter Dreitzel. Copyright © 1970 Diogenes. All rights reserved.

Excerpts from *Methodology of the Social Sciences* by Max Weber. Translated and edited by Edward A. Shils and Henry A. Finch. Copyright © 1949 Macmillan Publishing Co., Inc.

Excerpts from "Mother Right: A New Feminist Theory" by Jane Alpert. Excerpted from *Ms.* Magazine (August 1973). Reprinted by permission of the author c/o Wallace & Sheil Agency, Inc. Copyright © 1973 Ms. Magazine Corp.

INTRODUCTION

Some time ago I came to the conclusion that what a person needs to be happy is productive, creative work and love—a view I later found echoed in the writings of Erich Fromm and others.[1] At about the same time, the late 1960s, I was questioning what it meant to be a woman and a human in today's society. Many aspects of feminism attracted me. One was the goal of sisterhood to supplant the misogyny that women were socialized into accepting as a sign of exemption from "others" who were too trivial, stupid, or ignorant to realize that the company of females was to be tolerated only as a last resort. I also found compatible with my thinking feminist feelings about how stifling the old sex roles were for both sexes; feminism's relationship to a political critique of the equivalence-of-exchange style of relating to others, whereby one kept a mental balance sheet of debits and credits; and the exasperation about being taken for granted as objects to be used for pleasure, support, decoration, audience, or caretaking, especially by males who prided themselves on the impeccability of their politics.

Other aspects of the feminism of the time left me alienated or outraged. These included the rampant self-interestedness of some who used the banner of feminism to climb career ladders, or whose interest in women's studies arose because it provided opportunities to add items to résumés. I could not go along with the practice of some feminists of laying down laws for women to follow to be deemed "liberated": that all must either live communally or live alone; that one must be asexual, bisexual, homosexual, or heterosexual; that one must either despise and avoid males or go among them and raise their consciousnesses.

Back in 1970 I considered myself part of the women's liberation movement, but as a humanist-feminist. Men, as well as women, needed liberation from constricted roles—they were not the model to follow in the elusive search for that combination of creative work and love that I had found necessary. On the contrary, in many ways men were worse off than women because they were encouraged to dull their emotions and place economic success above all else. Yet many feminists were using male behavior as the gauge of what it meant to be human, a direction of the movement that left it square in the middle of this problematical male orientation. It was confusing to keep straight the political affiliations of those who seemed to be moving in this direction, for members of NOW and members of Weatherwomen were to be see here, along with what some are now calling women's righters (versus women's liberationists).

Along with the usual courses in fundamentals of sociology, I had begun, in the mid-1960s, to teach courses in sociology of the family. Part of the "family" material included Talcott Parsons's "Pattern Variables" [2] and Robert F. Winch's functional analysis of the family,[3] both based on the premise that emotionality and functionality were polar opposites: where one was present the other was absent. This explained why families that had few functions (such as production of goods or schooling the children) had a structure that allowed for a more intense emotionality, and vice versa. Parsons's pattern variables were used to detail this premise: one had to choose either polarity, along five specifiable dimensions, in any concrete action. For example, one could be either "affective" (express emotion) or "affectively neutral" (inhibit the expression of emotion). This seemed plain enough on the surface, and, as defined, the choices were set up as mutually exclusive.

My students were not so easily convinced. They kept asking, "Why?" Why not combine the emotional and the functional? This was actually another version of the goal that was becoming more compelling: the combination of productive work and love. Examples that accepted the duality of the two were becoming less definitive:

that friendship was threatened when two people became room-mates (because the need to perform and coordinate tasks "contaminated" the pure affection they shared beforehand) could no longer be taken as absolute law; that husbands could not teach their wives how to drive had no absolute validity. The students' questions, which at first had seemed naive, were on further study profound.

All sociologists face this hazard of taking preexisting explanations of social reality so for granted that they fail to investigate the reality. In this way, generation after generation of sociologists hand down clichés learned in their schooling to future sociologists. This practice is becoming increasingly hazardous today because the cult of experts is gaining power over the collective imagination, and the media rapidly disseminate the experts' latest pronouncements. Thus, whether emotionality and functionality are incompatible or not, the pervasive understanding is that the two cannot be happily mixed. But the "law" of duality of emotional and functional activities goes beyond an intellectual understanding. It is a commonplace insight of the sociology of knowledge that we collectively construct social reality, that what we define as real, is real. So if we believe that the heart and the head, or emotions and functions, are antithetical, we act on the basis of this definition and set up our lives in such a way as to confirm the belief. Our experience then provides further evidence that our definition is correct, and the duality goes on and on.

This discussion is directly related to the questions I was posing about the meaning of being female and being human in a society that assumes emotions and reason are not compatible, yet females are emotional and males rational. My involvement with the women's movement did not seem to be clarifying the problem as feminists made pronouncements that were inconsistent and contradictory. I began a foray into the sociological "wisdom" on functional-emotional dualism. I also started to look with "naive" eyes on the empirical social world, to try to find evidence that would cast doubt on the lawlike generalization about head-heart duality.

There were, indeed, ongoing endeavors that managed to combine friendship and task-concern in ways not accounted for by theories of dualistic inevitability. Obvious examples were underground newspapers, countercultural restaurants and shops, and various communal arrangements. In these endeavors there had to be enough practical, instrumental sense to pay bills, plan ahead, and so forth. Yet the rationale for setting up these enterprises was to permit the participants to experience, in a new way, earning their daily bread; they did not have to be emotionally cool, self-interested, and specialized, and individuals did not experience a split between public me and private me. True, these experiments sometimes resembled nuclear family structures, but unlike the nuclear family, with its sex and labor specializations, these new structures differed from what one might expect after reading the sociological wisdom. True, many of these enterprises were short-lived, others were taken over by "hip capitalists," and all involved small-scale operations; nevertheless, the viability of some of them challenged an easy acceptance of the law of dualism.

I became more interested in the question of duality. By now, variations on the theme included inspection of functionality-emotionality, reason-passion, public-private, and male-female. I thought of the issue as the instrumental-expressive puzzle, selecting that rather awkward terminology, which originated with Parsons, because it seemed sufficiently abstract to cover all variations and because I wanted to confront the Parsonian formulation on its own terms. (Later, I added a middle class–working class variation. Comparisons between the two class life styles always seemed to hark back to an instrumental-expressive classification, with middle-class life style embodying patterns compatible with the ethos of the modern instrumental world, and working-class style compatible with a traditional expressive order.)

At about this time I was finishing my graduate work and had to decide whether to write a dissertation or head for the Colorado mountains, which seemed a sure way to avoid the work-love contradictions built into the social world. My interest in feminism was also growing, and I began to participate in various organized activities. I decided to write my dissertation on something of significance to me, as well as something I thought would address important questions.

My plan was to research one of the new enterprises. I decided to focus on *RAT*, an underground newspaper taken over in 1970 by a feminist coup. The work I had already done with *RAT* suggested to me several general approaches for dealing with the instrumental-expressive dilemma that existed even on this radical New Left newspaper. I added material from a spectrum of women's groups, newspapers, magazines, and pamphlets, along with my participant observations of several feminist groups and information from interviews and conversations with feminists of varying persuasions. This research took four years, from 1970 to 1974. Since then, I have updated the material and have changed a number of my earlier interpretations.

A qualitative content analysis proved the best approach. My earlier exposure to the literature of feminism had suggested a number of inconsistent and contradictory premises about the good life, the ideal personality, and human nature. Most of the feminists I knew attempted to weave together antithetical assumptions, e.g., that females were biologically superior to males and that females could engineer a society where differences between the sexes (other than the genital difference) would disappear.

As I began to isolate certain themes, a pattern emerged. A major insight was that the dilemma I had set out to explore would itself serve as a major classification device. The instrumental-expressive dilemma was deeply entwined in sex roles, family life, and modern society. I isolated four ideal types of feminism—Instrumentalism, Expressivism, Synthesism, and Polarism—composites of themes about humanity, society, and the like, that hung together as clusters of consciousness. (All four types, by the way, were fairly evenly distributed throughout the issues of *RAT* published between February 1970 and August 1971.)

Awkward as the names of the four ideal types are, I have used them throughout the project because they serve two purposes. First, they sever the automatic connection of gender and behavior-temperament, a connection, grounded in our language and custom, that tends to obscure the real issues. We are so accustomed to equating "masculine" with rational-instrumental and "feminine" with emotional-expressive that it seemed a mistake to call the types Masculinism, Feminine-ism, Androgynism, and Anatomism, even though these names may at first appear more descriptive. "Masculinism," for example, is similar to the "male-oriented" solution of Sheila Johnson.[4] But Johnson misses the point by tacitly assuming that the instrumental role (rational, logical, emotionally disciplined) is a male role. She also refers to a "female-oriented" solution; I would use the term "expressivism." The taken-for-granted interchangeability of instrumental and masculine activity is the connection most feminists wish to sever. (One ideal type, Polarism, accepts a variation on this theme, however, as will become apparent in subsequent discussion.)

My second reason for using these names for the ideal types is to show how feminists are questioning the logic of duality. Although they never use the terms, feminist solutions to being pulled in opposite directions by social demands (what I call "marginality" or "caught-betweenness") challenge the "laws" of sociological convention that hold both orientations necessary for survival yet consider the polar opposites to be embraced in either-or fashion.

The present project, then, is intended primarily as an exercise in sociological theory. Even though a content analysis was the basis for the data, these empirical materials are used to bring out certain theoretical problems and themes. The analysis proceeds by means of the four ideal types, which were constructed with women's movement materials in view.

A word of explanation is necessary regarding "ideal type." For Max Weber,[5] an ideal type is a construct that accentuates certain essential features of a phenomenon so as to render it explicable.

This conceptual pattern [that is, ideal type] brings together certain relationships and events of historical life into a complex, which is conceived as an internally consistent system. Substantively, this construct in itself is like a *utopia* which has been arrived at by the analytical accentuation of certain elements of reality. . . . The ideal typical concept will help to develop our skill in imputation in *research*: it *is* no "hypothesis" but it offers guidance to the construction of hypotheses. It is not a *description* of reality but it aims to give unambiguous means of expression to such a description. . . . An ideal type is formed by the one-sided *accentuation* of one or more points of view and by the synthesis of a great many diffuse, discrete, more or less present and occasionally absent *concrete individual* phenomena, which are arranged according to those one-sidedly emphasized viewpoints into a unified analytical construct (*Gedankenbild*). In its conceptual purity, this mental construct (*Gedankenbild*) cannot be found anywhere in reality. It is a utopia.[6]

It is important to emphasize that ideal types, as conceived by Weber and as used in this book, are not intended as a complete, accurate description of existing reality. Weber further states:

[An ideal type] is a conceptual construct (*Gedankenbild*) which is neither historical reality nor even "true" reality. It is even less fitted to serve as a schema under which a real situation or action is to be subsumed as one *instance*. It has the significance of a purely ideal *limiting* concept with which the real situation or action is *compared* and surveyed for the explication of certain of its significant components.[7]

Perhaps the best-known example of Weber's ideal-type approach is his use of the writings of Benjamin Franklin and others in constructing the Protestant Ethic as an ideal type.[8] It is in a similar vein that I used feminist materials in constructing the four ideal types.

Briefly stated, the four feminist ideal types are as follows:

Instrumentalism. In addressing questions of world-view and meaning, Instrumentalism posits that humans are most authentic when rational, productive, and individualistic. It solves the marginality problem of being caught between opposing demands to be rational and emotional by eliminating the expressive, private sphere. Dualism will be replaced by an instrumental "monism."

Expressivism. The assumption of Expressivism is that the path to happiness lies in the emotional life. The opposite to Instrumentalism, Expressivism posits that communal, spontaneous relationships are the only legitimate ones; the ideal human is warm, supportive, and nonmanipulative. This ideal type would change the formula that equates female expressivity with inferiority and make it the superior orientation. It would "expressivize" everyone, males included. Females would not accommodate to the dominant instrumentality; males would change into expressive beings. This second ideal type would destroy dualism and its attendant marginality by eliminating the undesirable orientation.

Synthesism. This type assumes that the ideal human is a dialectical fusion of reason and emotion and that *any* division of self into roles is dehumanizing. It advocates the reorganization of society to eliminate the division of labor. The marginality struggle is to be solved by replacing dualism with a dialectic of head and heart. Sidestepping the either-or preoccupation, Synthesism advances a both-and solution. Both males and females must change, each having to integrate within themselves the orientation once thought of as the preserve of the "opposite" sex. The private-public division will have no purpose and will therefore disappear.

Polarism. The fourth feminist type posits an essential biological difference between females and males, but maintains that this has yet to be discovered. Polarism does away with the marginality struggle by eliminating the caught-betweenness felt by women with no clear-cut, liberated definition of what it means to be female. Polarism keeps the notion of duality intact—instrumentality and expressivity remain irreconcilable—but it proclaims that females and males must find their true gender essence and leave behind the caricatured roles that pass for femaleness and maleness in sexist society.

While some individuals and groups may identify strongly with one of the four types, all four can and do coexist in cognitive tension in any one person or group, over time or at the same time. As Weber remarks on the nature of ideal types:

> . . . those "ideas" which govern the behavior of the population of a certain epoch, i.e., which are concretely influential in determining their conduct, can, if a somewhat complicated construct is involved, be formulated precisely only in the form of

an ideal type, since empirically it exists in the minds of an indefinite and constantly changing mass of individuals and assumes in their minds the most multifarious nuances of form and content, clarity and meaning.[9]

The unrecognized mixture of these types in feminist groups helps explain why organizing attempts often degenerate and many programs perish. Members may agree about specific goals or tactics, but their views about authentic humanity and the good society may diverge widely. As an antidote, many feminists try to shift the focus away from these ill-understood differences to the sharing of personal experience in a consciousness-raising format. This sidesteps the larger questions because personal experience is considered valid in its own right and not to be analyzed and criticized. This focus may enable the groups to continue, as long as practical projects do not reintroduce the need for common definitions, goals, and tactics. For even a simple goal such as equal pay for equal work will not find favor with those who maintain that no one should be *paid* for work of any kind.

An ideal type as a construct is not to be taken literally or in a concrete sense. As a composite of qualities extracted from specific persons, an ideal type is not meant to correspond with any one person or group. It is inherent in the ideal-type approach to construct utopian concepts in order to bring out essential features of a given phenomenon. In this sense, then, the four feminist types or megathemes are "real" only as measuring rods or models against which real persons and groups can be compared.

The data show that much of the material manifests a multiplicity of types with inconsistent themes confronting and crisscrossing one another. The four types are useful devices for placing in context any pronouncements about the status quo, the vision of the good society, and so on. For example, if a group advocates rolelessness, as some do, certain other things would be implied that revert back to the megatheme as a cluster of consciousness. One can point out that rolelessness will not be compatible with a society wherein humans are viewed as plastic substances to be molded this way and that by conscious and implicit socialization.

The four types are also useful in assessing changes that might occur in a group over time. Further empirical study would be needed to determine the exact nature of the changes, but there is some evidence that many groups that started out strongly oriented toward an Instrumentalist outlook have begun to move away from this type (e.g., NOW and professional women's caucuses like Sociologists for Women in Society [SWS]). Thus, many groups can be classified as predominantly one or another ideal type only at given points in their history.

Obviously, ideal-type analysis focuses on the "idealist" rather than the "materialist" sociological perspective. I suggest connections between all four feminist types and the social context in which they are taking place, and some historical and structural reasons for embracing feminism at objective and subjective levels, but the analysis is not equipped to connect given social background characteristics of specific females with the four types. Such connections will have to wait for future empirical studies.

A number of limitations are inherent in this type of approach. As they stand, the four ideal types appear as detachable, free-floating clusters of consciousness because no attempt has been made to show which specific social bases are likely to generate which consciousness—a must for a full-fledged dialectical sociology of knowledge approach, an approach to which I subscribe as a general rule. Some hypotheses have suggested themselves in the course of the research. A feminist whose upbringing took place within a working-class life style, for example, is likely to be attracted to Expressivism because of the similarities in philosophical assumptions that underlie the two world-views. But this is merely a hypothesis. Another feminist might react against the Expressivist heritage of a working-class life style [10] and turn toward Instrumentalism.

Indeed, the study does not explain why any particular woman is drawn to feminism in the first place, except that all feminists seem to be recruited from the ranks of the "caught-betweens" or marginals. I find this explanation a valid one, although it may not be the rationale given by a woman for her participation in the movement. She may see her main reason for joining the ranks as the need for better child-care facilities, abortion reform, or a way to cope with her husband. Those looking for a connection between manifest and latent rationales for joining feminism will have to look elsewhere.

Perhaps the most severe limitation on their approach is that the four feminist types can be "reified," i.e., made into thinglike entities that are thought to have existence in and of themselves. (That would be especially ironic considering the exasperation many feminists feel toward conventional definitions of sex roles—male equals instrumental, female equals expressive—because these notions are reifications that construct more than they describe reality.) In other words, these four ideal types may re-create themselves in a self-fulfilling manner—leading one to declare, e.g., "I am an Expressivist" rather than a human being with ever-changing subjectivity and what phenomenologists would call intentionality.

Despite these limitations the approach is a necessary first step in approaching feminism and its implications for the future of society. Although my conclusions about the four types can be replicated by other researchers, these four are not the only discernible megathemes. A number of works on the women's movement have proposed a variety of classifications. My four types are useful in seeing the connections between feminism and larger social questions, and, on a smaller scale, in trying to unravel the tangle of feminist pronouncements.

Many changes have taken place since I began my research in 1970: the general political-economic climate has changed; more women are working; a higher divorce rate has prompted more public awareness of the precariousness of today's nuclear family; more women have rallied around issues relating to both sides of the Equal Rights Amendment, abortion laws, and homosexual rights; and a more vocal and well-organized antifeminist group has emerged. Perhaps most significant is the questioning of sex roles, by both women and men, for any change in sex-role expectations would affect both males and females. A state of uncertainty seems to have replaced the sure sense of sexual duality against which feminism struggled ten years ago.

Sociology and women's studies have changed too. The hard-

line dualism that characterized textbook discussions of family structure and sex roles can still be found, but numerous texts and
courses no longer accept sex-role specialization along instrumental-
expressive lines as a social law. Although some concessions have
been made on the dualism of sex roles, however, almost no attention has been given to the more pervasive issue of dualism along
instrumental-expressive lines in general.

Many social commentators have noticed the duality in modern
society between reason and emotion and between the public and
private spheres.[11] But relatively little attention has been paid to
duality itself, aside from the work of critical theorists,[12] the late-
1960s countercultural ethos,[13] and the writings of Alan Watts.[14]
If anything, duality has taken on a richer connotation as a result of
research on left-hemisphere (roughly instrumental) and right-
hemisphere (roughly expressive) thinking [15] and work relating to
differing styles of intelligence in females and males.[16] The notion
of a dichotomous development of intelligence has been used in
interpreting life-style differences and linguistic variations by a
number of researchers, notably Mary Douglas and Basil Bernstein.[17]
Although these researchers often take a critical look at duality,
viewing it as a social construction and not as an inevitable law,
most proceed to use duality as a given.

This book is written primarily for sociologists and those with
an interest in women's studies. Admittedly the approaches used by
these two groups are frequently considered antithetical. Sociologists are typically oriented more toward the instrumental pole
and women's studies people more toward the expressive pole.[18]
Sociologists often think of themselves as value neutral, detached,
and dispassionate. Women's studies people often opt for the experi-
ential, participatory, and value relevant. I have run into many
problems in doing research for this dual audience, but I hope I
have been able to combine the two interests in a way that does
honor to both. Both audiences generally accept the four feminist
ideal types as valid and useful, although sociologists not sympathetic to feminism have chided me for being "too gentle" with
feminists, and feminists on occasion have called me to task for
being too cynical. Moreover, many sociologists get exercised over

what they consider the unrealistic visions found in the feminist types, and many feminists point out that the use of conventional sociological wisdom usually ends up as self-fulfilling generalization.

Other interesting responses might also be noted. Almost all who hear of the four types immediately identify themselves as Synthesist (until they find out what the whole program would entail). In the eight-year span of my research, no one has claimed to be an Instrumentalist, although many identify their competitors, bosses, or enemies as Instrumentalist. This seems curious because evidence would lead one to conclude that the whole of modern society is moving toward the Instrumentalist pole as technocracy, scientism, and expertism gain an increasing hold on society and culture. I started this project eight years ago because of the alarm I felt about Instrumentalists; only in the last few years can I recognize aspects of Instrumentalism in my own world-view and come to terms with them.

NOTES

1. Erich Fromm, *The Art of Loving* (New York: Harper & Row, 1956). Among others, see also Rosemary Haughton, *Love* (Baltimore: Penguin, 1971); and Rollo May, *Love and Will* (New York: Delta, 1969).

2. Talcott Parsons, *The Social System* (Glencoe, Ill.: Free Press, 1951).

3. Robert F. Winch, *The Modern Family* (New York: Holt, Rinehart & Winston, 1963).

4. Sheila K. Johnson, "A Woman Anthropologist Offers a Solution to the Woman Problem," *New York Times Magazine*, 27 August 1972.

5. Max Weber, *The Methodology of the Social Sciences*, trans. and ed. Edward A. Shils and Henry A. Finch (Glencoe, Ill.: Free Press, 1949).

6. Ibid., p. 90.

7. Ibid., p. 93.

8. Max Weber, *The Protestant Ethic and the Spirit of Capitalism*, trans. Talcott Parsons (New York: Scribner's, 1958).

9. Weber, *Methodology*, pp. 95–96.

10. The Expressivist heritage of working-class life style is grounded in the following works: Basil Bernstein, *Class, Codes, and Control* (New York: Schocken, 1975); Mary Douglas, *Natural Symbols* (New York: Pantheon, 1970); Herbert Gans, *The Urban Villagers* (New York: Free Press, 1965); Lillian Breslow Rubin, *Worlds of Pain* (New York: Basic, 1976), Jack E. Weller, *Yesterday's People* (Lexington: University of Kentucky Press, 1965); and Betty Yorburg, *The Changing Family* (New York: Columbia University Press, 1973). It is developed more fully in a series of papers I am writing with Richard Butsch on the Portrayal of Social Class Lifestyles in Television Family Series, 1947–1977.

11. See, for example, Peter Berger, Brigitte Berger, and Hansfried Kellner, *The Homeless Mind* (New York: Random House, 1973).

12.   See, for example, Herbert Marcuse, *One-Dimensional Man* (Boston: Beacon Press, 1971); Jurgen Habermas, *Toward a Rational Society* (Boston: Beacon Press, 1971); and Trent Schroyer, *The Critique of Domination* (Boston: Beacon Press, 1975). Even in critical theory one will often find a bias toward the rational. On this point, Jessica Benjamin, "The End of Internalization: Adorno's Social Psychology," *Telos* 32 (Summer 1977): 42–64, is especially helpful.

13.   See Theodore Roszak, *The Making of a Counter-Culture* (Garden City, N.Y.: Anchor, 1969); and Charles A. Reich, *The Greening of America* (New York: Random House, 1970). Philip E. Slater, *The Pursuit of Loneliness* (Boston: Beacon Press, 1970), has bearing on the issue also.

14.   Alan W. Watts, *The Two Hands of God: The Myths of Polarity* (New York: Collier, 1969). Watts' *The Book* (New York: Vintage, 1972) and *Nature, Man and Woman* (New York: Vintage, 1970) are also relevant here.

15.   See Julian Jaynes, *Origin of Consciousness in the Breakdown of the Bicameral Mind* (New York: Houghton Mifflin, 1977).

16.   See Eleanor Maccoby, "Woman's Intellect," in *The Potential of Women*, ed. S. M. Farber and R. H. L. Wilson (New York: McGraw-Hill, 1963), pp. 24–38; and Carol Gilligan, "In a Different Voice: Women's Conceptions of Self and Morality, *Harvard Education Review* 47 (November 1977): 481–517.

17.   Bernstein, *Class, Codes, and Control;* and Douglas, *Natural Symbols.*

18.   A number of exceptions can be found, of course. Some recent work in women's studies would clearly follow Instrumentalist canons of science-scholarship; some sociological models (particularly critical theory) would seek out a dialectical rather than a dualistic approach associated with Instrumentalist positivism.

1

WOMEN AND DUALISM

I would roam through the Metropolitan Museum of Art looking
for one woman artist to show me the way. Mary Cassatt? Berthe
Morisot? Why was it that so many women artists who had re-
nounced having children could then paint nothing but mothers
and children? It was hopeless. If you were female and talented,
life was a trap no matter which way you turned. Either you
drowned in domesticity (and had Walter Mittyish fantasies
of escape) or you longed for domesticity in all your art. You
could never escape your femaleness. You had conflict written
in your very blood.

Neither my good mother nor my bad mother could help

me out of this dilemma. My bad mother told me she would have been a famous artist but for me, and my good mother adored me, and wouldn't have given me up for the world. What I learned from her I learned by example, not exhortation. And the lesson was clear: being a woman meant being harried, frustrated, and always angry. It meant being split into two irreconcilable halves.

—Erica Jong

The capacity to love is the strength women have developed and sometimes perfected through the ages, the gift we have grabbed out of the history of our oppression. But we are frightened by the distorted directions in which this power has sometimes led us. In its service we have been forced to neglect, even repress, our capacity for creative independence. So that in our polarized world, men and women alike stand as thwarted human beings.

But the struggle for unity has begun. The central problem for feminist therapists is the search for an androgynous understanding of personality. For in order to avoid the most ironic of defeats, in which we join the men in their form of half-life —autonomy at the expense of intimacy—we must be careful not to lose what we have.

—Jane Lazarre

What is the best way to understand the current feminist movement, its source, and its impact on society? Some suggest that feminism springs from the wrath women have accumulated over centuries of sexist oppression; others cite the "rising expectations" women experienced after their participation in the various human rights movements of the 1960s.

Both explanations have merit, but feminism is more a response to the crisis of consciousness created by modern technological society. Most people experience this crisis as a division of their emotional ("expressive") and rational ("instrumental") selves; a similar gulf separates their home ("private") and work ("public") worlds. The cutting off of the instrumental from the expressive and the public from the private is implied by the term *dualism*. The fragmentation that results from this dualism can explain why modern society is in crisis [1] and why women in particular have begun to challenge divided selves and divided worlds.

Traditionally, females have identified with the expressive-private realm and males with the instrumental-public one. As women increasingly have entered the public arena, they have been expected to take on instrumental qualities that clash with their traditional expressive ones. This clash between expressive and instrumental and between private and public orientations is one of "marginality," [2] of being caught between the margins of public and private worlds. Feminists are likely to be women who have one "foot" (or self) firmly planted in each world—home and work. The intuitiveness, gentleness, and supportiveness acquired through their expressive heritage clash with the assertiveness, competitiveness, and individualism expected in their instrumental work roles. From the vantage point of "caught-betweenness," feminists have begun to question the need for the wide gulf between public and private lives. Feminism is potentially the most radical social movement today because, in challenging the dualism of private-expressive and public-instrumental selves and worlds, it reaches to the roots of the crises of modern society.

Before considering dualism or marginality more carefully, let us see why feminism is more centrally a response to the crisis of modernity than, say, a response to sexist oppression. After all, most feminists define the "woman problem" as springing from sexism and have been successful in exposing many forms of sexist reality. Besides, feminism has provided women with an enemy—male chauvinism—that is concrete, recognizable, and fightable. But sexism and male chauvinism can be seen as no more than manifestations of the crisis of dualism diffused throughout modern society. Sexism symbolizes and aggravates the problem, but it, too, is a product of the instrumental-expressive dualism that has torn society since the dawn of the corporate-technological era.

Women's unhappiness goes beyond sexism to the crisis of consciousness that is a result of modernity. Nevertheless, in accepting this statement it is not necessary to join ranks with critics such as

Benjamin Barber, who insist that the feminist movement masks the real problem—life itself.

> Some feminists seem to expect of life not merely opportunity but fulfillment, not a lonely search for relative meaning but the final discovery of absolute truth, not a license for living but a guaranteed warrant for happiness. And then, when life is not forthcoming, a conspirator is conjured up from half-truths to explain the failure of these elaphantine expectations. . . . *It is life they* [the feminists] *fail to understand.*[3]

Such criticism is based on assumptions about human existence that can in no way be proved. Barber maintains:

> For *life*, even at its emancipated best, takes the form of *necessary, ineluctable tensions*, of poignant dilemmas confronting men and women with the painful hiatus between aspiration and achievement, between desire and fulfillment. Between the infant's fantasy world, which is but an extension of itself, and the mature being's comprehension of its own insignificance in an *indifferent cosmos* lies a *reality* into whose subtleties feminists have been unwilling or unable to enter. Hence they seem unaware that alienation is something other than a female disorder occasioned by the malice of men, that insufficiency and a sense of apartness have been our *species fate since Eden.*[4]

Barber presupposes unhappiness, ambiguity, and toil as the existential condition of humanity, a conception of life that figures in many criticisms of feminism. This type of criticism can be called "ontological criticism" or "original sin criticism"; it sees the crisis of contemporary life as inevitable because it comes from the human condition and not from the way society is arranged. In other words, feminism is railing against problems that are built into the human condition; it is not a response to a given, yet changeable, historico-economic reality. Anyone who criticizes feminism as a "scapegoat" or a "mask" for the problems inherent in "life itself" or "adulthood" or "maturity" or the "real world" falls into this category of critic.

Joan Didion's criticism is like this. Didion charges feminism with opting out of the struggle with the human condition of ambiguity:

> To those of us who remained committed mainly to the exploration of moral distinctions and ambiguities, the feminist analysis may have seemed a particularly narrow and cracked determinism. . . . The astral discontent [expressed by feminists] with actual lives, actual men, the denial of the real ambiguities and the real generative or malignant possibilities of adult sexual life, somehow touches beyond words. . . . These are converts who want not a revolution but "romance" . . . they also tell us, I suspect, that the women's movement is no longer a cause but a symptom.[5]

Didion goes on to charge feminists with seeking out a "childlike" sexuality—tender, delicate, and gentle—in order to avoid dealing with the "realities" of "adult" sexual life.

Didion's view is shared by Midge Decter, another critic of the women's movement.[6] Decter sees feminists as resorting to a pre-adult or childlike rejection of the responsibilities of adulthood. This includes a rejection of the "intrinsic" polarity that adult sexuality entails. For Decter, the repudiation and rejection of males presented in feminist ideology is a mask for feminists' real fear—adult heterosexuality. Decter sums up the movement as one in search of a "new chastity" built on fear and infantile regression rather than any real oppression of women.

Decter, Didion, and Barber contend that what feminists really want, as opposed to what they say they want, is an escape from freedom (not oppression) and an escape from dealing with life-as-it-is. These negative views of feminism stem from experiences of alienation in present society. These critics assume that such alienation is absolute and universal, and that no feminist wish will make it otherwise. They posit an antagonistic relationship between the individual and society and characterize as futile any attempt to create an alternative reality in which humans and society would be harmonious. For them, any social-change program, feminist or otherwise, that aims at transforming our present situation into a happier one is doomed to failure because "life," not "society," is the problem. Thus feminists fail to see that what make them unhappy are problems of universal human nature. For these critics, the problems that concern feminists must be confronted at the subjective level and not displaced onto society. According to this view, each of us is alone in our struggle.

Feminists and their "ontological" critics obviously see the issue of women's unhappiness from opposite vantage points. Oddly enough, neither side suggests confronting the problem at both the subjective and societal levels. For the argument at hand, let us agree that the root of women's unhappiness can be found at the societal level. But when feminism points at sexism as the enemy to be engaged, it deflects attention away from the real problem—what technocratic dualism has done to our lives. Some feminists wrongly believe that problems of identity can be solved by legalistic changes in the public realm (e.g., by passage of the Equal Rights Amendment), and by contracts that codify relationships and ensure equalitarianism in the private sphere (e.g., marriage contracts). Feminists of a more radical persuasion assume that if socialism or communism replaced capitalism, the "woman problem" would vanish. Capitalism does contain the most advanced form of dualism in evidence today, but any society that operates on technocratic premises dooms women to unhappiness. (Men suffer, too, but their pain is more effectively masked by the power and privilege they get in the bargain.) Soviet women (and men) also must face the problems of dualism that are built into technocracy. The issue is not capitalism per se. Technocracy creates and nourishes the dualism in our lives, and as a particular form of this dualism, the modern version of the gulf between men and women.

In the shift from traditional to modern society a number of significant qualitative changes occurred. The Appendix contains a theoretical discussion of the nature of this shift, but one specific point can be noted here. If nothing else, modern life ushered in an era of increasing (instrumental) rationalization and fragmentation. We see this continual rationalization of life in many ways: as a product of the development of capitalism or Calvinism; as the rise of the modern state or the bourgeoisie; as the emergence of bureaucracy, industrialization, urbanization, technology, and science; or as all these things in relationship to one another.

Benjamin Nelson's analysis is most to the point in understanding how the character of the social fabric changed with the passing of traditional society.[7] Like Max Weber, to whom much of Nelson's analysis is indebted, Nelson sees the massive transformation from traditional to modern society as originating in consciousness (the Protestant reformation of Luther and Calvin) and later becoming solidified in social structure (the economy—capitalism). Nelson makes a persuasive case for the effect that disposing of the religious "logics" of the day had on dualizing social life. He maintains that the Protestant Reformation made possible a splitting of the interdependent "logics" for moral action (belief and behavior) by disposing of the Court of Conscience and the causistry that penetrated all aspects of human action and involvement, both public and private. This change in religious consciousness prompted institutional changes so vast that social life was no longer considered to be of one piece. The fragmentations—religion v. world, "private ethic and logic of conscience" v. "public ethic and logic of consequences," ecclesiastical v. civil, sacred v. profane—originated in the realm of consciousness (what Nelson calls "regulative rationale systems"[8]) but became sedimented in social structure. The legacy of the modern world is a series of fragmentations made possible only after these decisive changes in consciousness and social structure had taken place. Thus a series of dualities entered into everyday life concomitant with all the other changes that marked the passing of traditional society.

Technocracy implies a social order in which all things are accommodated to the needs of science and technology—and their by-product, bureaucracy. Such a society finds itself more and more bureaucratized and run according to the dictates of scientism. In a technocratic society a cult of experts gains influential adherents, and ever larger areas of life are drawn into its scope. Child rearing, lovemaking, sexuality, face and body language, ways of arguing, and similar "human" concerns are handed over to the expert for diagnosis and prescription.

The technocratic society harbors the mentality that "business is business" or "that's politics." In doing so, it grants license to rampant self-interest in the public arena. Under this scheme of things, it makes perfect sense that business and pleasure don't mix. Yet the truth of that statement springs not from any essential opposition between business and pleasure. Business (instrumental) and pleasure (expressive) simply do not mix in this particular historical creation called technocracy. Some cultures (e.g., that of the Tasaday) recognize no division between work and play, which certainly suggests that our belief that the two are incompatible cannot stand as a universal social "law."

Technocracy legitimates the notion that science should serve productivity and bureaucratic administration by concentrating on the prediction and control of human behavior. It provides sophisticated rationales to mask the use of humans as "objects" in research. But these rationales accept a view of human behavior that is intrinsic to a technocratic world-view—that all human processes can be explained, predicted, and controlled by scientific investigation and technological manipulation. Moreover, technocracy implies the pervasive influence of instrumental orientations. What genuine expressivity remains in a technocracy must be more and more instrumentalized. Private and public spheres alike are approached technocratically. Sex therapy, fight-training techniques, behavior-modification techniques, marriage contracts, and child-rearing manuals reflect the acceptance of instrumental assumptions in our everyday lives.

The technocratic society splits selfhood into the instrumental and expressive self; it divides social life into public and private spheres. It presupposes polar opposites. An increase in one's instrumentality *must* mean a decrease in one's expressivity, and vice versa. The assumption that this choice must be made is the crucial logical link to conventional views about male and female roles, for males are assumed to be instrumental creatures and females expressive ones.

Is sex-role duality also a modern invention? There is conflicting evidence here. Some would argue that instrumental-expressive sex duality antedates modern society, citing a public-private separation between the sexes that can be traced back at least as far as ancient Greece.[9] Others suggest that the specialization of women in domesticity and motherhood is a modern, particularly middle-class, phenomenon; not until home and work were separated, and wages were paid for work, was housework considered as something other than productive labor.[10] With the split of the household from the economic realm, the woman's role became one of specialized activity that had no economic value. Still others find it impossible to get a true reading on male-female duality because, having been raised in a dualistic setting, they see the data through a dualistic lens, gaining at best a distorted reflection of life.[11] The issue is far from settled. Differences in class, culture, and history, as well as what aspect of instrumental-expressive duality one was using, would all affect any answer on sex-role duality in modern society.

The general philosophical assumptions that underlie the modern world-view assume that human nature is context-free—we are all equivalent in our humanity; ascribed characteristics such as race, age, and sex have no bearing on this equality. Yet we have a heritage of sexual dualism in consciousness (e.g., proverbs, jokes) and institutions (e.g., different pay scales, division of labor). We train young women expressively, then expect them to perform instrumentally (in school or on a job). Females are caught between clearly contradictory expectations because the modern world is set up that way.

Moreover, modern life is characterized by the dominance of the instrumental ethos. The dualism that characterizes modern society is less a situation of separate but equal spheres than a matter of hierarchy, with the instrumental, public realms engulfing the expressive, private ones. So a sense of urgency pervades the dilemmas that women face, for personal peace of mind as well as for the future of society.

Females have long been portrayed as expressive creatures. On the positive side, we hear that women are passionate, personal, perceptive, intuitive, and passive. On the negative side, they are irrational, illogical, fickle, and unable to view matters objectively. Good or bad, these are all expressive traits. Males are portrayed in their instrumentality. In positive characterizations they are rational, logical, abstract, analytical, active, assertive, and achieving. They are negatively depicted as cold, aggressive, insensitive, impersonal, and tactless. All these traits are instrumental ones. The following illustrations point up the pervasiveness of the male-instrumental and female-expressive dichotomy in the everyday world: [12]

Man for the field and woman for the hearth:
Man for the sword and the needle she:
Man with the head and woman with the heart:
Man to command and woman to obey:
All else confusion.

—Alfred, Lord Tennyson

Women have great talent, but no genius, for they always remain subjective.—*Arthur Schopenhauer*

A woman who is guided by the head and not the heart is a social pestilence: she has all the defects of a passionate and affectionate woman with none of her compensations; she is without pity, without love, without virtue, without sex.—*Honoré de Balzac*

Women, in general, want to be loved for what they are and men for what they accomplish. The first for their looks and charm, the latter for their actions.—*Theodor Reik*

Women are usually more patient at working at unexciting, repetitive tasks . . . Women on the average have more passivity in the inborn core of their personality. . . . I believe women are designed in their deeper instincts to get more pleasure out of life—not only sexually but socially, occupationally, maternally —when they are not aggressive. To put it another way I think when women are encouraged to be competitive, too many of them become disagreeable.—*Benjamin Spock*

The assumption that instrumentality is masculine and expressivity is feminine ensures the persistence of personal dualism in modern society. These gender divisions make it impossible for people to become whole, because few can endure the label of "deviant" for acting in ways that are reserved for the "opposite" sex. The corollary assumption that males are breadwinners, adventurers, warriors, and thinkers, whereas women are homemakers, soothers, listeners, and emotionalists ensures a dualistic social world.

The subtle and complex debate over instrumentality and expressivity has fascinated social philosophers for as long as there have been philosophers. Today it is of central concern to sociological interpreters of the crisis of technocratic society. When this debate is resolved in favor of dualism, a dualism grounded in gender, the personal and political implications are profound.

If males are the instrumental half of the species, and females the expressive opposite half, an individual's humanity is reduced to that one-half of the behavioral spectrum deemed appropriate for the gender of the person. Like racism, agism, or classism, sexism restricts both women and men from developing their humanity fully.

To illustrate: I happen to be female. This "fact of life" decrees that I be expressive and not instrumental—in our society, one *or* the other must be chosen. Should I slip out of the appropriate behavior, I will quickly find myself sanctioned. I may even begin to doubt my "normality." After all, I *must* be expressive, it is my nature. If I rebel against this, I am either "crazy," "abnormal," or "deviant." At the same time, I am expected to do well in school and come to terms with the modern (instrumentalized) world. Is if any wonder that I am "caught-between," "marginal," and a feminist?

INSTRUMENTAL—EXPRESSIVE DUALISM

Both the rational (instrumentality) and the emotional (expressivity) are needed if personal and social life are to thrive. Even though commonplace, this assumption is a highly problematical one and must be explored to see the relationship of feminism to the crisis of technocracy. Some see the relationship between "head" and "heart" as a dialectical one; the two are bound together in a unity, with each acting back upon the other. Others consider reason and emotion inevitably dualistic; when one comes into play, the other vanishes. Although both notions can be found in any era, the dualistic assumption dominates the modern, technocratic world-view: being emotional and being rational are antithetical modes of relating to the world.

In the everyday world one hears the bromides "Don't mix business with pleasure" and "When you work, work, and when you play, play." These sayings presuppose that being instrumental and being expressive are incompatible ways of acting—it must be "either-or," or disaster will follow. Each of us probably has a reper-toire of these "truisms": surgeons "cannot" operate on members of their families, teachers "must not" become emotionally involved with their students, nurses "should not" consider their patients as anything other than patients. The mass media are permeated with examples.[13] One banking commercial on television shows a per-son literally split into two—the "human" side and the "business" side. Another commercial, advertising a restaurant, has the female owner of a boutique saying that "business is business" but that lunch with "the girls" is "different." The model for *Ms.* magazine's March 1978 cover story was depicted as split down the middle: her left side dressed in a gray flannel blazer and skirt and her left hand holding on to a briefcase; her right-side clothed in casual slacks and T-shirt and her right hand holding a toddler's. This illustrated a series of articles titled "Can Women Really Have It All?"[14] Taking their cue from Talcott Parsons,[15] some sociologists also generalize that instrumental and expressive activities are anti-thetical but necessary orientations if personality, social, and cultural systems are to remain in equilibrium. This presumed inevitable duality of mind and heart is the base on which the explanation of sex-role dualism rests. Before we look at the logic of this, a few definitions are needed.

For Parsons, instrumental behavior includes an emphasis on

task fulfillment, productivity, and efficiency. A person who is acting instrumentally in a social relationship would typically inhibit emotions, act from self-interested motives, rely on standardized or "objective" codes for judgment, evaluate others in terms of performance or achievement, and display involvement with the other that is limited to specific aims. Any instrumental relationship is construed as a means to an end.[16] Expressive behavior, on the other hand, emphasizes such integrative goals as emotional fulfillment, group cohesiveness, and stability. A person who is acting expressively would typically show emotion, be oriented toward the collective interest, rely on personal relational criteria for the evaluation of others, judge others in terms of their personal qualities, and show a wide interest in the other. Here the relationship is an end in itself, to be enjoyed for its own sake and not because of a specific interest.[17]

The present book defines instrumentalism and expressivism in a more encompassing sense than one would gather from Parsons's usage. In addition to his right-side (instrumental) pattern variables (affective neutrality, self-orientation, universalism, performance-achievement, and specificity) the composite of instrumentalism includes various connotations usually associated with modern, middle-class life styles: an emphasis on individualism, active mastery approach to the world, achievement-progressivity orientation, and competitiveness. It also includes a rationality in which both means and ends are subject to calculation for self-interested purposes, and relationships are viewed as means to ends. For Parsons, expressivism entails pattern variables of affectivity, collectivity-interest, particularism, quality-ascription, and diffuseness. Taken together, they usually reflect qualities found in traditional and working-class life styles. In addition to these five variables, the present book includes in expressivism an emphasis on familism, cooperativeness, fatalism, mysticism or superstitions, and symbolic interconnectedness.

Many sociologists say that small groups require both instrumental and expressive activities in order to remain in equilibrium.[18] According to Parsons, an exclusive emphasis on such instrumental activities as pushing forward the work of the group evokes negative responses in the group. To prevent or curtail hostility, ex pressive outlets are called for—the group needs to release emotions, feel a sense of solidarity, and have ruffled feelings soothed. The picture of the group that Parsons paints is one in which instrumental and expressive activities *follow* one another in a continual sequence.

Because he considers the two modes of behavior antithetical, Parsons generalizes that *two* "leader" roles must be elaborated to assure the presence of the two modes. He bases this contention on the premise that instrumental behavior in itself evokes hostility.[19] For Parsons, the instrumental leader could never be the "most popular" member of the group (or "expressive" leader) because instrumental leadership is hostility-inducing.

Instrumental leaders are concerned with problem solving ("chairman" or "executive" types). Expressive leaders are concerned with group members' feelings and group cohesiveness ("best liked" or "most popular" types). One of Parson's colleagues describes the expressive leader as follows:

> Such a man [sic] can be warm, receptive, responsive, and rewarding, can "conciliate" and "bind up the wounds," without diverting the movement of the system too far from the kind of movement in the instrumental-adaptive direction which is also felt to be necessary. He can do this because he does not assume the "responsibility" for the movement in these directions, but leaves this to the technical or executive specialist.[20]

The masculine referent was used intentionally in the quote to describe the expressive leader. The Parsonian research circle used same-sex small groups in their experimental work. Expressive leadership, which is considered necessary for group survival and success, would thus have to be taken on by a male in an all-male group. All well and good, but how, then, does Parsons connect the instrumental-expressive dichotomy to sex roles?

The link can be found in Parsons's assumption that the nuclear family was a small group—with one important distinction. After looking at cross-cultural data on family life, Zelditch (another of Parsons's associates) concluded that it was a *universal* of family structure that the instrumental role be played by the husband-father and the expressive role be played by the wife-mother. Parsons generalized that the "normal" nuclear family would always be characterized by such role allocation. His rationale was that the mother's physiological bond with the child, established prenatally, would continue after birth to cement the mother's responsibility as child rearer within the family. This private-expressive responsibility of the wife-mother would require the husband-father instrumentally to negotiate family survival with external systems, such as the economy and polity. In this way, instrumental-expressive specializations became linked with parental roles.[21] The next step of this logic was that most human beings had continuous intimate relationships with an instrumental father and an expressive mother. Parsons and company conclude that these role specializations are generalized by the child to all males and females. Mother's expressive behavior became "female" behavior, and father's instrumental behavior became "male" behavior. In sum, instrumental and expressive roles were internalized early in the life of the child as male and female roles. In the Parsonian scheme, sex-role differentiation along instrumental-expressive lines had its origins in the family's structure and its persistence in the socialization of the young.

A number of sociologists questioned Parsons's conclusions. Philip Slater, reinterpreting data from the small-group studies, challenged the assumption that instrumental and expressive behaviors were negatively related.[22] For example, Slater doubted a son would be able to identify with a father who played the instrumental role strictly as an emotionally distant disciplinarian. Slater also argued that Parsons's duality was not suited to the "de-differentiated" family that is emerging in advanced techno-industrial society.[23]

George Levinger accepts instrumental-expressive duality as far as parental roles are concerned but challenges its application to spouse roles.[24] Although one spouse may be more active in initiating expressive interaction, Levinger argues that marital satisfaction requires mutuality. He also finds that both husband and wife are instrumental specialists and that neither is an expressive specialist, at least in the middle class. Both marital partners show similar needs: interdependence, and giving and receiving nurturance. Levinger adds that these expressive needs "are conventionally suppressed in the general environment particularly by men; in marriage, these needs are given preference by *both* partners over other more achievement-oriented desires." [25] He concludes that marriage allows both partners to indulge expressive needs that are inhibited in the public sphere.

This brings us to another duality, that between the public and the private spheres, with its attendant specializations of instrumental and expressive activities. The shift from family-as-a-system to family-as-a-*sub*system in the larger social system presents theoretical problems in the Parsonian schema. Recall Parsons's view that each system requires both instrumental and expressive orientations to survive, but because the two orientations are antithetical, they must be performed by separate individuals. Like Levinger, Parsons views the family as an expressive refuge. Parenthood, for Parsons, functions as an outlet for adults of both sexes to act out what he calls the "regressive" emotional needs that began in childhood.

. . . the principal stages in the development of personality, particularly on its affective or "emotional" side, leave certain "residua" which constitute a stratification (in the geological sense) of the structure of the personality itself with reference to its own developmental history. Partly *these residua of earlier experience can constitute threats to effective functioning on adult levels,* the more so the more "abnormal" that history and its consequences for the individual have been. But partly, also, they have important positive functions for the adult personality. *To express and in certain ways and contexts "act out," motivational systems and complexes which are primarily "infantile" or "regressive"* in their meaning is, in our view, by no means always undesirable, but on the contrary *necessary to a healthy balance of the adult personality.* At the same time the dangers are very real and regulation of context, manner and occasion of expression is very important. . . . We suggest then that children are important to adults because it is important to the latter to express what are essentially the "childish" elements of their own personalities.[26]

Berger and Kellner offer a similar way of looking at the family's function with respect to the public sphere.[27] They see the family as an "enclave" that facilitates a sense of meaningfulness and order, what they call "nomos." Uncontrollability and incomprehensibility surround people in the public sphere. Therefore, the private sphere, where the family figures significantly, becomes the area where a sense of control over one's own life, active involvement, and happiness can be realized. For Berger and Kellner, the nuclear family is infused with an ideology that stresses expressivity in the extreme: romantic love, sexual fulfillment, and self-discovery and realization through love and sexuality. The family functions as a safety valve for nomos, and protects (as Parsons would see it) the instrumentality of the public sphere.

> . . . the narrow enclave of the nuclear family serves as macrosocially innocuous "play area" in which the individual safely exercise his world-building proclivities *without upsetting any of the important social, economic, and political apple carts*. Barred from expanding himself into the area occupied by those major institutions, he is given plenty of leeway to "discover himself" in his marriage and his family. . . .
>
> The marital adventure can be relied upon to absorb a large amount of *energy that might otherwise be expended more dangerously*. The ideological themes of familism, romantic love, sexual expression, maturity, and social adjustment, with the pervasive psychologistic anthropology that underlies them all, function to legitimate this enterprise.[28]

The latter two descriptions of the family as specializing in expressive orientation in the private-public duality cast doubt on Parsons's position that instrumentality and expressivity are necessarily polarized. If the husband-father is the instrumental specialist within the family, how can he act out the expressive elements that

Parsons sees as protecting the pure instrumentality of the public sphere? Does the husband-father behave both expressively and instrumentally, thereby providing his children with a bipolar role model? But this contradicts Parsons's analysis of family structure, as well as the origin and persistence of sex roles.

Problems such as this appear whenever Parsons shifts the system level of analysis. That is, all systems require two antithetical orientations, but because they are antithetical, specialization is necessary. In the shift from personality to social and cultural system levels, one can see the dilemma: what of the instrumental specialist in a family seen as expressive subsystem in the larger society? Parsons's work is highly subtle and complex, and within the parameters of dualistic thinking his analysis holds. Even if his version of structural functional analysis is being challenged, his underlying dualism is shared by many theoreticians today.

Throughout Parsons's work one finds shifting nuances of definitions, ongoing qualifications of points previously made, and reworkings of ideas that make it seem as if a simple duality was the last thing Parsons intended. For example, in his pattern variables he has offered five choices that are involved in every social action, no matter how trivial or significant it may be. This fivefold schema is presented as sets of polar choices:

Affectivity	v.	Affective Neutrality
Collectivity-Interest	v.	Self-Interest
Particularism	v.	Universalism
Quality (Ascription)	v.	Performance (Achievement)
Diffuseness	v.	Specificity [29]

Each action, role, or social system must come to terms with these five sets of choices. (In the present book instrumentality and expressivity embody the right and left sides of the pattern variables just presented, along with additional connotations derived from other theorists.) Because Parsons proposes five choices rather than one, we might assume that there is a great deal of flexibility. One might mix and match these choices at will across the great divide of instrumental and expressive orientations. Parsons gives examples of cases where such mixing is possible, and says, for example, that both aspects may be present in a role, although one is primary or "more present." Even if we grant the possibility that instrumental and expressive aspects may be mixed in a given role, we are still left with a dualistic situation: one must choose *either* one *or* the other aspect in any given subcontext.

> . . . the variables we have stated are dichotomies and not continua. In a series of concrete actions, a person might be partly "affective" and partly "neutral." But this series would be composed of dichotomous choices; no specific choice can be half affective half neutral. The same is true of the other pattern variables. One who has carefully read the definitions and discussions will see that each concept sets up a polarity, a true dilemma.[30]

This was written in 1951; in 1960, Parsons reiterated the point in an article entitled "Pattern Variables Revisited." [31] He purposely set up the variables as polarities requiring an either-or choice. Thus, although the husband-father behaves both instrumentally and expressively (as Parsons shifts levels of abstraction) in the family, he does not do so at the same time, but sequentially.

Is the Instrumental-Expressive Dichotomy "Real"?

When levels of analysis and abstraction change, it becomes difficult to keep straight what either-or choices are being made. For example, if the focus is on the individual as the unit of analysis, it can be assumed that both males and females have some experience and adeptness with both instrumental and expressive behavior. If the focus is on the social role, and we assume specialization (as Parsons does), a combination of instrumental and expressive behavior is possible if one mixes equal numbers of either. For example, a female might mix four expressive roles (wife, mother, hostess, and family nurse) with four instrumental ones (accountant, engineer, club treasurer, and mayor).

A problem remains at the level of social role. In the example above, it is apparent that the "wife" or "mother" role is very imprecise. For instance, the wife role involves all kinds of social role behavior: lover, homemaker, cook, chauffeur, budget maker, bookkeeper, neighbor, social secretary, daughter-in-law, and so on, each of which can be further broken down into smaller units of action.[32] Thus these conventionally recognized expressive roles entail instrumental activities. This is not a startling insight, but it is important in pointing out the analytical difficulties encountered in the Parsonian conception of instrumental-expressive duality.

This discussion may appear to be academic nit-picking. Many academicians dismiss the issue by saying the instrumental-expressive dichotomy is simply an analytical device—it may hold true theoretically or stereotypically, but it cannot be applied empirically. We come now to the rub. Our definitions of reality are not innocent, isolated entities that have little interplay with the empirical world. The dialectical model wherein ideas are derived from the social and material base, and ideas act back upon that material base, is appropriate here. The cognitive habit of thinking in either-or categories is part of the change in consciousness that allowed for the introduction of sacred v. profane, private v. public, and the like that Nelson talked about in his discussion of modernity. The shape of the social world effects ways of thinking about that world. In turn, our conceptions become part of that social world insofar as we act toward things in terms of how we think about them. This is the connection between social perceptions and the way people actually behave.

As people, and as social scientists, we continually create our social world and in turn are created by it. Our ideas, theories, and perceptions interact with, and act back upon, how we think about ourselves and how we relate to others. Dichotomized sex roles, the case in point, have been internalized as real by many people in modern society, regardless of whether they exist "really." Whether the socially constructed roles are perpetuated by sociology texts,

psychotherapists, advice-to-the-lovelorn columnists, television characters, pastoral counseling, jokes, relatives and friends, or whom or
whatever, they exist and affect all of us, constructing and con-
trolling our behavior.

The Relative Nature of
Expressive-Instrumental Dualism

Parsons and others like him perpetuate the reality of dualism by
elevating a specific, relative condition to the status of law. When
Parsons proclaims instrumental and expressive activities to be antithetical modes, he is simply stating as fact his own taken-for-
granted assumptions about the two modes. His experience comes
from the everyday world and from the world he observes in the
"role" of "sociologist." His observations are grounded in what is
"real" to him (and therefore historically specific and relative); he is
not uncovering some absolute, universal law. All sociologists, like
all other human beings, take the base assumptions of their society
for granted in the lives they lead. The taken-for-granted character
of these assumptions cannot be overemphasized. "Taken for
granted" is meant literally. These assumptions are rarely exposed to
examination.[33]

If a society is structured so that instrumental and expressive
activities cannot be performed compatibly, and if the society has
a rigid separation between public and private spheres, we can expect the society to elaborate explanations (a "world-view") that
make sense out of the dichotomized reality people experience first-
hand in the everyday world. The world-view in turn "acts back"
upon the social structure to enhance the dualities further.

To illustrate: We hear from the person-on-the-street that "business and pleasure don't mix." We also hear (if so inclined) from the
academician that "instrumental and expressive activities fall along
a polar axis." The experience of the person-on-the-street suggests
that business and pleasure should not be mixed. (For example,
the person remembers when a friend lost out on a promotion for
getting "too friendly" with a competitor and giving out compromis-

ing information). In like manner, the sociologist's experience in professional observations of people in the everyday world and in the laboratory suggest that instrumental and expressive activities are incompatible. In this one sense, then, everyday and professional generalizations made about the instrumental-expressive dichotomy are accurate statements of the reality observed. But what most sociologists proceed to do at this point is to assume that there is nothing more to say in the matter, that they have uncovered some universal "code" about human behavior.

Recently, the "sociology of sociology" discipline has begun to explore the relationship between sociology and the *creation* of social "reality." One intriguing thesis is that sociology legitimates the status quo by describing what it finds there in "lawlike" terms. That is, by describing what they see (the "is") and proposing a generalization about what they have observed, sociologists give further "weight" to the preexisting situation. For generations, sociologists have accepted the lawlike "universality" of the nuclear family's need for dual parental roles and, by extension, dual sex roles. Recent work on role differentiation within the family has called into question the generalization that the wife-mother is the expressive "specialist" and the husband-father the instrumental "specialist." [34] Such challenges in part reflect the promptings of feminist sociologists, whose experience with sex roles in their everyday worlds does not permit them to take for granted male-female duality.

Feminists are becoming more outspoken in their charge that sociologists have legitimated sexism by defining as "normal" and "necessary" the dualism of male and female roles. An example is instructive: After observing changes in sex-role expectations over decades, social researchers concluded that a trend toward greater assertiveness was emerging among women. They referred to this trend as a "masculinization" of the female role.[35] Notice that a behavioral trait—assertiveness—was intertwined with gender identity—male. The finding itself took on an emotional-laden, judgmental tone. The researchers could have labeled the trend an "instrumentalization" of the female role, or another such sexually irrelevant term. Instead they said that females were becoming masculinized. With our society's knee-jerk fear of sex-identity fuzziness, such a description puts pressure on women to retain their "femininity," meaning of course, to stop being assertive (and competing with, and thereby threatening, males). Yet males are "threatened" in this schema only because of the notion of a single "instrumental leader" in a small group. In a small group of two, if the female becomes more assertive, the male must "give up" his monopoly and take on a more expressive cast to his behavior. Under these premises, the male trend could be characterized as "de-masculinization."

Sex-role duality is thus "explained" in sociological terms. Contrary to claims that sociology is neutral ("value free"), sociologists have provided a legitimation, indeed an ideology, for justifying the status quo of sexual dualism. By describing the male-instrumental and female-expressive dichotomy as a "fact" found universally in the "normal" nuclear family, they are also saying that any other arrangement is "deviant."

Parsons and his colleagues have explicitly characterized various deviations from the male-instrumental and female-expressive patterns as matters open to ridicule. For example, Zelditch writes that most people consider the expressive male as "having too much fat on the inner side of his thigh." [36] Although Zelditch writes that *people* say such things, it is Zelditch who perpetuates the stigma by accepting the characterization uncritically. As another instance, Parsons describes females who enter the labor force as "following the masculine pattern." [37] Surely the entry of females into the labor force could have been described without putting a gender label on the trend.

A depiction of males as the embodiment of instrumentality and females as expressivity personified has dominated the field of the sociology of the family, at least until recently. Six widely used texts in this field assume the male-instrumental and female-expressive dichotomy in all discussions of sex-role differentiation [38]—another instance of sociologists taking for granted the "given" sexual dualism and thereby closing off any further discussion.

In summary, as sociologists' descriptions of the "is" under observation have been transformed into "ontological" statements, sexual dualism has become an absolute, context-free universal of human existence rather than an outgrowth of a specific historical-economic reality. Sociological pronouncements about the "universality" of, and "necessity" for, sexual dualism have legitimated the status quo. Such pronouncements have established a "social scientific" rationale for a linkage existing in the modern world between gender and behavior orientations. Thus, as females have begun to behave more instrumentally by becoming more assertive or independent, their behavior can be labeled an act of defiance against nature, society, and True Masculinity.

FEMINISM AND MARGINALITY

Women who identify with feminism are usually those who are firmly caught in the gulf that separates the expressive-private realm from the instrumental-public one. Although all people—males and females, old and young, black and white—find their lives divided in two in a technocratic society, middle-class college-educated women experienced the plight of marginality earlier than most, and became feminists. They were bombarded with the double message to be assertive, creative, independent (all "instrumental"), and supportive, sensitive, gentle (all "expressive"). Few of these women found institutional structures that would integrate home and work worlds. They tried to juggle both roles, shifting back and forth between the sweet, deferring girl and the independent, quick-witted woman. Little wonder, then, that these women asked, "Who am I?" and "What am I supposed to do to be happy?"

For example, a working mother is regularly confronted with such incompatibilities as that between the working hours of her job and the school holidays of her children, or between her need to be "stroked" after a day's work and her role as "stroker" of her husband at the end of his workday. Moreover, as she acts instrumentally she is warned that she better not "lose" her femininity. Then she looks around and discovers that "femininity" (more appropriately, "expressivity") is not highly valued in the public realm, and is in fact often derided in an instrumentalized society.

In the 1940s, a majority of college women reconciled this double message by taking the middle ground between "modern" (instrumental) and "feminine" (expressive) roles.[39] But the "middle-of-the-road personality" that emerged was achieved only by scaling down instrumental demands. By the late 1960s, many college-educated women found such a solution intolerable. Nor was this feeling limited to women with college degrees.

In the last few years the women's movement has reached into the ranks of working-class women, especially those who have jobs outside the home. Granted, many of these women see the movement as a lobby for better pay, better working conditions, and better-quality child care. But they were recruitable into the movement in the first place because they were caught between instrumental-public and expressive-private realms. They, too, were forced to confront an incompatibility between the worlds of home and work that society created.

Feminist Solutions

Feminists agree that women feel oppressed, unhappy, and unfulfilled. Individual women identify with the feminist movement because they are dissatisfied with present-day society; in this sense the feminist movement may be thought of as a single movement. In the sense of expressing this dissatisfaction and proposing solutions, this common motivation is molded into four different ideological types and resembles four separate movements. Although most feminists avoid emphasizing differences within the movement in order to present a united front to critics, an understanding of these four divergent types is essential because the movement is pivotal in the crisis of consciousness in today's society. The manifest understanding feminists have of the movement as one, animated by a common definition of the situation—women are oppressed, women are sisters—must be placed in a perspective that goes beyond the woman's role to the whole of technocratic society.

Each of the four types this book cites as found within feminism is radically different from the others in its view of what the "woman problem" is, who is responsible for it, what goals should be pursued, and what image of humanity is presupposed. The contradictions within these four types explain why many feminist meetings avoid questions of theory and stress instead the common psychological plight of women ("the personal is political"). They also explain why many feminist groups are short-lived, as well as why many feminists, in groups and as individuals, do not heed the call to "sisterhood" as they might. These differences are also important in understanding why attempts to start or finish practical political projects often fail, and the women's group involved returns to personalized "consciousness-raising" activities.

What, then, are the four feminist "solutions" to the crisis of dualism in modern society? A chapter of the present book is devoted to each of the four—Instrumentalism, Expressivism, Synthesism, and Polarism. The reader might note in these chapters that feminists themselves frequently slip into the habit of equating behavioral orientations with gender identity. The habit is understandable because it is so deeply entrenched in the everyday world.

NOTES

1. Many critiques of modern society share the view that dualism in one form or another is at the heart of the crisis. For an interpretation of dualism and the crisis of modernity, see Richard J. Butsch, "The Technological Ethos: Modern Life as Dualistic Rationalization." (Ph.D. qualifying essay, Department of Psychology, Rutgers University, 1973). Mimeographed.

2. "Marginality," a term derived from sociological analysis, is developed more fully in chapter 6.

3. Benjamin Barber, "Man on Woman," *Worldview*, April 1973, pp. 20–21. Italics added.

4. Ibid. Italics added.

5. Joan Didion, "The Woman's Movement," *New York Times Book Review*, 30 July 1972, pp. 2, 14.

6. Midge Decter, *The New Chastity and Other Arguments Against Women's Liberation* (New York: Coward, McCann & Geoghegan, 1972).

7. Benjamin Nelson, "Conscience and the Making of Early Modern Cultures: The Protestant Ethic Beyond Max Weber," *Social Research* 36 (Spring 1969): 4–21; and idem, *The Idea of Usury* (Chicago: University of Chicago Press, 1969).

8. Nelson, "Conscience and the Making of Early Modern Cultures," pp. 10, 15, 17.

9. Marilyn Arthur, "Early Greece: The Origins of the Western Attitude Towards Women," *Arethusa* 6 (Spring 1973): 7–59.

10. See Tamara K. Hareven, "Modernization and Family History: Perspectives on Social Change," *Signs* 2 (Autumn 1976): 190–206; and Joan Scott and Louise Tilly, "Women's Work and the Family in Nineteenth Century Europe," *Comparative Studies in Society and History* 17 (January 1975): 34–64.

11. Compare Claude Levi-Strauss's view on the distorted reflection soci-

ology is able to get of the modern era because of its being epistomologi-
cally rooted in a single given historical moment. See his Preface to *Structural Anthropology*, vol. 2, trans. Monique Layton (New York: Basic,
1976).

12.   Robin Morgan, ed., *Sisterhood Is Powerful* (New York: Vintage,
1970), pp. 31–36.

13.   There is some indication that the reason-emotion split is beginning
to spawn escapist alternatives in TV series. For example, "The Waltons,"
"The Little House on the Prairie," and "Eight Is Enough" show some acceptance for the idea that home and work lives are compatible. These
shows may represent vicarious escape from an increasing dualism in public and private life.

14.   *Ms.* 6 (March 1978): 47–51.

15.   The major sources for Parsons's views are: Talcott Parsons, Robert
F. Bales, and Edward A. Shils, *Working Papers in the Theory of Action*
(Glencoe, Ill.: Free Press, 1953); and Talcott Parsons and Robert F.
Bales, *Family, Socialization and Interaction Process* (Glencoe, Ill.: Free
Press, 1955).

16.   Instrumental behavior is captured in Parsons's "pattern variables"
of affective neutrality, self-orientation, universalism, achievement or performance and specificity. See his *The Social System* (Glencoe, Ill.: Free
Press, 1951).

17.   Ibid. Expressive behavior is described by the left-side variables:
affectivity, collectivity-orientation, particularism, quality and diffuseness.

18.   These generalizations about small-group dynamics derive primarily
from the work of Robert F. Bales on same-sex groups brought together
for the first time in a laboratory setting.

19.   The contention that productivity and popularity are incompatible is
fairly widespread. For example, one frequently hears teachers who pride
themselves on their "hardness," legitimating their lack of popularity with
students as evidence that they must be doing a good job of "imparting
knowledge." Colleagues who get along well with students are judged as
"soft" or "easy graders."

20.   Parsons and Bales, *Family, Socialization*, p. 148.

21.   The linkage to spouse roles is more complicated. A number of critics

have suggested that this is the weak link in the argument that family structure explains instrumental-expressive specialization. See especially George Levinger, "Task and Social Behavior in Marriage," in *The Family*, ed. Norman W. Bell and Ezra F. Vogel (2d. ed. rev.; New York: Free Press, 1968), pp. 355–67.

22. Philip E. Slater, "Parental Role Differentiation," *American Journal of Sociology* 67 (November 1961): 296–308.

23. Ibid., pp. 307–8.

24. Levinger, "Task and Social Behavior in Marriage."

25. Ibid., p. 363.

26. Parsons and Bales, *Family, Socialization*, pp. 20–21. Italics added.

27. Peter L. Berger and Hansfried Kellner, "Marriage and the Construction of Reality," in *Recent Sociology Number Two*, ed. Hans Peter Dreitzel (New York: Macmillan, 1970), pp. 49–72.

28. Ibid., p. 65. Italics added.

29. Parsons, *The Social System*. It must be noted that Parsons's Collectivity v. Self Interest variable is one of the more problematical ones for classification into expressive-instrumental terms. In some places in his analysis, this variable can involve either expressive or instrumental orientations (see pp. 143–50). But by and large, the variable in question is aligned at higher system levels as I indicate and as is so interpreted by those who work with Parsons's model (e.g., the value of individualism—self-orientation in some respects—is usually taken as part of the modernity composition of instrumental values).

30. Talcott Parsons and Edward A. Shils, *Toward a General Theory of Action* (New York: Harper Torchbooks, 1964), p. 91.

31. Talcott Parsons, "Pattern Variables Revisited: A Response to Robert Dubin," *American Sociological Review*, August 1960, pp. 467–83.

32. See, for example, Jessie Bernard, *Women and the Public Interest* (Chicago: Aldine, 1971), pp. 67–85. Bernard lists six functions performed by women in contemporary society: reproductive, homemaking, child-rearing, glamor, emotional support, and industrial production.

33. For a discussion of the influence of "background assumptions" on theory, see Alvin W. Gouldner, *The Coming Crisis in Western Sociology*

(New York: Equinox, 1971), esp. chap. 2; and Robert Friedrichs, *A Sociology of Sociology* (New York: Free Press, 1972).

34. Cf. Joel Aronoff and William D. Crano, "A Re-Examination of the Cross Cultural Principles of Task Segregation and Sex Role Differentiation in the Family," *American Sociological Review* 40 (February 1975): 12–20.

35. See Ferdinand Lundberg and Marynis F. Farnham, *Modern Woman: The Lost Sex* (New York: Harper & Brothers, 1947); and Helene Deutsch, *The Psychology of Women,* vols. 1 and 2 (New York: Grune & Stratton, 1944–45).

36. Morris Zelditch, Jr., "Role Differentiation in the Nuclear Family: A Comparative Study," in Parsons and Bales, *Family, Socialization,* p. 339.

37. Parsons, Bales, and Shils, *Working Papers,* p. 75.

38. See Carol Ehrlich, "The Male Sociologist's Burden: The Place of Women in Marriage and Family Texts," in Sexism in Family Studies, a Special Issue of *Journal of Marriage and the Family,* 33 (August 1971): 421–30. The survey is based on the texts of Goode, Kephart, Kenkel, Udry, Leslie, and Saxton, all published since 1964.

39. See Mirra Komarovsky, "Cultural Contradictions and Sex Roles," in *Selected Studies in Marriage and the Family,* ed. Robert F. Winch et al. (New York: Holt, Rinehart & Winston, 1962), pp. 126–33.

INSTRUMENTALISM

Instrumentalism (often shortened to I-type in this chapter) is the ideal type feminists are least likely to identify with, despite the fact that it is the reigning media stereotype of the "women's liberationist," and despite the fact that feminists often incorporate a form of Instrumentalism in their consciousness because modern society has been largely based on it.

Instrumentalism is the embodiment of the extremes of modern consciousness: rationalistic, self-interested, emotionally managed. It stresses the work orientation of human activity. The individual is most human when doing productive work—efficient, rational, assertive, and ambitious. The following tenets would be found in the I-type person's cluster of consciousness:

Work is life.

Rational, logical activity supersedes emotional, intuitive activity.

Technical skills (and executive competence) are superior to conciliatory skills.

Possessive individualism and self-interest are keys to success; ambition, achievement, and assertiveness are measures of self-worth.

Decision-making roles are superior to supportive ones.

Getting things done is more important than making people feel good.

Productive creativity is superior to popularity.

Any skill can be learned.

Any problem can be solved with knowledge of appropriate strategies.

The superior way of relating to others involves coolness, assertiveness, a codification of what is expected, mutual attention to performance, awareness of self-interest, segmentation of aspects of involvement.

Individualistic, self-motivated effort is life-directed; collective, other-motivated work is life-lessening.

Objective standards are superior to subjective ones.

Life must be understood as a sequence of exchanges of benefits and costs. Altruism is a disguised form of egoism.

All activities can be performed rationally and professionally, be they practical or emotional tasks.

Experts can solve all human problems.

The ability to speak well is measured by one's adherence to rules of correct procedure and codes of acceptability.

Instrumentalism includes the rational, progressive ethos of technocratic society; the exchange ethos of capitalism; the individualistic, objectivistic ethos of Ayn Rand; the modernistic outlook of the middle class; and the assertive self-interestedness of the archetypical male.

Instrumentalism is one response to the fragmentation of the self. As an ideal type, Instrumentalism solves the dualistic dilemma by deemphasizing, if not eliminating, the expressive, emotional side of human beings and society. This ideal type proclaims the rational, productive, achieving side of the self. In the technocratic Utopia envisaged by Instrumentalism, there will be no male-female division in behavior and world-view; there will be, instead, equivalent and interchangeable "humans." To Instrumentalists, the woman or man who is detached, objective, self-assertive, self-oriented, aggressive, and achieving is the model personality.

The character of Mr. Spock in television's "Star Trek" comes to mind. Mr. Spock, the chief science officer of the *Enterprise*, is half-human, half-Vulcan. He is portrayed as totally oriented to logic —a Vulcan trait. He is critical of humans for their preoccupation with emotional aspects of their natures, which he maintains are the source of all their problems. His human half occasionally breaks through, allowing some emotions, so perhaps he is not a pure Instrumentalist after all.

Within the feminist movement, the woman who identifies with an organized group that has career advancement as its highest goal and as a yardstick of self-worth would be exhibiting Instrumentalist traits. (NOW illustrates such a group in several, but not in all, respects.) The Instrumentalist feminist might assume that overcoming her "fear of success" is the solution to the problems she faces in the business world. Her interpersonal relationships, including marriage, would be defined and lived contractually; her social contacts would be calculated as "experience counting." She would judge her life by cost/reward calculations.

At present, the image of the Instrumentalist woman in the public imagination ranges from the manipulative "career woman" (somewhat like those women portrayed in 1940's films by Rosalind Russell or Bette Davis) to the dedicated, goal-oriented Madame Curie or Joan of Arc. The image also ranges from the "masculine" one of the female villain caricatures in the James Bond films, to the "feminine" one of the "Cosmo Girl" in the magazine—it emphasizes manipulation and rational calculation in order to strike a good "exchange" on the sex-and-marriage market.

Instrumentalism defines the good society as one in which features of the modern social structure are carried to their logical extremes. Thus Instrumentalism accepts as good what some humanist social critics decry as alienating and dehumanizing—functional rationality, specialization, expertise, task orientation, and emotionally neutral objectivity. In the Instrumentalist view, however, present-day society is far from "modern" in its definition and treatment of women because it prevents women from becoming fully instrumental by forcing them into the inferior expressive mold.

It must be remembered that Instrumentalism is an ideal type, a composite of qualities that is not meant to correspond with any one person or group. The reader should not be misled into thinking that specific persons can be accurately fitted into an ideal type. No one is the embodiment of "pure" Instrumentalism. As an ideal type, Instrumentalism represents an ethos that implies certain things about human nature, about desirable personality styles, about relationships with others, and about the shape of social structure.

IDEAL PERSONALITY

For Instrumentalist feminists, to be expressive is to be less than human; to be instrumental is to be fully human. As one feminist expresses it:

> The role I must fill [as a full human being] meant I had to do well in school, be strong, aggressive, a winner intellectually. Plus I had to help humanity and change the world. The problem was that, according to all the cultural norms, these were the goals of a man.[1]

Strength, aggressiveness, achievement, and world-building proclivities all figure into the picture of what I-type feminists opt for in their personalities. They deplore the present situation because females have not been given the opportunity to become instrumental. For them, the male monopoly on instrumental behavior must be broken if females are to enter the human species as full-fledged members.

For example, *Working Woman*, practically an Instrumentalist's bible, features articles on how to play the game the way males do and how to use other people as business contacts, along with step-by-step instructions for learning such skills.

> Making contacts has long been part of the male repertoire. Meeting for drinks after work, sharing a tennis court, getting acquainted over lunches where the discussion is 10 percent business and 90 percent football—these are connection-building processes with which men feel comfortable and have been using to advantage for years. . . . Through the use of contacts you often get an opportunity to sell yourself that you might never otherwise have. . . . Everyone is a potential connection. A dedicated connection-seeker is, in an inoffensive way, always on the prowl. . . . A thorough job-hunt is a sophisticated research project. You are at point A, sitting without a job or in one which you've outgrown. Point Z is your ideal job. A creative job-hunter is a detective trying to get from A to Z through the most efficient network possible. Contacts not only can speed your way, they can help to create a path for you. Use them well. . . . Once you have succeeded in getting a job, don't stop pursuing connections. This is the time to cultivate a new batch.[2]

These are typically Instrumentalist values: relationships as means to ends, logical calculation, planning and efficiency, and relentless onward-and-upward aspirations.

> The Instrumentalist ethos reappears in the following:
> Women are also learning to strategize and plan their careers. . . . As one young woman executive who has moved rather quickly up the ladder of a major multinational firm puts it: "I used to think it wasn't 'nice,' that it was 'using' people, to make friends with someone because of his or her job or because of their possible usefulness to me later, but I've learned to do it in order to develop my contacts, enlarge my options, build my networks." She has also learned to be tough-minded about

her career; to consider clubs in terms of professional development, not as social gatherings; and to appreciate business associates for their job-related abilities, without feeling they have to become her best friends. Basically, it's not a case of "using" people for your own ends. It's exchange for *mutual* benefit, the trading of information, ideas, and favors. . . . Talk to everyone you possibly can in your organization, from the mailroom clerks to top management. Small talk and pleasantries can sometimes turn you on to opportunities to enlarge your network.[3]

I-types place emphasis on the need for young girls to be socialized exactly as young boys are; in this way, as women they will end up, as men do, in instrumental work roles. They also advocate a thorough resocialization program for adult women so that their conditioned expressivity can be eradicated and replaced by instrumentality. They consider all male occupations to be superior to female ones, but a middle-class careerist bias is discernible. Thus, although women are encouraged to train for jobs as electricians, carpenters, plumbers, and locksmiths, a much stronger emphasis is placed on careers in the professions, business management, and academia. Consider, for example, the following protest launched by female workers against *Newsweek:*

Almost all of the forty-six [*Newsweek* female employees] are "editorial assistants." That's the prestige title for a researcher, someone who checks the facts in the news stories written by an almost exclusively male writing staff and approved by a spotlessly male editorial board. Besides checking sources, the researchers are *office wives* to the men writers, ordering their coffee, making travel arrangements, tidying their papers. The women are satisfied enough about their salaries for this *elegant slavery;* they are simply asking for the chance to be writers after a reasonable stint at "research." . . . The writing staff that they hope to *integrate* presently consists of fifty men and one woman.[4]

Acceptance of the present occupational hierarchy is a theme
of particular importance in understanding Instrumentalism. In the
above quote we find that a magazine writer's job is, and should be,
higher in pay and prestige than a magazine researcher's because
the researcher job includes such expressive duties as making coffee
and tidying papers. Instrumentalists would judge a capable secretary as hopeless if she considered such expressive duties in any way
satisfying and did not opt for a decision-making position. Instrumentalism does not question the occupational hierarchy (the other
three ideal types do), nor does it challenge the premises by which
expressive jobs are ranked below, and paid considerably less than,
instrumental ones. Instead, Instrumentalism aims at *integrating*
women into the existing occupational hierarchy, particularly at the
higher ranks.[5]

All male occupations, however, are coveted by I-type feminists
because of an unrecognized confusion over the male-instrumental
equation—whatever males do must be instrumental. Of special interest is the attempt to bring women into occupations currently
dominated by males.

> We all know that the rock scene is male-dominated, as most
> other areas of creative work. But no other area is so totally
> male as music. Has anyone reading this article ever met a
> woman electric guitarist, woman drummer? I doubt it. And if
> you have, it's one or two, and maybe you had to think about it
> for a few minutes.[6]

Notice the tacit acceptance of the male-instrumental equation here
and in the previous *Newsweek* quote. Both writing and popular
music are assumed to be instrumental worlds—because the writing
staff is "almost exclusively" male and because the rock music scene
is male-dominated. In other words, instrumental activity translates
as any activity in which males engage and females do not. Yet
music and writing are not strictly instrumental in orientation.[7]
This is the logical contradiction mentioned earlier—assuming instrumental activity is sexually neutral, but defining it in terms of the

male model. Thus, in order to become instrumental, females must imitate males.

So far, we have seen that the desirable personality, for the I-type, emphasizes achievement and aggressiveness and aims at providing women with roles that will enable them to rise in the existing occupational hierarchy. We turn now to Instrumentalism's characterization of the traditional expressive female personality style.

For Instrumentalism, the expressive style traditionally associated with women encompasses traits that keep women from experiencing authentic humanity. In the words of one feminist:

> Society encourages women to become addicts of every kind, to deny themselves the kind of vitality that would make them demand *real lives*. No one is disturbed to see a mindless, passive woman; in fact, *the more mindless and passive, the more "womanly."* [8]

Here Instrumentalism accepts the traditional female style as inferior. The contempt for passivity is explicit. I-types characterize the entire female expressive style as humiliating and degrading. Another feminist says:

> As women our needs are defined in terms of the needs of the men whom we relate to, without any regard for us as independent people. We are taught we are weak and passive—that we are nothing and can do nothing without a man. We are made dependent on men for economic and emotional security. If we dare to step out of our role as "mother" or "girlfriend" or "wife" and make demands for ourselves we are ignored, ridiculed and otherwise repressed. We are treated like uppity slaves who must be contained. [9]

The picture of the expressive woman is painted in wholly negative terms. I-types would, for example, generalize the negative aspects of "All in the Family's" Edith Bunker to any woman whose personal style is expressive, no matter how subtle or sophisticated the form. Expressivity implies mindlessness, frailness, and insipidness—it is a sham, a substitute for authentic living. The following quote implies far worse:

> Women are not the only prostitutes, but somehow people feel that a person's selling her/his own body for another's sexual gratification is an *essentially feminine* act. Prostitutes really do live out one side of what being "feminine" means. Every woman is taught that she has to be sexually exciting to many men in order to feel like a *real woman;* that if she pleases a man, he will pay her way in exchange for her companionship. As one sister who has worked as a hooker wrote, "All the prostitute has done is eliminate the bullshit." [10]

In this quote financial dependency and sexual attractiveness are characterized as a latent form of prostitution. Frail, mindless Edith Bunker, then, is really a hooker in disguise; she aims at pleasing Archie in exchange for his financial support.

Instrumentalism rejects the positive aspects of expressivity as well. I-types feel contempt for gentleness, supportiveness, intuition, tenderness, and self-sacrifice. These latter aspects of expressivity are revealed as poor substitutes for women's needs for achievement and success as creative, independent individuals. For example, Gloria Steinem once characterized romance as a displacement of a woman's longing for success.[11] To Instrumentalist feminists, romance is an "opiate for females" that dulls their failure as real persons and allows them to live parasitically through the human identity of an instrumental male:

> [Monogamous] relationships are usually built around weakness and dependency. . . . Women identify themselves through their men and usually get introduced as someone's girl. Monogamous relationships are set up because people see them as the only way to feel secured and loved.[12]

In sum, Instrumentalism posits that expressivity must be eradicated from the personalities of women because it prevents them from concentrating on their instrumental development. Softness gets in the way of ambition, supportiveness robs one of self-assertiveness, conciliatory behavior dulls aggressive drive, and passions interfere with efficiency. Backing away from careers into lives of domestic tranquility is an Instrumentalist fall from grace.

THE INSTRUMENTALIST CRITIQUE

Instrumentalism represents itself as pro-woman and in favor of sisterhood. How, then, does it justify its contempt for expressivity, which traditionally has been associated with females? It does this by rejecting any male-female division of personality, as well as rejecting the notion that both instrumental and expressive orientations are necessary in a society.

How, then, did women get to be expressive? According to Instrumentalists, women have been conditioned to be weak, petty persons by the socialization process of a sexist society.

> The family structure restricts the liberties of a young girl and curtails her development as a *full human being*. . . . Parents can maintain control over her activities, in the guise of protection, until she is delivered into the hands of a husband. The qualities *instilled* in her for her future role as wife and mother are *dependence, passivity,* and *self-denial*. . . . That their [women's] "crimes" are directed mainly against themselves is a reflection of the *self-hatred* women are made to feel from earliest childhood.[13]

Thus the family is an agent in the process of stunting the human (i.e., instrumental) potential of young girls. Under the guise of female protection, it instills the self-hatred I-types say most women experience. Expressive traits of dependence, passivity, and self-denial are in no way linked with female nature (Instrumentalists recognize no such thing as "female nature") but are products of the social structure.

For Instrumentalism, the entire social structure induces women to accept an inferior expressive life and persuades them that something is wrong with them if they do not.

> As a woman, forced to accept the whole male structure, I accept the idea that I [as an individual] have a problem, rather than realizing that I as a woman am forced to function in a male supremacist structure and that I cannot function as a *human being* when I am constantly being knocked down, forced to have meaningless relationships with men because I am afraid of the consequences if I don't, forced to submit to a life of educational tracking—and then told I am *sick* when I refuse to put up with any more of the shit. . . . From age three I was dragged to shrink after shrink because I was "*too aggressive.*" Meaning I was not acting *like a little girl should.* I hit boys and talked back.[14]

Familiar Instrumentalist themes: woman is kept in expressive "chains" and expected to find her identity through what is basically an inferior set of activities; a woman who attempts to break out of these confines will run headlong into the barrier of discrimination, be prevented from achieving her aims, and likely to be labeled "abnormal." In the quote, however, the Instrumentalist feminist shares with feminists of the other three ideal types a refusal to continue defining female identity problems as matters for individual psychotherapy. The "woman problem" is generated by social definitions.

Along with sexist barriers entrenched in the social structure, which prevent women from developing instrumentally, I-type feminists deplore the sexism found in interpersonal relationships between males and females.

> Male chauvinism is basically the way men see women as sex objects who can't either think very well or fight. We are some-

thing to be laughed at and protected if we are weak or put down and fought against if we are strong.[15]

Sexism must be placed within the logic of this ideal type, however. The following quote illustrates one Instrumentalist definition of sexism:

> Like racism, sexism was the unconscious, taken-for-granted, unquestioned, unexamined, and unchallenged acceptance of the belief that the world as it looked to men was the only world, that the way of dealing with it that men had created was the only way, that the values men had evolved were the only ones, that the way sex looked to men was the only way it could look to anyone, that what men thought women were like was the only way to think about women.[16]

For this ideal type, the charge of sexism (or "male supremacy" or "male chauvinism") is not focused on a repudiation of "male" values, because these are instrumental values. Here again the male-instrumental inconsistency surfaces. Instrumentalists focus the charge of sexism on those male values that define women as expressive-bound, inferior sex objects. The world "as it looks to men" (excluding their perceptions of women) is, for this ideal type, the authentic world for both men and women.

Sexism is not restricted to male attitudes and practices that keep women locked into an inferior, expressive style. In the Instrumentalist view, women may constitute "the enemy within":

> Women are also male chauvinist in the ways they view themselves. Men's image of women reinforces the image women have of themselves, and the image women have of themselves reinforces the image men have of them. The problem is to break into this cycle.[17]

Thus women are also "carriers" of sexism, having internalized those social definitions that equate "female" with "expressivity." I-type

feminists argue that expressive women are "their own worst enemies"—but only because society has socialized them this way:

> Women are socialized to see themselves as frail, delicate and
> defenseless. We are taught to look to men for protection; and
> since we are kept emotionally and physically unprepared to
> defend ourselves, we remain vulnerable to confrontations. . . .
> Much of our self-contempt is determined by the values we ab-
> sorb from the mass media. We spend an enormous amount of
> time and energy trying to reach the unattainable image of the
> "ideal" white, wealthy, beautiful woman. Since we judge our
> worth by how well we meet this standard, we tend to think
> little of ourselves.[18]

Some women have been socialized so well that they serve as cen-
sors and make it difficult for any female to break out of the expressive mold into instrumental authenticity. I-types are especially
dismayed when other feminists do not accept their instrumental
world-view:

> Before we got it from men; now we're getting it from our sis-
> ters—and often from those who espouse the pro-woman line
> most strongly. . . . *Achievement or accomplishment of any kind*
> *would seem to be the worst crime.* Write a book, publish an
> article, appear on TV, be interviewed in the newspapers, start
> a theatre group dedicated to feminist principles, make a film,
> be asked to give a lecture and do it well so that you're asked
> again or referred to other places. Do anything, in short, that
> every other woman secretly or otherwise feels she could do
> just as well—and baby, watch out, because you're in for it. If
> then, God forbid, you should also have what is generally de-
> scribed as a *"forceful personality,"* if you *"come on strong"* even
> if you're talking about potato chips . . . if, in short, you do not
> fit the conventional stereotype of a *"feminine"* woman—if you
> are a bitch—forget it baby, it's all over. . . .[19]

Thus Instrumentalism identifies sexism as both the enemy within and the enemy without—anyone responsible for the inferior expressive existence in which women today find themselves.

SOCIAL CLASS AND POLITICAL ORIENTATION

Although the Instrumental ethos is most compatible with a middle-class, establishment-legitimating world-view, I-type feminists are not restricted to any one social class or political orientation. With regard to social-class variability, one feminist says:

> Everyday experiences in high school are a microcosm of the oppression of women in our society. From being tracked, not only are women from poorer families convinced that they are stupid, but they are aware they are being led into their future dull jobs as secretaries and clerks (by their business courses), homemakers (by sewing and home economics), and as wives (by being encouraged and forced to escape from total boredom, alienation, and oppression by fantasizing about how great marriage will be.[20]

And in the same vein:

> I chose to try and become middle class, but the only movies, books, or real life class climbing, success story heroes were working class men so I totally identified with that image. . . . I couldn't stand the female role in the working class family and was a total flop anyway. I couldn't do the male thing in my class, and I didn't succeed in class climbing. Soon the belief set in that "I couldn't do anything." I was absolutely awful at anything females were supposed to do and I didn't dig men.[21]

Here working-class women suffer the same plight as middle-class women. Both are confined in inferior, expressive identities regardless of their class position.

Politically, feminists who espouse Instrumentalism may identify with a liberal, establishment-oriented ideology (e.g., members of NOW) or a radical, New Left ideology (e.g., Weatherwomen). Regardless of political orientation, Instrumentalist feminists share in common the belief that instrumentality alone can authenticate human existence.

Establishment-based I-type feminists approach the institutional order by adopting the style of establishment males: they are cool, rational, competitive, self-assertive, and self-interested. Revolution-oriented I-types of course, would overthrow the established order, but they adopt the style of radical males in the "counterinstitutional" order: they are serious, capable of policy and decision making, committed, courageous, and display a bravado (*machismo*) that includes a willingness to use any means to advance revolutionary goals.

Whatever their political affiliation, then, I-type feminists share the goal of co-participating with males in an existing set of social arrangements. These feminists do not seek to create a new order (or counter-order for the revolutionaries); they simply want the old order to stop excluding women and exploiting their labor. They seek a change in personnel, not a massive reorganization of the work world. A refusal to make the coffee or do the typing for the organization is typical, whether the ultimate aim is becoming a bank president or blowing up the bank.

THE INSTRUMENTALIST PROGRAM

"Let Us In" best describes the Instrumentalist's banner: integrate women into the existing instrumental order. The basic project of I-types is the abolition of sex-role socialization so that males and females both develop instrumentally. Discard the female expressive role; permit the "male" sex role to remain intact, but re-define it as sexually neutral. Retrain females so that they can compete with males, and reform the opportunity structure so that it is accessible to these newly instrumentalized females.

Institutionalized sexism is to be abolished in both public and private spheres—at work and in the home. Thus all humans will be encouraged to act instrumentally at all times—in family life, in sexual union, in child rearing, on the job, in the political arena, at play.

For politically radical Instrumentalists (a type especially prevalent in the late 1960s), strategy entails training women in skills and techniques of street fighting, in self-defense (usually karate or judo), in the handling of weapons and explosives, and in physical and emotional discipline. For politically liberal Instrumentalists, strategies include an emphasis on reforms that will provide inexpensive, accessible training facilities in educational, employment, and political skills and that will ensure equality of opportunity for women. These feminists are likely to support the Equal Rights Amendment; affirmative-action programs to prevent discrimination against women; class-action suits against public facilities that exclude women (e.g., all-male clubs, bars, athletic teams); and workers' organizations that reflect the interests of female employees.

Of course, these strategies (excepting the radical ones) are not exclusive to Instrumentalism. The other ideal types use similar strategies. But the motive in the strategies is Instrumentalist: the elimination of sexist barriers that interfere with the full, equal participation of females in the instrumental order.

The family looms as the strategic battleground for combating sexism in the private sphere. The family must be restructured so that it allows women to engage, freely and fully, in activity outside the home. Basic strategies here would include the elimination of sexist legal definitions concerning wives' property rights; a revision of divorce statutes so that they reflect a female's basic right to independence and autonomy; the establishment of facilities for birth control and abortion counseling; and the instituting of inexpensive, good-quality child-care centers.

Within the family, the husband-father's monopoly of the instrumental role will be broken by means of several strategies, including marriage contracts and paternity leaves. (The drawing up of marriage contracts by individual couples is clearly a technocratic innovation. Relationships are now to be placed on a formalistic, rational level and construed in cost/reward terms.) In the future envisaged by I-types, expressive (female) work will be performed instrumentally. For example, cooking, cleaning, and child care will form a residual category subsumed under the instrumental style.

> Housewifery, when done with grace and style and caring, requires as much ambition and self-discipline as the practice of law or the corporate climb and is, for those of us who have been there, the most demanding and least recognized of noble professions.[22]

In advocating paternity leaves for husbands, Instrumentalist feminists do not imply that males should take on aspects of the expressive role. Child care, as all other formerly expressive tasks, will be reorganized so that it is rational, efficient, and contractual; it will be shared by both spouses. One is reminded of the father in *Cheaper by the Dozen,* a time-and-motion study expert, or the parent who raises children "by the book," which is, written, of course, by a child-development "expert."

The importance of planning and plotting one's life course is an Instrumentalist theme that permeates the fabric of everyday life. A version of this as related to child care is the following excerpt from *Working Woman:*

> As a mother you are entitled to put a market value on the time with your child. Like a bolt from the blue, it suddenly occurred to me: Time is the key. It had been managing me. Now I would manage it. I put a meter on every minute of my life and made several discoveries that have cut chores to a minimum. ... Children like to cook and clean. Washing dishes, especially, should be encouraged. A self-reliant, competent child is well on the way to being a happy child. . . . Create a Playtime

Litany to make the time you have together seem longer, "Remember the time we . . ." Talk about it over and over, like a bedtime story . . . one adventure is usually good for several weeks. . . . A nasty trick I have, which won't last forever is setting the digital clock in my kitchen (the only one Alex can read) ahead 20 minutes. By doing so I can appear to make concessions and still enforce an 8:00 p.m. bedtime. I'm a firm believer in bedtimes. It's important to have time to yourself.[23]

Instrumentalist traits come through clearly: a cost-accounting attitude toward relationships, time-money-efficiency considerations, a highly manipulative attitude toward others, and a clear sense of self-interestedness. Housework makes for happy children; bedtimes are important for mother's needs.

Instrumentalist feminists grant that some tasks have less prestige than others. And some tasks are downright boring: repairing a toilet hardly compares with drafting a political position paper. Nevertheless, I-types assume that all tasks can be performed instrumentally by instrumental people. High-status and low-status tasks within the family will be allocated in equal shares to husband and wife.

In the realm of sexuality, emphasis must be given to the women's equal right to orgasm. The "fair play for women" ideology repudiates the notion that woman's role in the sex act should be passive, submissive, or surrendering (all expressive). Women are to be redefined as fully active, aggressive sex partners. Many Instrumentalist feminists, citing clinical research data on the multiple orgasmic capacity of women, define female sexual capacity as superior to male. This belief reflects a tendency to outperform males in those areas that traditionally have been dominated by them. The technocratic ethos is manifested in an emphasis on sexual technique and performance measurement (sex "by the book"), as well as in the quantification of sexual satisfaction by orgasm counting and recording. The exchange ethos shows up in an emphasis on a contractual relationship based on equivalence of pleasure given and received.

Since sexism is entrenched in consciousness as well as in social institutions, Instrumentalism devotes much time and energy to "consciousness raising." Although used by all feminists, consciousness raising in this case means resocializing adult females into the new instrumental style, and resocializing adult males away from their sexist attitudes toward women.

Interpersonal relationships between males and females must also be changed. One-to-one male-female relationships are seen as a microcosm of males' oppression of women. The slogan "The personal is political" is directed at those encounters with males who would define and treat women as expressive. The formation of men's consciousness-raising groups is lauded by I-types if these groups are addressed to redefining women as instrumental.

Instrumentalism places particular emphasis on childhood socialization practices. Girls and boys are to be presented with identical expectations and career aspirations. Sexist imagery must be removed from children's books, toys, clothing styles, athletic programs, and so on.

PHILOSOPHICAL ASSUMPTIONS

The themes embodied in the four ideal types are built on fundamental philosophical assumptions about human nature and society. Instrumentalism is founded on an antibiologistic premise: biological differences are irrelevant to basic human nature. According to Instrumentalists, humanity is universal and transcends such biological particulars as sex-gender, race, or age. Further, the present significance and "noticeability" of biological distinctions are artificial products of social definition; they are dehumanizing to all individuals and are productive of sexism, racism, and agism.

Instrumentalism also rests on anti-ascriptive premises, repudiating social differences as well as biological ones. Thus wealth, ethnicity, beauty, religion, and other ascriptive differences are "accidents." They should have nothing whatever to do with an individual's social destiny.

Another assumption of Instrumentalism is the near-total plasticity of human nature. Individuals are almost infinitely malleable, taking shape through the sculptings of those social systems in which they are located. Social destiny may be changed by changing the social structures. Social character can be constructed along desirable lines if appropriate structures are provided, either by altering present ones or inventing new ones. Thus, Instrumentalism is also based on environmental determinism.

These premises must be placed in context with Instrumentalism's major evaluative assumption: to be fully and completely human is to be instrumental; expressivity is a demeaning, degrading version of human potential. The ideal human is rational, ambitious, powerful, independent, and emotionally disciplined. Instrumentality and expressivity are antithetical orientations and, as such, are dualistically related. Since an individual cannot orient himself or herself to two opposing orientations simultaneously, one must "become" either of the two. And, since the instrumental orientation represents authentic humanity, the choice for Instrumental feminists is clear.

Instrumentalism assumes that the good society can be constructed through rational planning and human engineering. Human effort can be brought to bear in changing society and history. Progress toward a better society is presupposed as long as the appropriate techniques can be called into play.

Taken together, these presuppositions describe what is encapsulated in the modern world-view: ascribed differences are irrelevant; there is a basic equality and equivalency of human nature that underlies its plastic potentiality; the rational, instrumental life is dualistically related to the emotional, expressive one; and the good society can be constructed by human effort.

Instrumentalism is, then, an extreme version of modern consciousness. It entails a liberal, universalistic, rationalized definition of human nature. Instrumentalism, however, adds sex-gender to the list of particularizations that should be deemed irrelevant to human formation and opportunity. Sex-gender is an artificial, socially constructed category that alienates women from their basic instrumental selves.

Instrumentalism perceives human beings as basically interchangeable, context-free, and instrumental in public and private institutional realms. The Instrumentalist view reflects the growing technical-rational approach to intimate relationships exemplified by computerized dating services, fight-training clinics, sexuality-sensuality tutoring, child-rearing manuals—all attempts to rationalize subjectivity. This "seepage" of instrumental rationality into the private sphere has been interpreted by several social critics as a source of dehumanization and alienation. Yet what Instrumentalism is advocating is compatible with the ethos and interests of modern technological society.

NOTES

1. "Jewish Consciousness Raising," *RAT*, no. 18 (12–29 January 1971): 6.

2. Sally Koslow, "Connections—How to Use Them to Pull Strings," *Working Woman* 3 (March 1978): 42–45.

3. Patricia Brooks, "Plugging into the Old Girl Network," *Working Woman* 2 (July 1977): 26–29.

4. "*Newsweek,* the Man's Media," *RAT*, no. 5 (4–18 April 1970): 4. Italics added.

5. The aim of integrating women into the occupational hierarchy has implications for social structure that are discussed in chapter 7.

6. Arlene Brown, "Grateful Dead," *RAT*, no. 5 (4–18 April 1970): 26.

7. The popular music field is perceived differently by the other ideal types. For example, Expressivisim characterizes current popular music as "cock rock," which women cannot relate to, and suggests that women orient music to expressivity.

8. "Why Are Women Arrested?" *RAT*, no. 17 (17 December–6 January 1970–71): 9. Italics added.

9. "International Sisterhood," *RAT*, no. 18 (12–29 January 1971): 9.

10. "Why Are Women Arrested?" p. 9. Italics added.

11. See Stephanie Harrington, "Ms. versus Cosmo," *New York Times Magazine,* 11 August 1974.

12. A Weatherwoman, "Inside the Weather Machine," *RAT*, no. 1 (6–23 February 1970): 5.

13. "Why Are Women Arrested?" p. 9. Italics added.

14. Nadine Miller, "Shrunken Woman," *RAT*, no. 10 (26 June–10 July 1970): 20. Italics added.

15. Weatherwoman, "Inside the Weather Machine," p. 5.

16. Jessie Bernard, *Women and the Public Interest* (Chicago: Aldine, 1971), p. 37.

17. Weatherwoman, "Inside the Weather Machine," p. 5.

18. "International Sisterhood," p. 9.

19. Anselma dell'Olio, "A Plea to the Woman's Movement," *Liberated Guardian,* 11 March 1971.

20. "Letter to RAT," *RAT,* no. 17 (17 December–6 January 1970–71): 24.

21. "Starting to Think about Class," *RAT,* no. 24 (2 August 1971): 13.

22. Bill Davidson, "Marriages That Work: Norman and Frances Lear," *Family Circle* 91 (1 March 1978): 134. The excerpt is by Frances Loeb Lear, a feminist and women's employment specialist, as quoted by author from an unidentified *Newsweek* article.

23. Nancy Hechinger, "Time and the Working Mother," *Working Woman* 3 (January 1978): 43–46.

EXPRESSIVISM

The second feminist type, Expressivism, is a mirror image of Instrumentalism. Where the Instrumentalist is rational and calculating, the Expressivist is emotional and spontaneous. Expressivism wants to eliminate those characteristics that predominate in the technological era. Gone will be rational calculation to optimize self-interest. "What's in it for me?" will become "What good will it achieve for the communal well-being?" Emotional reserve and coolness will give way to emotional involvement and passion. Considering people as objects to be used for ulterior ends will be replaced by a new consciousness about human subjectivity. The glorification of winning, of profit, of productivity for its own sake will be no more. The glorification of abstraction, generalization, and syllogistic logic—keystones of a rational-scientific-technological world view—will vanish. In short, the antirationalist Utopia envisaged by Expressivism will turn present-day society on its head.

What kind of person is the Expressivist? In pure form the E-type (as Expressionists are often called in this chapter) embodies today's archetypical or ideal woman. But in an Expressivist future, this kind of personality would have no gender connotation. All people would be expressive, and only expressive—males as well as females. Sex differences in personality would disappear; dualism would be supplanted by sexual monism (i.e., one-dimensional development).

At first, the E-type seems to be an easygoing, relaxed, "let it all hang out" person. But Expressionists are highly complicated, with personalities as subtle as those of Instrumentalists. Emotionality varies in its expression, intensity, and positive and negative aspects. So does the E-type, the embodiment of emotionality. Expressionists can be affectionate, compassionate, gentle, loyal, sensitive, warm, and understanding; they also can be hateful, spiteful, rage-filled, jealous, thin-skinned, hot-blooded, and stubborn. E-types are likely to be intense, volatile; they laugh and cry easily. Such people, their hearts on their sleeves, have little capacity for concealing their feelings. They may be rude in situations where others may be tactful, for Expressionists freely express anger, grief, annoyance, or distaste.

Because face and body movements register clearly, however, E-types are fluent in nonverbal communication. They tend in fact to eschew verbal communication because many people (particularly I-types) use it to mask real feelings. But when writing or speaking, E-types are likely to invent new expressions—in order to avoid what they consider a rigid style of communication.

To Expressivists, personal relationships are ends in themselves, involving the whole person. Each relationship is also viewed as unique, having its own history and shared experiences. Thus the E-type does not have standard-operating-procedures (scripts, roles and formulas) for social situations and relationships. This stress on the unique and particular, rather than the general and universal, makes learning and understanding dependent on experience alone. To understand another means one must "walk in similar shoes." Engagement, not dispassionate intellectualizing, is the key to understanding for E-types. Intuition, not logic, leads to wisdom. The Expressivist universe is a mystical one; fate and chance must always be reckoned with.

What kind of feminist is most likely to embody these qualities? Jill Johnston is a well-known feminist who has approached the E-type. (Remember, however, that no human being can be captured in a type; it is merely that Johnston's work illustrates many E-type themes.) In the *Village Voice* column she had until recently, Johnston wrote freely and fully of her personal experiences—her passion, her sexual attractions, her dreams, her joys and fears. Her writing was very E-style; lower-case letters throughout, little punctuation, neologisms, satiric plays on words ("midevil" for medieval), and erratic abbreviations gave her stream-of-consciousness technique an explosive concreteness.

Here is one example, in which she is talking about another writer, Tom Wolfe:

> . . . i was dazzled by wolfe but then left feeling the tedium of a certain unrelieved dazzlement. all that glittered was the gold of style and the discovery of new subjects and the excitement of doing something different in newspapers and after enough of that i wanted some sense of the dross of the man who was covering all this stuff. the man seemed really above or outside the events he was recording with such a clamorous realistic fervor. eyes he dare not meet in dreams in death's dream kingdom possibly. for me he remained the Cool Objective Male, notwithstanding his little devices of sticking himself in the narrative . . . or alluding to himself in the third person. . . .[1]

Johnston's writing darts in and out of the argument, "working circles within circles, like the quadriga, the four horsed chariot, constantly returning to its point of origin."[2] It is Expressivist in tone as well as in subject matter.

In her book *Flying*,[3] Kate Millett also gave indication of an

Expressivist orientation. This work explored her feelings about events in the year following publication of her first book, *Sexual Politics* [4]—the memories, fears, joys, doubts, and pain of becoming a public figure and having it known that she was bisexual.

Flying was the antithesis of Millett's scholarly *Sexual Politics*, and touched off waves of criticism in the feminist community. Instrumentalist feminists were enraged because, in their view, Millett had betrayed the Instrumentalist faith and had converted to Expressivism. One critic put it this way:

> I find *Flying* as pitiful as I found *Sexual Politics* brilliant: a pointless, tangled self-revelation as the other was a genuine intellectual achievement. . . . Millett could think it through, but won't. She will only tell how it feels: shitty. "Thinking" for her is no more. It is something she left behind at Columbia with *Sexual Politics* which she explicitly and repeatedly—and tragically—disowns. . . . It is not the real Kate Millett that wrote the book in the first place, she claims, but an academic impersonator. This splintered, quicksilvery, suffering soul, rushing from meeting to meeting, from bed to bed, from shore to shore, jotting down "everything," is really me. [5]

Clearly the critic, Elinor Langer, was upset by Millett's rejection of the rational tradition, her disowning a book that Langer considered a work of Instrumentalist genius. In her Instrumentalist critique of the Expressivist *Flying*, Langer continued:

> Writing a book is a professional activity, like running a dress shop or a kennel. It is a business. . . . A book is a work of language, nothing else. It is not flesh and it is not time. It is not life. . . . confession, self-revelation, and subjectivity, all instruments of insight and development and experimentation when they occur within small groups, or writing classes, or are explored in private journals, can look shabby—even indecent—when they appear on the public shelves, where both literary and moral-political judgements must be made if the public side of life is to have any integrity at all. . . . It is inadequate to scorn

high standards as "male," for published writers to take refuge in internal Movement techniques, or to pretend that one is the other.[6]

Replying to Langer, Millett shows us the Expressivist type in feminism:

> All that *Sexual Politics* has come to stand for in the four years since its publication: respectability, erudition, objective and theoretical impersonality . . . all this is overturned, and for the rigid-minded like Langer even "betrayed" by the absolute *personality of Flying*.[7]

More Expressivist themes emerge as Millett continues:

> The trouble with *Flying* is simple: it's the personhood; not the sweeping generalities of patriarchal society but the private and unique case. . . . Langer expected *Sexual Politics* again and instead found me. And she turned in disgust, rather as, I expect, she would have turned from herself. "Men repress, women confess," she lectures. Perhaps it would have been clearer to say, "Men repress, women express." In any case, she clearly feels that I should have repressed, I should have shut up. I have no more intention of doing so than do my sisters. Those days are over.[8]

To Millett, the personal is what counts now. Abstraction and generalization have worsened women's plight and driven them away from shared personal truth. In examining and expressing their feelings, each in her own unique and special way, women will touch what is human in others. To disassociate themselves from the personal, to blot out feelings, is an abomination.

Their Expressivist orientation caused Johnston and Millett to announce publicly that they are lesbians. It could be no other way: to be "in the closet" *and* an Expressivist was not possible. Expressivists must share their personal feelings with others. Expressivist feminists need not be lesbians, of course. Nevertheless, an affinity between radical lesbianism and the Expressivist type exists, which is discussed later in the chapter.

Robin Morgan is another feminist whose work contains Expressivist themes. In her introduction to *Sisterhood Is Powerful,* Morgan recalls the personal feelings she had while editing the book—how reading personal accounts of other women gave her insights into her own life and sharpened her feminist consciousness. No dispassionate literary introduction, this. She says about the style of the anthology:

> There is also a blessedly uneven quality noticeable in the book, which I, for one, delight in. There is a certain kind of linear, tight, dry, boring, male super-consistency that we are beginning to reject. That's why this collection combines all sorts of articles, poems, graphics, and sundry papers.[9]

Morgan's references to male-style communication and the female alternative to it easily translate into instrumental and expressive terms. What identifies her as an Expressivist here is the putting down of the Instrumentalist way of writing and the obvious attraction for the Expressivist style.

Morgan was one of the original members of the feminist collective that took over and for eighteen months published *RAT,* an underground newspaper. *RAT's* authors embodied all four feminist ideal types, but much of its style was Expressivist. Here is Morgan writing in the first feminist issue of *RAT*:

> Goodbye, goodbye forever, counterfeit Left, counterleft, male-dominated cracked-glass-mirror reflection of the Amerikan Nightmare. Women are the real Left. We are rising, powerful in our unclean bodies; bright glowing mad in our inferior brains; wild hair flying, wild eyes staring, wild voices keening; undaunted by blood we who hemorrhage every twenty-eight days; laughing at our own beauty we who have lost our sense of humor; mourning for all each precious one of us might have been in this one living time-place had she not been born a

woman; stuffing fingers into our mouths to stop the screams of fear and hate and pity for men we have loved and love still; tears in our eyes and bitterness in our mouths for children we couldn't have, or couldn't *not* have, or didn't want, or didn't want *yet*, or wanted and had in this place and this time of horror. We are rising with a fury older and potentially greater than any force in history, and this time we will be free or no one will survive. Power to all the people or none. All the way down, this time.[10]

Aside from Johnston, Millett, and Morgan, few well-known feminists consistently exhibit an Expressivist image (although most feminists are Expressivist in orientation from time to time, this being the whole point of the argument). Two characteristics of E-types may explain this. First, most Expressivist feminists eschew the individual achievement-recognition-stardom syndrome. Instead, they put their energies into collective efforts and frequently write anonymously, or simply as a member of a collective. Second, Expressivist writing is highly unconventional. It is freewheeling, gutsy, personal (embarrassingly so at times), sometimes incoherent, and always anti-Instrumentalist.

Because it is the antithesis of the literary style that predominates in the media, few conventional publications give serious consideration to contributions submitted in Expressivist style. (For the same reason, many students, expecially female or black or working-class ones, flunk courses for submitting work in Expressivist style, which is considered nonprofessional and contemptuous of academic standards.) Thus the Expressivist way of writing is rarely found "aboveground." Expressivist themes, clothed in customary language, at times do appear.

Expressivist-style writing gets published in underground feminist newspapers—in *RAT*, *It Ain't Me Babe*, *Up From Under*, and *Off Our Backs*.[11] For example, two statements by CLIT (Collective Lesbian International Terrors), a group of New York lesbian separatists, were published by *Off Our Backs* even though the OOB collective anguished over the dissension caused by

CLIT by writings permeated with hatred of men, straight women, the aboveground media, and the dominant culture. CLIT, by the way, exhibited all four ideal types in the articles, but the style in which they are written is Expressivist. Here is an excerpt:

> The C.L.I.T. Collection is written by C.L.I.T.s. We intentionally prefer not to write under our own names for these reasons: We are trying to put into practice some of our sentiments about breaking the star-system described in C.L.I.T. Statement No. 1. We don't want to make a name for ourselves as thinkers or whatever you think we are. . . . The pseudonym also has a freeing effect. We can write whatever we want in any style without the fear of someone telling us we are *bad* writers. So we have more room to experiment with writing. It takes a lot of weight off most of our shoulders who are nervous about writing.[12]

A discussion of male-female approaches to language gives another example of Expressivist style and content:

> Women communicate intensely in a complicated way without speaking. Men cannot and this scares the shit out of them. And when women talk, they wouldn't think of speaking without mixing emotions with words, unless they are imitating men (the professional woman) or doing straight seduction numbers which is the way you operate with men—it's the only thing that turns them on—artifice. Men freak when women speak emotionally simply because women are on a higher existence level that men could not reach even with a ladder. So men trash speaking with emotional intensity and make their nontalent into a social virtue—the ability to speak ridiculous mindfucking stale languages (legal, business, doctor) that are like them—they attempt to sound important but mean nothing. They try to make women feel stupid for not understanding these languages that are essentially meaningless (Watergate talk.) [13]

These examples should give some idea of what the E-type is like. But, again, no feminist embodies any ideal type. By definition, the ideal type is a pure form and cannot be found in reality.

EXPRESSIVE FEMINISTS AND CONVENTIONAL WOMEN

The Expressivist feminist is an embodiment of the archetypical woman or female principle. But feminism is a movement whose members are united in their dissatisfaction with the lot of females in today's society. What relationship exists, then, between what Expressivists consider the ideal human personality and what is usually thought of as feminine? First, E-types do not equate the female principle (i.e., expressivity) with our society's traditional female role. At the same time, however, Expressivists and traditional females resemble one another because both revert to the same principle—the emotional rather than the rational governs human existence.

So the Expressivist and the traditional female are similar in some respects and unlike in others. Both are emotional, sensitive, and nurturing; but the Expressivist sees the conventional woman as forced to define herself as inferior in comparison with male instrumentality. Expressivists feel that males have taken advantage of females' expressivity, turning female supportiveness into a device for their enslavement. Expressivity has been transformed into a mockery of itself—passivity becomes servility, mysticism becomes superstition, lightheartedness becomes triviality, and passion becomes sexiness when instrumental males have their way.

Further, the Expressivist sees herself as different from the conventional woman by virtue of the pride and strength she derives from being expressive. Many conventional women think they are inferior to instrumental males because they are expressive. Much of the Expressivist's energy is directed toward upending the instrumental-expressive hierarchy with variations on the theme that "expressive is beautiful; instrumental is devilish." (The parallel to the "Black is Beautiful" theme is noticeable here.) E-type feminists hope to convince women to stop their self-hatred and begin to identify with all other women as superior expressive humans who will be able to show males the way to authentic humanity.

> All the female culture traits are defined as negatives by the dominant world male culture. We do not believe them to be so. . . . We are proud of the female culture of emotion, intuition, love, personal relationships, etc. as the most essential human characteristics. It is our male colonizers—it is the male culture —who have defined essential humanity out of their identity and who are "culturally deprived." [14]

Many Expressivist feminists feel that males also suffer from instrumentalization and need to be shown the way out of their misery. But the Expressivist position on males is a complicated one and will be taken up later in the chapter.

A further parallel between the traditional woman and the feminist E-type is that both share a personal, subjective approach to social relationships. That is, the E-type does not favor treating everyone alike, according to some fixed social rules. E-types avoid standard procedures—such as like treatment for *all* students, *all* patients or *all* job applicants. Standardized codes of this kind are replaced by responding to another in terms of the unique relationship. The following diary excerpt illustrates the personalistic approach:

> When I show a friend one of my sculptures I feel best when he says, "I enjoy looking at it," "That makes me feel very relaxed" or "That makes me feel uncomfortable and threatened." I hate it when he says, "This is better than your other one," "That's great," or "It is very well done."
>
> The first reaction is honest subjectivity, the second is a reaction, a detached pretense of "objectivity."

When I feel tempted to criticize the work of another, I know
I am not allowing myself to experience his work.

My son brings home his paintings from nursery school. They
cover our den wall. To say which is "best" would be impossible.
Each is a distinct and special part of himself he has trusted
me to share.[15]

Both traditional women and E-type feminists view others in
personalized terms, and each relationship fits within a particular
configuration of shared history. As in the example, both female
types would be apt to judge a friend's work in such a way as to
take into consideration the friend's fears of inadequacy, what this
work means to the creator, and the special ways of relating to each
other that have built up over the history of the relationship. Instead
of casting a dispassionate, critical eye on the work, as an art critic
or English professor (both of whom are likely Instrumentalists)
might, the Expressivist (traditional or feminist) relates to the work
as a uniquely personal creation and responds to it with great emotional involvement. This emotion could be intense anger, as well
as joy.

Personalized criteria are also illustrated by the statement
"You are beautiful to me," rather than "You have the most beautiful body in the world." The latter statement implies some universal
or objective standard against which the one who is judging measures
the object in question. (Women who were socialized from birth
to the subjectivist rather than the universalist approach are sur-
prised to find that many males consider it perfectly acceptable to
sum up a woman's looks with a coded classification, such as a 3 or
7 on a ten-point scale.[16] Expressivist feminists aim to convince
both males and females that such a practice is barbaric.) The
subjective approach to beauty implies that every person is unique;
because this is so, rating beauty is meaningless at best, dehumanizing at worst.

The conventional female might not be inclined to protest a
universalist approach to the world, but the Expressivist feminist
would stop it right away. For example, in a heated discussion

between a male and a female, when voices are raised (and some-times even before), females often begin to take the matter per-sonally. If the man is yelling, he must be angry at them. Males frequently respond by bellowing in exasperation, "Why must you take everything so personally? Can't I have a decent intellectual conversation without your getting all emotional about it?" Tradi-tional females usually do not contest this attitude—older women probably say resignedly, "You men are all the same," and younger ones may break into tears and feel inadequate for not being men's equals. Expressivist feminists are a different story altogether. If they still have the patience to interact with males at all, they prob-ably bellow back: "You idiot, every argument is personal; there's something wrong with you if you can cut off your emotions when you discuss something. If you think your yelling has nothing to do with me as a person, that you are only getting carried away with the debate, then I pity you, because you have lost all touch with your own emotions and with me as another human being."

Another quality that the traditional female and the E-type feminist have in common is that of being a "stroker"—one who makes people feel good, boosts egos, and is generally supportive. A traditional stroker is captured in this portrait of the southern woman:

> From the moment you enter her house, you will be treated like royalty. Whatever you do, whatever you want, she will make you feel you are always right. . . . Her skills for keeping the surface of life smooth are legendary. If any unpleasantness should arise, her duty is to pretend it doesn't exist, and to con-vince everybody else of its nonexistence. Perhaps you fling your coat petulantly to the floor. Mrs. Stephens will pick it up, or see that it is picked up, and in such a way to make it appear that all guests habitually fling their wraps to the floor. She may even remark playfully, "You dropped something!" Her eyes, cruising continually over the well-being of her guests, are light-ning-quick to anticipate anything that might detract from this well-being: an almost empty glass, a needed ashtray, an awk-ward turn in the conversation. Any signs of rough seas will be

promptly, charmingly quashed by her deft intervention. She will
minister, forestall, deflect, prevaricate, suffer martyrdoms of discomfort herself, before she will ever allow the uninvited guest of
"Unpleasantness" in any shape or form to cross the threshold
of her living room.[17]

The difference between the Expressivist feminist and the traditional woman as strokers comes from the feminist's attitude toward
herself and the kind of society she envisions in the future. As described above the southern woman loses track of herself and her
needs in her quest to put everyone at ease. This happens easily
because others (particularly males) are on the receiving end of her
ministrations. The roles become fixed: one is stroker, the other is
strokee. In the Expressivist future, feminists would not allow such
role fixation. All people would be strokers. Everyone would be
looking out for the other's feelings. All would be sensitive, intuitive,
gentle—stroking.

There is another important difference between this the traditional woman as stroker and the E-type feminist stroker. The
feminist applauds the expression of all emotions, negative as well
as positive; her goal is not to cover up unpleasantness. In the
southern scenario just described, the Expressivist feminist might
yell at the coat-thrower, "Pick your damn coat up!" if she were
feeling angry. The Expressivist feminist may be a stroker, but she
also can be a bristler. In her way of seeing things, no emotions
should be inhibited.

Whether or not she is familiar with confrontation therapy, the
Expressivist feminist advocates open, direct expression of unpleas-
ant emotions: anger, sadness, rage, and so on. But this does not
mean that behavior usually associated with the "macho" stereotype
is acceptable. Quite the contrary. The E-type feminist would not
agree that Expressivity is contained in the swaggering, sometimes
violent aggressiveness of the macho style. She would say that such
behavior evidences "contaminated" Expressivity. The outward
manifestation of emotions mask or deflect the underlying true
feelings. The macho style, the Expressivist feminist would say,
masks fear with swagger, vulnerability with toughness, and insecur-

ity with cockiness. Thus Expressivism has an implicit model of emotional health; not *any* emotional expression is approved, only those that are "authentic." Expressivism implies a match between behavior and subjectivity, between outer manifestation with inner feeling. This model, however, is not at all systematized in the Expressivist world-view. E-type feminists often advocate the expression of all emotion, hoping that everything will somehow turn out all right and not result in violence and aggression. As one such feminist put it:

> When I was married, I thought my role was to be endlessly agreeable, to always compromise, to never nag or bitch. As a result, I became so stony and passive that E.H. [author's ex-husband] was impotent to get a reaction from me. I drove him out of his mind.
>
> Now I am expressing anger freely and it feels good to me, and I think it is a lot fairer to others, too.[18]

Not only will it be for the greater good of self and others, but, when expressed, anger dissipates:

> I am still amazed at how in expressing my hostility toward E. H., I have lost it. The only way to let go is to allow yourself to feel, guiltlessly and without analyzing your feelings.[19]

From such experiences with anger and hostility the Expressivist feminist concludes that the best way to deal with emotional dissension is to acknowledge it, for in doing so, one makes room for happier feelings. If one is allowed to express only positive emotions, an inauthenticity sets in, and stroking promotes alienation from self.

Some Expressivist feminists consider anger the vehicle for women's liberation. The theme "Anger is changing our lives" is voiced time and again by E-types. It is a theme initiated by the feminist theater group "It's All Right to Be Woman Theatre," and is included in all their performances. E-type feminists encourage women to show anger, to stop smiling when they don't feel happy, to stop the conditioned agreeableness that glosses over real feelings. Shulamith Firestone even recommended a "smile boycott, at which declaration all women would instantly abandon their 'pleasing' smiles, henceforth smiling only when something pleased *them*." [20] The following description of positive anger is taken from an informal theatre workshop put together by feminists:

> One woman becomes angry and pounds the floor and then suddenly another hears her and recognizes it and then all the women are angry. From an inarticulate moaning and pounding comes an angry fury as they rise together chanting "No! No! No!"–"No more shame. . . ." [21]

The Expressivist is readily recognized here as the angry feminist who frightens some males with her "stridency", the one who is prompted to write articles titled "I Am Furious (Female)." [22] Her anger is a way of energizing women's emancipation from present-day strictures, so that women can usher in an emotional paradise where all will soothe one another, where all negative feelings –once released–will help in self and social renewal.

EXPRESSIVISM AND THE WORKING CLASS

The Expressivist feminist has several characteristics in common with the working-class person. (Again, note that the "working-class person" described here is ideal typical.) This does not mean that the worker never does anything instrumental. To be sure, there is probably nothing more instrumental than factory work. This is not the point, however. The E-style of the working class has its roots in the historical communities and the rural and ethnic traditions out of which it emerged and is in marked contrast to the instrumental-universalist style of the middle class.

Researchers disagree in their interpretations of the working-class life style, but many point out its tendency toward Expressivism. For example, Gans finds members of the working class "person-oriented," in contrast to a middle-class "object-orientation." [23] Bernstein characterizes working-class language as "particularistic," "restricted," or "public," as compared with the "universalistic," "elaborated," and "formal" code of middle-class communication.[24]

Person-orientation implies emotional, personalized involvement of the whole person in relationships that are considered ends in themselves. Its opposite, object-orientation, entails impersonal, rational ways of relating to others with universalistic, self-interested aspects predominating. This style of interacting involves the manipulation of others in relationships that are considered means to an end.

Because of their personalized, subjective involvement, both E-types and working-class persons experience severe discomfort when dealing with bureaucracies, which are seen as cold, unfriendly, and rigid. But though both respond expressively, their responses differ. The working-class person typically feels inadequate, cowed by the effects of social-class hierarchy.[25] The E-type's response typically is belligerent. To her the problem is the bureaucratic form, not her inability to cope with it. She sees her inability to cope with such "barbarism" as a sign of her humanity.

E-types and working-class persons also share a way of communicating. Basically this style emphasizes such extraverbal components as rhythm, stress, pitch, gestures, body language, muscular tension, and facial expressions.[26] This communication is usually found where the participants share common meanings, identification, and empathy—where the "we" is more important than the "I." [27]

Basil Bernstein says that the language code found in the working class will emphasize verbally the communal rather than the individual, the concrete rather than the abstract, substance rather than elaboration of process, the here and now rather than exploration of motives and intentions, and positional rather than personalized forms of social control.[28]

This is the opposite of what Benjamin Nelson was getting at with his notion of the "universal otherhood" that pervades modern social consciousness,[29] and also of the characteristic researchers found in a study of middle-class life, *Crestwood Heights,* where children learn early how to compete while maintaining a friendly, cooperative exterior.[30]

One point is worth exploring as far as the evaluation of such a "restricted" language code goes among social scientists. For the most part, this way of communicating is hardly recognized. The usual practice is to see it as a lack of verbal ability, as verbal impoverishment—inadequate when compared with the middle-class model of instrumental, universalistic communication. Bernstein maintains that the working-class code has been undervalued. Such a language code "will tend to develop a metaphoric range of considerable power, a simplicity and directness, a vitality and rhythm." [31] Nevertheless, Bernstein refers to this code as "restricted" (as opposed to the "elaborated" middle-class code) because it *limits* its users insofar as school and work success are concerned and also in their ability to be introspective. That is, one does not have the conceptual equipment with a restricted code for personal liberation. This is a highly loaded interpretation, even in the face of his more positive remarks about the code.

E-type feminists would disagree. They maintain that those who speak in the "elaborated" code of the middle-class instrumental world are "restricted" in their ability to communicate because they must depend on words alone to convey their messages and meanings. The E-type is wholly comfortable with silence. In an E-type gathering you will find all manner of nonverbal styles. Two or three people may sit smiling and nodding, unruffled by any pressure to start a conversation. A couple may glower in silence at one another. Yet another may embrace each other with gentleness and concern. The emotions communicated nonverbally run the gamut from joy to misery.

Because she is nonverbal, the E-type experiences pride and a sense of superiority over I-types. The working-class person who is nonverbal experiences shame and inadequacy because she or he is not able to cope with the dominant style of communicating.

Another parallel between the E-type feminist and the working-class person is suggested by Frank Riessman's work on the life style of the lower-class child and the middle-class school world.[32]

He concludes that the world of the school, run on middle-class principles, is the antithesis of the world of the lower-class child. Transposing his research into the terms of this book the lower-class child's world is expressive, and the middle-class school is instrumental. Riessman summarizes the differences as follows: [33]

Life Style of Lower-Income Child	*Middle-Class School World*
Physical and visual	Aural
Content-centered	Form-centered
Externally oriented	Introspective
Problem-centered	Abstract-centered
Inductive	Deductive
Spatial	Temporal
Slow, careful	Quick, facile
Games and action	Tests
Expressive orientation	Instrumental orientation
One-track thinking	"Other-directed" flexibility
Words as related to acts	Word-bound

The characteristics that summarize the life style of the lower-income child match the composite Expressivist type. E-types and working-class persons have much in common. The social-change potential of the E-type is radical, for what these feminists advocate is a repudiation not only of Instrumentalism but also of the middle-class life style.

OTHER CHARACTERISTICS OF EXPRESSIVISM

Antielitism and structurelessness are two other characteristics of Expressivism. The E-type has much in common with the collective principle described by Elizabeth Mann Borgese. Drawing insight from the work of Bachofen and Baumann, Borgese contends that women as a type and the masses as a type are similar (men and elites are her corresponding types).

> The affinity between the feminine and the collective seems to have penetrated man's unconscious and to reflect itself in language and art, in myth and faith. . . . The essence of this unity, of this collective, was woman—as bee-like as possible. The shelterer, the nourisher, the life-giver, the priestess and the witch, the medicine woman, the potter of cosmic vessels, the spinner of the threads of life. . . . For *nous*, mind, and *nomos*, rational law that can be grasped by mind, are masculine; whereas *tyche*, chance or fate, is feminine.[34]

The precedent of pairing "feminine" or women in general with larger cultural entities stretches far back in social thought. Tonnies, a classical sociological theorist, has offered a throughgoing parallel between women and *Gemeinschaft*, or what is inadequately translated as community. For him, women are aligned with the spontaneous and the passionate.

> . . . women are usually led by feelings, men more by intellect. Men are more clever. They alone are more capable of calculation, of calm (abstract) thinking, of consideration, combination and logic. . . . If the privilege of cleverness is attributed to the man, it must be kept in mind that cleverness is by no means the same as general intellectual power. On the contrary to the extent that intellectual power is productive or synthetic, the female mind excels. . . . All activity which expresses itself in a direct manner, either originally or from habit or memory, as consequence and expression of life itself, belongs to the realm of the woman. Thus, all expressions and outbursts of emotions and sentiments, conscience, and inspired thoughts are the specific truthfulness, naivete, directness, and passionateness of the woman, who is in every respect the more natural being.[35]

Translating Tonnies's thesis to fit our expressive-instrumental terminology, he concludes that women's expressivity makes them the
more natural beings, but that as women enter the public arena they
too will become instrumentalized. Comparing woman and the proletariat, Tonnies speculates that it is possible that the consciousness of women may develop in such a way as to forestall the erosion of expressivity (what he called *Germeinschaft*). [36] This is
exactly what the E-type has in mind.

The association of the "female principle" with larger cultural
entities is also found in the work of Shulamith Firestone, a contemporary feminist theoretician. Firestone would divide cultural
history into two modes, which correspond to the female principle
and the male principle. The female principle flowers in the Aesthetic Mode, which for her, is idealistic and humanistic. The ma-
terialistic, scientific Technological Mode stems from the male principle.

> . . . the aesthetic response corresponds with "female" behavior.
> The same terminology can be applied to either: subjective, in-
> tuitive, introverted, wishful, dreamy or fantastic, concerned
> with the subconscious (the *id*), emotional, even tempera-
> mental (hysterical). Correspondingly, the technological re-
> sponse is the masculine response: objective, logical, extroverted,
> realistic, concerned with the conscious mind (the ego), rational,
> mechanical, pragmatic and down-to-earth, stable.[37]

In sum, Expressivists are a composite of traditional females,
working-class persons, communalists, antielitists, and unstructured
anarchists.

EXPRESSIVIST UTOPIA

The impulse to classify, categorize, abstract, and generalize would
be done away with by the Expressivist feminist. In addition,
science, technology, the academy, and all institutions run on

universalist principles would have to go. The world as we know it today, dominated by Instrumentalist patterns, would be radically changed. For example, art would no longer be judged by universalist standards, but would stress the personal and the emotional. Quilting, embroidery, macramé, ceramics, and other handicrafts usually thought of as women's art would be the height of artistic expression because they touch human life at its most genuine—in the heart, at the hearth, in the home. Expressivist feminists would have no patience with computer art, mathematical art, or any abstract or conceptual art that is not expressive in form and content.

Along with objective standards and measurements would go individual luminaries and experts. Everybody would be a "star" in his or her own right, and an expert as well. In this view, if no one is judged on a scale that runs from best to worst, no one risks having a particular contribution reduced to an object that can be measured. Expressivist feminists would make all people singers, poets, artists, and storytellers—no matter what the results. In the Expressivist world, no one would determine who is *best,* what is worth *more,* how *good* is it by popular reckoning.

In the E-Utopia, all would have emotional freedom. The world would be one in which people could expect direct, open feedback on all actions and moods. Fulfillment would be found in human relationships—in the communal unit.

The Utopia imagined by Expressivism would combine elements of the 1960s counterculture, mysticism, romanticism, socialism, and anarchism. E-type collectives give evidence of many of these patterns. While not all feminist collectives are Expressivist, many are founded on Expressivist ways of ordering the world. E-type collectives are usually loosely structured and try to avoid freezing people into group roles. Rotating leadership and work roles eliminates the chances that elitism and specialization will develop. Such groups involve everyone in decision making. This can be an inefficient, if not chaotic, way of doing things. The charge that lack of structure is inefficient does not dismay the E-type; efficiency is a value that the Expressivist hopes to eliminate. Yet the E-type's value system may make it impossible to get the revolution going, for it tells her that whatever will be, will be. The revolution may simply have to happen.

This fatalism has its advantages, however. E-types can concentrate on life in the here-and-now, a prime value for an Expressivist. She can involve herself in her collective life and avoid brushes with the outside, instrumental world. The separatist, isolationist tendencies of the E-type emerge in her refusal to go to doctors or consult lawyers, except in dire emergency. Even then, she tries to find a female professional in the hope that she will escape the instrumentalization in the public realm. The same holds true for other specialists. E-types encourage women to learn how to do plumbing, electrical, and auto repairs, to become communally sufficient.

Here, however, is another contradiction in Expressivism. All task behavior is usually thought of as instrumental because of the customary logic that dualizes task and emotional behavior. Dualists believe they can either work or play, be efficient or be sensitive, but not do both at the same time. The E-type feminist begins with this either-or logic with regard to instrumental and expressive activity but does not accept that both types of behavior are necessary for group survival. What happens to tasks in the Expressivist Utopia? All things are encompassed by the Expressivist ethos. Tasks are done, but they are done expressively. Efficiency, productivity for its own sake, rationalization, and similar Instrumentalist values are eliminated. This being the case, it doesn't matter to the E-type that it takes forever to get a job done—as long as feelings are expressed, communication emerges, and human growth takes place.

Approaches to work vary in E-type collectives. In one, work may be done in an atmosphere that encourages the open expression of irritation and anger. In another, members approach work differently on different occasions: one member washes dishes while yelling, another paints walls while singing, a third sweeps the floor while dancing.

EXPRESSIVIST FEMINISTS AND MEN

The E-type wants to expressivize all people, including males, of course. But another contradiction surfaces. The E-type emphasizes the personalistic. An E-type feminist locates problem sources in concrete, face-to-face relationships. She often finds males, rather than some abstraction called sexism, directly and personally responsible for her oppression. Males make Expressivists unhappy; at the same time, there is nothing inevitable about males' instrumentality, so they, too, can be brought into the Expressivist light. The E-type believes nurture, not nature, determines how people turn out. If males are encouraged to be expressive as boys, they will grow into expressive men.

The E-type also maintains that we learn by experience however. Each of us becomes what our experience dictates, and we are alike only insofar as we have common experience. Where, then, does this leave men, whose lives have been an accumulation of instrumental attitudes and practices? Can they erase this experience and accept expressive resocialization? Some E-types say yes, and seek out males in order to provide them with the encouragement and support to develop their expressive humanity more fully. Other E-types avoid males completely, as dangerous carriers of instrumentality.

To protect themselves against contamination, some E-type feminists join collectives that aim for unit sufficiency. Many E-types are found among radical lesbians because both groups share the conviction that males represent the concrete form of the problem—the instrumental style. Radical lesbianism is a pure form of female self-sufficiency. Homosexual E-types forego the struggle with males and find an ideal lover in another woman.[38] Heterosexual E-types could renounce sexuality (as some feminists have done), but most feminists have no wish to renounce sexual feelings and sexual expression. They must await the day when male Expressivist lovers are widely available.

PHILOSOPHICAL ASSUMPTIONS

What assumptions about humanity, gender, and the individual's relationship to society are fundamental to Expressivism? It must be remembered, first, that the E-type lives in the modern technocratic world. Even though the E-type feminist represents a reversal of values about people and society, she nevertheless draws upon technocratic ideas.

For example, the idea that people turn out as they do because of social conditioning and not because of biological or sexual determination is associated with Enlightenment philosophy—one of the foundations of the Western rational, liberal ethos. When E-type feminists insist that males can be resocialized into expressivity, they are calling upon clearly rationalist presuppositions. Yet, another part of the rationalist tradition upon which Expressivism draws is the notion that all people are interchangeable at birth, that people are shaped socially by their social placement. This being so, male adults probably have lost the capability to eradicate their instrumentality and remold themselves into the expressive orientation.

Besides the antibiological, social deterministic theses associated with the modern world-view, the E-type also draws on the traditional world-view. Expressivism is similar to the Romantic Conservatism movement in Germany, described and interpreted by Karl Mannheim, a classical sociology of knowledge theorist.[39] Romantic Conservatism stressed the qualitative over the quantitative, the concrete over the abstract, and the personal over the objective. Both Romantic Conservatism and Expressivism can be seen as reactions to the encroaching rationalism and the expanding technological ethos in their respective eras. Both stress the emotional level of understanding; both are likely to seek for solutions in back-to-earth movements.

But the two are also very different. Unlike Expressivism, Romantic Conservatism looked backward to a former era for a model of the good society, to the time of a clear-cut hierarchy of status and authority, one wherein all people had and knew their places. E-types reject such notions. They long for the chaos of spontaneous emotional expression.

NOTES

1. Jill Johnston, "Write About Face," *Village Voice*, 9 June 1975, p. 26.

2. Jill Johnston, *Lesbian Nation* (New York: Simon & Schuster, 1973), p. 11.

3. Kate Millett, *Flying* (New York: Knopf, 1974).

4. Kate Millett, *Sexual Politics* (New York: Avon Equinox, 1970).

5. Elinor Langer, "Confessing: Forum," *Ms.* 3 (December 1974): 70.

6. Ibid., pp. 70–71.

7. Kate Millett, "The Shame Is Over: Forum," *Ms.* 3 (January 1975): 27.

8. Ibid.

9. Robin Morgan, "Introduction," in Robin Morgan, ed., *Sisterhood Is Powerful* (New York: Vintage, 1970), p. xvii.

10. Robin Morgan, "Goodbye to All That," *RAT*, no. 1 (6–23 February 1970): 7.

11. Of the feminist newspapers mentioned, only *Off Our Backs* is still publishing and available in metropolitan areas across the country. Many newsletter-type local papers are available, but these do not have the in-depth articles of feminist protest associated with underground papers in the early 1970s.

12. Anonymous Member of CLIT, "Introduction," *Off Our Backs* 4 (July 1974): 12. CLIT did not try to publish its papers in the above-ground press because, in an earlier statement of its political position, it said it would have nothing to do with the straight press.

13. Ibid. This excerpt borders on a Polarist theme: males are essentially different from females, now and forever. The Expressivist maintains that males are redeemable and that young boys can be socialized to be expressive.

14. Barbara Burris, *Fourth World Manifesto* (New Haven, Conn.: Advocate Press, 1971), p. 12.

15. Jan Fuller, *Space: The Scrapbook of My Divorce* (Greenwich, Conn.: Fawcett, 1973), p. 157.

16. The variety of codes used is large, as far as the specifics of the rating categories go, but the principle is the same. Somehow all the uniqueness of a person can be translated into a standard classification. This principle is also at work in much of the research of conventional social science, and of the other sciences as well. Even this present work of finding ideal types within the feminist movement goes against the grain of the Expressivists.

17. Gail Godwin, "The Southern Belle," *Ms.* 4 (July 1975): 49–51.

18. Fuller, *Space*, p. 54.

19. Ibid., p. 139.

20. Shulamith Firestone, *The Dialectic of Sex* (New York: Bantam, 1970), p. 90.

21. Anonymous, "Our Hands—Our Feet—Our Bodies—Our Minds Are Tools for Social Change," *RAT*, no. 24 (12–29 January 1971): 13.

22. Anonymous, *I Am Furious (Female)* (Detroit: Radical Education Project, n.d.).

23. Cf. Herbert Gans, *Urban Villagers* (New York: Free Press, 1965).

24. Basil Bernstein, *Class, Codes, and Control* (New York: Schocken, 1975).

25. Cf. Richard Sennett and Jonathan Cobb, *The Hidden Injuries of Class* (New York: Knopf, 1972).

26. Bernstein, *Class, Codes, and Control*, p. 126.

27. Ibid., pp. 146–47.

28. Ibid., p. 143. *Personalized* here means a universalized personableness in which a person can communicate in a flexibly friendly way with any other person. The working-class person typically does not feel at ease with strangers and thus may appear unfriendly, whereas the middle-class person typically can talk with strangers in a friendly, "personable" way. The working-class individual, however, may actually be acting more genu-

inely personable than the middle-class individual, whose universalized friendliness may belie genuine personableness.

29. Benjamin Nelson, *The Idea of Usury* (Chicago: University of Chicago Press, 1964).

30. John Seeley et al., *Crestwood Heights* (New York: Wiley, 1963).

31. Bernstein, p. 136.

32. Frank Riessman, "Cultural Styles of the Disadvantaged" (New York, 1964), p. 3. Mimeographed. Cf. also Frank Riessman, "The Strategy of Styles," *Teachers College Record* 65 (1964): 484–89.

33. Ibid.

34. Elizabeth Mann Borgese, *The Ascent of Woman* (New York: George Braziller, 1963), pp. 53–55.

35. Ferdinand Tonnies, *Community and Society* (New York: Harper Torchbooks, 1963), pp. 151–53.

36. Ibid., p. 166.

37. Firestone, *The Dialectic of Sex*, p. 175.

38. Cf. Ingrid Bengis, *Combat in the Erogenous Zone* (New York: Knopf, 1972), pp. 166–94, for a discussion of some of the implications of choosing women rather than men as lovers. One of Bengis's friends puts the matter this way: "Do you want to spend your whole life teaching men how to be human?" Ibid., p. 184.

39. Karl Mannheim, "Conservative Thought," in Kurt H. Wolff, ed., *From Karl Mannheim* (New York: Oxford University Press, 1971), pp. 132–222.

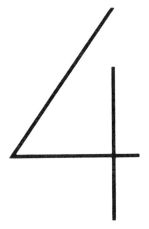

SYNTHESISM

Synthesism, the third feminist ideal type is a fusion of Instrumentalism and Expressivism. The ideal Synthesist is instrumental *and* expressive. The idea of being simultaneously instrumental and expressive may be beyond the understanding of most people, who were raised on dualistic principles about self and society and saturated with experiences that confirm the belief that one cannot be rational and emotional at the same time.

Synthesism may be almost impossible to imagine, yet, on hearing brief descriptions of the four ideal types, most people classify themselves as Synthesists! The goal of being rationally and emotionally competent is a popular one, and a superficial reading of Synthesism leads people to believe that it entails any combination of instrumentality and expressivity. Confirmed male supremacists (both male and female) and philosophical conservatives both have declared Synthesism to be a great idea, a way to *human* liberation. Among these self-defined Synthesists are some archetypically dualistic people, thoroughly technocratic in their worldview, people whose lives are models of the public-private and head-heart split that Synthesism decries.

Why do so many people readily identify with this ideal type? Perhaps it is because Synthesism's ideal human seems to represent what people call the well-rounded person—the one who does many different things well, things drawn from both the emotional and rational realms. The Synthesist and the well-rounded person are similar in that both give play to instrumentality and expressivity, yet they are far from identical. The well-rounded person segregates the two kinds of activities, performing them in sequence; the Synthesist performs them simultaneously. Being well-rounded might simply mean that a person plays out a variety of life roles well. For example, if you can balance four expressive roles (wife mother, lover, and hostess) with four instrumental ones (lawyer, politician, club president, and writer), you are indeed well-rounded. But as long as these roles are kept separate from one another, you are not what feminists of this third ideal type mean by Synthesist.

Synthesism desires something very different from having males add to their instrumental repertoire such expressive activities as writing poetry, stroking egos, or telling stories to their children; or having females go back to work, repair toilets, service their cars, or become sexually aggressive. Synthesism is not the sum of adding up compartmentalized activities. What Synthesism requires is the transformation of a dualistic world into a dialectical one. If your self and your world are so organized that you cannot get things done and make people feel good at the same time you are not in touch with your authentic humanity.

A similar confusion arises between Synthesism and what is called sociological ambivalence. In one of his theoretical pieces,

Robert Merton describes the doctor's role as one of "detached concern."[1] At first glance, this resembles the fusion S-types (as we also call Synthesists) have in mind. But Merton refers to the combination of detachment (instrumental trait) and concern (an expressive trait) as a perfect example of sociological *ambivalence* in that it involves an oscillation between conflicting norms:

> ... the therapist role of the physician ... calls for *both* a degree of affective detachment from the patient and a degree of compassionate concern with him. ... Since these norms *cannot be simultaneously expressed* in behavior, they come to be expressed in an *oscillation* of behaviors: of detachment and compassion, of discipline and permissiveness, or personal and impersonal treatment.[2]

Instead of a dialectic wherein each opposite fuses with the other, we have here a dualistic oscillation and a resultant ambivalence. The doctor in Merton's view is first detached, then concerned, in a chronological sequence of stops and starts, dashing back and forth between polar expectations. This is not what Synthesism has in mind.

Another major confusion that should be cleared is the relationship between Synthesism and the marginality that throws women into an identity crisis. A college-educated woman, for example, is marginalized by discrepant social expectations: she should be instrumentally productive and do something with her life, yet her primary mission in life is to be a good wife and mother. Such a woman is treated officially in much the same manner as a man; she is given the same assignments, graded on the same scale, expected to try her best. Yet the unofficial message, confirmed by her own social experience, is that she will be unhappy if she does not defer to the male and stroke, prop up, and inflate his fragile ego. She finds that most people mistrust her if she moves too far away from her expressive focus, and that the majority of males resent the slightest challenge to their leadership in instrumental situations.

The college-educated female, especially if she holds down a job, has experience in acting instrumentally and expressively, but she rarely achieves Synthesism's ideal fusion. Frequently she fails to become even well-rounded. Society gives the higher prestige to instrumental activities, yet she learns to apologize for her success in this realm. Instead of being well-rounded, many college-educated women become confused and nervous from oscillating between society's conflicting demands, and achieve a state closer to "cultural schizophrenia" than synthesis.

SYNTHESIS AS A DIALECTICAL PROCESS

How can instrumentality and expressivity be expressed at the same time when all our experience indicates that the two are incompatible? The Synthesist says these opposites can be joined through a dialectical process. In this respect the Synthesist feminist often sounds as mystifying as Hegelian logic. But, simply put, for the Synthesist the authentic human being is a unity of opposites. Instrumentality is completed by its antithesis, expressivity, so that the two merge and become indistinguishable.

For example: My instrumentality gives a hardness and a crispness to my expressivity, which in turn gives a softness and a resilience to my instrumentality, and on and on in a continual process of dialectical becomingness. Each infuses and transforms the other. This results in a continual transcending of one opposition by the other, in a continual struggle of the two for change and equilibrium. We have in Synthesism a call for something other than a simple addition process whereby instrumental and expressive activities are performed separately, one after the other. On the contrary, in the Synthesist view instrumentality and expressivity abolish one another in coming together. The transcendence of one by the other is something altogether different from the two placed side by side in an either/or capacity.

SYNTHESISM IN THE EVERYDAY WORLD

What is the Synthesist personality like? Synthesist feminists say that at present she is one of the few "together" people in society. (In the future all people will be like this, they add.) She is one whose warmth infuses her drive and whose strength gives substance to her gentleness. She has reconciled the two opposites in such a way as to inspire and yet soothe those around her. Her instrumental-expressive unity is so rare and so striking that her presence both disturbs and exhilarates. She avoids the excesses of both extremes.

To those who would say that this personality description is wishful thinking, the Synthesist feminist would reply that a few concrete models can establish the credibility of the S-type. They mention instances where many of us may have experienced moments of synthesis; for example, in a crisis our powers of compassion and productivity may fuse so that either transforms the other. Or a unity of emotions and intelligence may take place in a time of terror. For example, some kidnap victims attest to a coming together of their sense and reasoning capabilities, which saved them from disaster. Or a fusion of head and heart are possible in sexual love, at such moments as those in which concentration on self and other is indistinguishable. Or synthesis may occur in collective work—be it political, religious or community-based—when the distinctions between self-interest and collective-interest are overcome, and a separate public-me and private-me has no meaning.

Synthesism and Charisma

Synthesist feminists often point to the charismatic leader as a model of Synthesism. Sociologists describe this leader as one who exudes a special grace or charisma.[3] The charismatic presence makes any situation a special one. The interplay between leader and followers is highly charged emotionally, yet the followers are committed intellectually to getting done whatever work is called for by the leader. Thus the charismatic leader fuses the instrumental and the expressive; he or she pushes the work ahead and at the same time makes people feel good. The instrumental-expressive dichotomy that many sociologists point to in studies of leadership in small groups is overcome by the charismatic leader.

Most sociologists use the term charisma to refer to extraordinary people (e.g., Jesus Christ, Ghandi, Hitler, John F. Kennedy, Martin Luther King, Eleanor Roosevelt). Sociologists also describe charismatic authority as antithetical to everyday life and thus unable to be incorporated into the institutional framework. The logic here is that something extraordinary cannot become routinized; if it were, the charisma would vanish and be replaced by other forms of authority.

Contrary to the sociologists' interpretation of charisma as out of the ordinary, anti-everyday, and characteristic of a handful of special people, Synthesism holds that all people can and will become charismatic in the Synthesist Utopia. They also say that the extraordinary and the everyday dichotomy will be overcome through a dialectical unity. Synthesist feminists point out that charismatic leadership can be found in ordinary settings; examples would include teachers who are loved by their students; yet manage to bring forth creative work; doctors whose devotion to their patients' needs gives fullness to necessary medical skills; lawyers whose personal involvement in their clients' lives infuses and enhances legal skills; and bosses who can make instrumental demands because of the emotional tie that exists with their employees. Further, the growing popularity of the charismatic (Synthesist) type in the media is cited by Synthesist feminists to refute the charge that it is unthinkable to fuse emotional and rational orientations. More and more television dramas involve charismatic (or Synthesist) types: Dr. Marcus Welby, lawyer Kate McShane, high school teacher Lucas Tanner, policeman Columbo, boss Lou Grant, and career woman Mary Richards are but a few of these characters.

Synthesism and Black Women

Synthesist feminists point to black women as possible models of Synthesism. For the worst reasons, slavery and racism, the black woman was forced to develop her instrumentality while holding on to her expressivity. The black man was considered a threat to white society, so jobs were nearly impossible for him to get, either in small towns or large cities. The black woman had to earn a living, or failing that, to apply for welfare. She could move more freely through white society than black males could. At the same time the black woman had to retain her expressivity, in part so that she, too, did not become a threat to white society, but mostly because she was the one who raised children, nurtured them, and gave them the support to carry on in the face of adversity. She had the key role in child rearing as the two-parent family structure disintegrated for many black people in a racist society. The black woman's expressivity also resulted from her socialization into the female role as defined until recently in both the black and the white community.

Many black women keep their instrumental and expressive behavior separated in dualistic fashion, some with a sense of being well-rounded, others feeling schizophrenic.[4] But black women who manage to attain Synthesis emerge from suffering and oppression with a stamina that infuses gentleness, with a spine that gives shape to resilience, and with a sensuousness that softens efficiency.

Synthesism and Single Parents

Another possible model of Synthesis used by S-type feminists is the single parent. Like black women, single parents (male or female) are often required to exercise their instrumental and expressive selves. Children have to be provided for, economically and emotionally. Conservative sociologists still claim it is bad for children not to have two parents to play out the gender-connected roles of instrumentality and expressivity—an instrumental father and an expressive mother. Because these sociologists are dualists, they assume that one parent cannot fill both roles, that instrumental and expressive responsibilities are antithetical and clear-cut specialization is needed if the family is not to go under. This once popular way of looking at the family is no longer dominant. With more families emerging through divorce as one-parent families, the stigma on the single parent has all but disappeared.

Single parents are as apt to be dualists as they are Synthesists, but their children have different role models from children in a conventional two-parent household. Consider this scenario: Your mother is your only parent, so you do not share with children of more conventional families the assumption that females are specialists in expressive activities. Were that the case, your parent and you would likely starve or be evicted. As your one parent must make do instrumentally and expressively, you get to see one adult performing both kinds of activities, without reference to gender appropriateness. Granted, you still are indoctrinated by the larger society, which says that women cannot be instrumentally adequate, that women need to be rescued from instrumental problems by men (whether to change a tire, pick out a detergent, fix a leaky faucet, or keep the boss in line). The shining knight dream-myth hangs on in the culture. But even though you may succumb to cultural pressures to define women as expressive and males as instrumental, your family life will affect your self-image. If it is a happy family life, you will be more likely than a child from a conventional dualized family to experience a merge of instrumental and expressive orientations.

HUMAN NATURE IN SYNTHESISM

Human nature is a dialectical unity of opposites. In a natural state male and female are transcended in "human." Both sexes share the same existential conditions. Synthesist feminists often quote Simone de Beauvoir's insistence that humanity is one:

The fact that we are human beings is infinitely more important than all the peculiarities that distinguish human beings from one another. . . . In both sexes is played out the same drama of the flesh and the spirit, of finitude and transcendence; both are gnawed away by time and laid in wait for by death, they have the same essential need for one another; and they gain from their liberty the same glory.[5]

Synthesism says that male-female duality has violated the wholeness of human nature, splitting humans into half-people. Society has denied the total humanity of all people, so they end up trying to experience their lost selves through the "opposite" sex. One feminist describes the process this way:

He is playing masculine. She is playing feminine.

He is playing masculine *because* she is playing feminine. She is playing feminine *because* he is playing masculine. . . .

If he were not playing masculine, he might well be more feminine than she is—except when she is playing very feminine. If she were not playing feminine, she might well be more masculine than he is—except when he is playing very masculine.

So he plays harder. And she plays—softer. . . .

He desires her for her femininity which is *his* femininity, but which he can never lay claim to. She admires him for his masculinity which is *her* masculinity, but which she can never lay claim to. Since he may only love his own femity in her, he envies her her femininity. Since she may only love her own masculinity in him, she envies him his masculinity.

The envy poisons their love.

He, coveting her unattainable femininity, decides to punish her. She, coveting his unattainable masculinity, decides to punish him. He denigrates her femininity—which he is supposed to desire and which he really envies—and becomes more aggressively masculine. She feigns disgust at his masculinity—which she is supposed to admire and which she really envies—and becomes more fastidiously feminine. He is becoming less and less what he wants to be. She is becoming less and less what she wants to be. But now he is more manly than ever, and she is more womanly than ever. . . .

So far, it has all been very symmetrical. But we have left one thing out.

The world belongs to what his masculinity has become. The reward for what her femininity has become is only the security which his power can bestow upon her. . . .

She is stifling under the triviality of her femininity. The world is groaning beneath the terrors of his masculinity. . . .[6]

Thus polarization, envy, resentment, denigration, and power imbalances are the legacy of sex duality.

People try to recover their lost half by bonding with the opposite sex, but they end up fearing and hating their opposites, resentful of their otherness. The war of the sexes is really the war of the self:

In these combats where they [male and female] confront one another, it is really against the self that each struggles, projecting onto the partner that part of the self which is repudiated; instead of living out the ambiguities of their situation, each tries to make the other bear the abjection and tries to reserve the honor for the self.[7]

Synthesist feminists say sexual dualism brutalizes males and females, but women suffer more because they are at the powerless, trivialized bottom of the hierarchy. Males put up with alienation from self and from the opposite sex just as females do. But females also are made to feel inferior and treated in a subservient way. In addition to the scorn opposite halves feel toward one another, females are feared because they encapsulate the dreaded expressivity everyone considers inferior:

Man is concerned with the effort to appear male, important, superior; he pretends so as to get pretense in return; he, too, is aggressive, uneasy; he feels hostility for women because he is afraid of the personage, the image with which he identifies himself. What time and strength he squanders in liquidating, sublimating, transferring complexes in talking about women, in seducing them, in fearing them! He would be liberated himself in their liberation. But this is precisely what he dreads. And so he obstinately persists in the mystifications intended to keep woman in her chains.[8]

Males need liberation, too, says Synthesism, but their power and privilege mystify their oppression and keep them from seeking a change in the status quo.

SYNTHESISM AND ANDROGYNY

The concept of androgyny (from the Greek *andros* 'male' and *gynos* 'female') is frequently used by Synthesist feminists to refer to the human personality they consider ideal. The term is in some ways unfortunate because it reintroduces the confusion about the link between gender and behavior that most feminists wish to eliminate. Instrumental behavior is not inherently male, nor is expressivity essentially female, but when S-types speak about fusing the two polarities of behavior, the term they use, androgyny, is gender-based.

What is meant by androgyny in Synthesism? In the words of one feminist:

> . . . androgyny is visionary—it's not an absolute or final goal, but it is a view of how life could be better, freer, more whole. It's a vision of a sex-roleless society, comparable in utopianism to a classless society. We see no clear way to get there, except that it seems to involve some kind of dialectical process where the best of the traditional male role and the best of the traditional female role synthesize into a new entity, a new wholeness.[9]

Here again are the themes that humanity is a totality and that opposing behavioral traits will be brought together in a dialectical unity. Although the term androgyny is not used in the following quote, it captures this notion of wholeness well:

> I am beginning to have a sense of myself in my new identity. From the "half-person" I felt in my marriage, I am now beginning to fill in that other half, not with another person but with myself. I can be both a giver and a taker, logical and spiritual, aesthetic and practical, strong and vulnerable. I realize that no traits are mutually exclusive. I am beginning to feel whole within myself. It is beginning to fall into place. All of it.[10]

In the quote that follows, "androgynous" describes the kind of person who will overcome sexual dualism:

> Some of the most interesting poems in the book are those in which [Adrienne] Rich imagines an androgynous creature who transcends conventional maleness and conventional femaleness and walks through the city like a stranger. . . . This stranger-poet-survivor carries "a book of myths" in which her/his "names do not appear." These are the old myths of patriarchy, the myths that split male and female irreconcilably into two warring factions, the myths that perpetuate the battle between the sexes. Implicit in Rich's image of the androgyne is the idea that we must write new myths, create new definitions of humanity which will not glorify this angry chasm but heal it.[11]

Some people assume that androgyny (i.e., synthesis) would blur physical distinctions between males and females (desexualization) or entail a combination of male and female features (a kind of hermaphroditism). Most Synthesists deny that this is what they mean by androgyny. The union of instrumental and expressive characteristics will not be reduced to physical synthesis. They would agree with the following concrete illustrations of androgyny only if the closing sentence on physical features was removed:

> Was it, perhaps, not just that they [Brando and Garbo] dom-

inated members of the opposite sex, but that they contained ingredients of the other sex within them; was it not their androgyny, as much as their brilliance, that made their partners superfluous?

This is not unusual. Certain stars, like certain people, seem to reconcile sexual opposites. Chaplin and Mae West, Dietrich and Mick Jagger, are only the most obvious ones. And Garbo and Brando. They understand, intuitively, what it is to be "feminine" and "masculine," and they explore these qualities while remaining just within the boundaries of their sex, i.e., without being "gay" or "butch." Chaplin can be delicate, flirtatious, and coy, while Mae West is never less than forthright. Garbo is fearless in the transactions of love, while Brando hesitates in vulnerable self-defense. He is more sensitive than the women he loves, while Garbo makes the men to whom she devotes herself look indecisive and weak. Physically, too, they unite or borrow opposite sexual characteristics.[12]

Synthesism's goal is a sex-roleless totality. What, then, would be the basis for male-female relationships if each individual enjoys an instrumental-expressive wholeness? What of the adage that opposites attract? Synthesists reply that when males and females no longer need to seek completion through the opposite sex, they can relate to one another in healthy ways. Synthesism is nonetheless tolerant of a variety of options for human sexuality. Asexuality, bisexuality, and homosexuality seem likely to appear in their Utopia, along with heterosexuality. But these notions as they are now understood will disappear because they are founded on dualistic premises about human nature. Sexuality is a human trait to S-types, not a trait of "males" and "females":

. . . in the primary sexual response of the body, there is no differentiation between man or woman; there is no "man," there is no "woman" (mental images), just a shared organism responding to touch, smell, taste, sound. The sexual response can then be seen as one part of the species' total response to and participation in the environment. We sense the world

with our sensitive bodies as an ever-changing flow of relationships in which we move and partake.[13]

To the charge that Synthesis and androgyny mean that everybody will be alike, and bored, S-type feminists reply:

> Androgyny doesn't mean that everyone will be alike; actually
> it should lead to more variety. It means that everyone won't
> be rigidly polarized. It should lead to more equality, better
> communication, fewer power plays, and more love—therefore,
> ultimately, better sex.[14]

The reason Synthesis will lead to greater variety among human
beings than exists at present is that every human being will fuse the
emotional-rational contradiction in a unique way:

> This process [of synthesis] will be experientially different for
> each individual because each of us has a unique split between
> what we experience in ourselves as masculine and feminine
> (depending on different real-life models, cultural values, and
> personal inclinations). Different people will emphasize differ-
> ent aspects of the process: for some women androgyny means
> getting more in touch with their "masculine" side, for some it
> means getting in touch with their "feminine" side, and for some
> it's affirming both sides instead of feeling shame about one or
> the other.[15]

Mary Daly's sentiments summarize what feminists of this ideal type
see in Synthesism:

> By becoming whole persons women can generate a counter-
> force to the stereotype of the leader, challenging the artificial
> polarization of human characteristics into sex-role identifica-
> tion. . . . The becoming of androgynous human persons implies
> a radical change in the fabric of human consciousness and in
> styles of behavior.[16]

SYNTHESIS AND DUALISM

Being feminist, Synthesis's primary concern is with sexual dualism. But it regards any manifestation of dualism as abominable:

> Masculine/feminine is just one of such polarities among many, including body/mind, organism/environment, plant/animal, good/evil, black/white, feeling/intellect, passive/active, sane/insane, living/dead. Such language hardens what is in reality a continuum and a unity into separate mental images always in opposition to one another.[17]

Some blame males for dualism:

> Masculine society has insisted on seeing in sexuality that same sense of conflict and competition that it has imposed upon its relation to the planet as a whole. From the bedroom to the board room to the international conference table, separateness, differentiation, opposition, exclusion, antithesis have been the cause and goal of the male politics of power. Human characteristics belonging to the entire species have been crystallized out of the living flow of human experience and made into either/or categories. This male habit of setting up boundary lines between imagined polarities has been the impetus for untold hatred and destruction.[18]

Others see dualism as endemic to modern capitalist society. But, whatever the cause, polarization is at the root of social malaise. Oppression and domination are inherent in dualism:

> All oppression takes the form of domination and subservience, submission and control; men over women, whites over blacks, bosses over workers, the U.S. over the Third World. Those in positions of power see others not as humans but as objects to be used. Hierarchy is established to keep us in line so that

we never see others as our equals, as sisters and brothers, but as either above or below us. Power is concentrated in the hands of a few elite rulers while the people fight among themselves to grab what little power they can instead of seeing that freedom comes in destroying power, domination, hierarchy and elitism.[19]

Synthesists say that all forms of dualism lead to hierarchy and then to domination of one "half" by the other. Every duality must be struggled with so that genuine unity can occur within and between persons. The following quote about social-class antagonisms within feminism reflects yet another way in which polarization creates disunity:

> . . . when I feel real class antagonism from my middle class sisters, I start seeing things totally in class terms. I start defining a class war and lose sight of any feminine consciousness I have. It's a dichotomy I know is not real but appears because we have not dealt with class in any but a superficial way. Somehow that dichotomy for me has to be broken and the class differences among us have to be dealt with, struggled with, so that our oneness is real, not just the result of ignoring the parts that don't fit.[20]

The classless society is a goal of every Synthesist. Synthesism aims at a unity of life that will overcome all role fragmentations. Then there will be no "males" or "females," no "husbands" or "wives," no "rich" or "poor," no "children" or "adults"—at least as these roles are understood now. There will be only unified selves.

THE SYNTHESIST UTOPIA

The social program in Synthesism can be summarized by the slogan "Reunite Us." All people will be made whole in the simultaneous fusion of instrumentality and expressivity. Relationships between males and females will be open and wholesome; freed from the fear and contempt built into sexual dualism. With the elimination of dualism, hierarchy and domination will collapse. Gone too will be fragmented, rigid roles. People will relate to the world as an all-at-once totality, not as a series of parts strung together sequentially.

One would not restrict subjective experience to such identity labels as "wife," "mother," "worker," or "friend," but would experience personhood in all these things in all contexts. For example, the student-teacher role pair would no longer exist in its present form. If I had formerly thought of myself as "teacher" in a classroom setting, in the Synthesist Utopia I would be teacher and student simultaneously, learning while sharing my knowledge and experience with others who would be doing the same thing. The "classroom" would also vanish. There would, of course, be rooms in which knowledge could be shared, but many other activities would also go on here, following the model of some open classrooms.

Another central thing the Synthesists look forward to is the coming together of public and private selves and institutions. Gone would be the chasm between work and home life. It would be a regular thing to find children in the "workplace." While not precisely Synthesist, a sense of this was foreshadowed when *Ms.* magazine devoted an issue to the idea of children at the office. The central article was about Alix, the daughter of one of the staffers, who began her career at the *Ms.* editorial offices at the age of one month. Reactions to her presence were favorable. As one staff member said:

> If I had a child, I'd definitely bring her into the office. Why not? Alix doesn't disrupt work—if people stop to play with her, they just work later. That's the way the whole office works, anyway. Alix reminds you that you're people. You're rushing around like a maniac, like everyone else in New York City, and then you see Alix and just slow up for a minute and become human again.[21]

This particular reply is not derived from a Synthesist world-view. Dualism comes through in the notion that working and playing are separate activities; one must stop one to start the other. The Synthesist flavor is clearly discernible in the response of another staffer:

> It's a very human thing to have a child around. You don't keep your two lives separate: your family life here, with warmth and caring, and your business life over there, strictly without those elements. Having a child in the office makes you realize that both areas of your life can go on at the same time, that you don't have to shut off whole areas of experience from morning till night.[22]

But Synthesism has a much more drastic plan for social change than bringing children to the office. S-types, in fact, would have no "offices." No specialized place for conducting "business" would exist in this Utopia. Images of "me-at-work" (productive and instrumental) and "me-at-home" (relaxed, expressive) would fuse into "me-anywhere." There would be no more parceling of self into this or that specialized role. The whole conception of a division of labor as we now experience it would be abolished. The Synthesist worldview resembles what Marx had in mind for utopian communism:

> . . . in communist society, where nobody has one exclusive sphere of activity but each can become accomplished in any branch he wishes, society regulates the general production and thus makes it possible for me to do one thing today and another tomorrow, to hunt in the morning, fish in the afternoon, rear cattle in the evening, criticize after dinner, just as I have a mind, without ever becoming hunter, fisherman, shepherd, or critic.[23]

In Marx's model there is some sense that activity would be performed sequentially, since all activity mentioned is time-bound. But one's identity does not get frozen on some branch of the division of labor. I may rear cattle, but this act does not label me "cattle-rearer" and prevent me from living my productive life in other terms. Synthesism agrees with the Marxian thesis that rigidified role fragmentations (occupational, sexual, age-based, etc.) are tied to the economic division of labor in a reciprocal way. If one is eliminated, the other will fall, too. The future hoped for by Synthesism will be one with no strict economic division of labor, no divisions of sex, race, age, class, or ethnicity. It will be a society that has overcome sexism, classism, racism, and and agism.

Most work will be done in collective settings in order to bring about the highest individual creativity. The excitement engendered by this overcoming of the self-communal dichotomy is caught in the following description:

> It's so exciting to create something collectively. I used to write poetry when I was seventeen and then I stopped. I'm feeling creative like I did then, but it's also very different because what is being created now is an expression of our group spirit. The ideas and images are by us all, and so the voices have a totally different richness and power.[24]

The merge of feeling with functionality is also best accomplished in a collective setting:

> . . . the skit really happened to us organically. No one knew from the beginning what would come out—the scenario wasn't given. I think that we are all shocked in a sense at how our involvement with each other in the project has actually produced something this good! . . . the way we were moving was really changed; the sounds more subtly together with the movement; the movements more complex and the whole development from one individual to another far more communicative and organic. Though I had been feeling more together about the women, I was surprised at how clearly it showed in the way we worked.[25]

Synthesists point out that people already have had glimpses of a world where the work-play fusion is a reality. Painting parties, grocery shopping with friends, cooking communally, working with friends on political programs—these activities hint at the Synthesist future.

PHILOSOPHICAL ASSUMPTIONS

Like Expressivism, Synthesism rejects the modern social world. Both share with Instrumentalism the idea that human beings are essentially context-free (i.e., one's humanity exists apart from one's ascribed status) and that gender has nothing to do with behavior and temperament. All three ideal types assume that the good society can be brought about, that society can be changed if enough energy and commitment are applied to the project. These assumptions are modern philosophical ones, ideas that serve as part of the technocratic foundation. That Expressivism and Synthesism are derived from modern premises yet stand in opposition to the modern, technological world must be emphasized.

Even though derived from modern premises, Synthesism strikes at the roots of technocracy and capitalism in its repudiation of dualized selves and social institutions. In advocating an end to the present division of labor, in refusing to accept the necessity of role fragmentation and role distance, and in denying the need for a public-private split, Synthesism clashes head-on with the modern world.

Synthesism differs from Instrumentalism and Expressivism because it has a definite conception of human nature. Instrumentalists and Expressivists see human nature as plastic, as able to be molded in any number of ways, depending on available social-conditioning devices. But Synthesists see human nature as a unity of oppositions that is in continual dialectical becomingness. People are viewed as having an essential wholeness that exists beneath, and often in spite of, attempts to fragment it. For Synthesism, basic human nature suffers if the wrong social structures surround it. Human nature is not the predictable by-product of given social structures. So the Synthesists' social program is not one of providing structures that will fashion human nature into a desired shape, but one of taking away structures that pervert authentic human nature. Synthesism's goal is an almost total destructuring of society by eliminating divisions and specializations.

NOTES

1. Robert K. Merton and Elinor Barber, "Sociological Ambivalence," in *Sociological Theory, Values and Sociocultural Change,* ed. Edward A. Tiryakian (New York: Harper Torchbooks, 1967), pp. 91–120.

2. Ibid., p. 96. Emphasis added.

3. Cf. Max Weber, *The Theory of Social and Economic Organization,* ed. Talcott Parsons (New York: Free Press, 1964), pp. 358 ff.; and Max Weber, *From Max Weber,* ed. Hans Gerth and C. Wright Mills (New York: Oxford University Press, 1958), pp. 247 ff.

4. Black women who keep instrumentality and expressivity dualized are most likely in the ranks of those seeking to redefine the black woman's role as one of expressivity alone. But one factor must be kept in mind: the work that most black women get is difficult and low-paying, far from the heights of instrumental expression. The goal of staying home, caring for husband, children, and house, would be attractive to anyone in oppressive work conditions.

5. Simone de Beauvoir, *The Second Sex,* trans. and ed. H. M. Parshley (New York: Bantam, 1961), pp. 685–86.

6. Betty Roszak, "The Human Continuum," in *Masculine/Feminine,* ed. Betty Roszak and Theodore Roszak (New York: Harper & Row, 1969), p. 304.

7. de Beauvoir, *The Second Sex,* p. 685.

8. Ibid., p. 677.

9. Irene Reville and Margaret Blanchard, "The Controversy over Androgyny," *Women, A Journal of Liberation* 4 (Winter 1974): 58.

10. Jan Fuller, *Space: The Scrapbook of My Divorce* (Greenwich, Conn.: Fawcett, 1975), p. 99.

11. Erica Jong, "Visionary Anger," a review of Adrienne Rich's *Diving into the Wreck: Poems 1971–72, Ms.,* July 1973, p. 34.

12. Molly Haskell, "The Woman in the 'All-Man' Legend," *Village Voice*, 21 June 1973, p. 85.

13. Betty Roszak, "The Human Continuum," p. 305.

14. Reville and Blanchard, "The Controversy over Androgyny, p. 59.

15. Ibid., p. 58.

16. Mary Daly, *Beyond God the Father* (Boston: Beacon Press, 1973), p. 15.

17. Betty Roszak, "The Human Continuum," p. 304.

18. Ibid.

19. Anonymous, "International Sisterhood," *RAT*, no. 18 (12–29 January 1971): 9.

20. Anonymous, "Starting to Think About Class," *RAT*, no. 24 (2 August 1971): 16.

21. Anonymous, "Alix at Ms." *Ms.* 3 (March 1975): 55.

22. Ibid., p. 94.

23. Karl Marx and Friedrich Engels, *Basic Writings on Politics and Philosophy*, ed. Lewis Feuer (Garden City, N.Y.: Doubleday, 1959), p. 254.

24. Anonymous, "Our Hands–Our Feet–Our Bodies–Our Minds Are Tools for Social Change," *RAT*, no. 24 (2 August 1971): 13.

25. Ibid.

POLARISM

Polarism, the most complicated of the four feminist ideal types, is a composite of themes and subthemes that center around the idea that males and females are polar opposites. Polarists say that sex differences in personality and outlook stem from precultural sources. They believe in an inherent difference between females and males, regardless of their culture. This innate sex difference corresponds with the instrumental-expressive dichotomy. Males and females are separate subspecies of humanity specialized along instrumental and expressive paths. But this sounds exactly like the sexist ideology feminists reject. Why, then, is Polarism a feminist ideal type?

Above all, Polarism must be considered feminist because feminists say these things themselves or quote with approval those who see the world through Polarist lenses.[1] All four ideal types presented in this book are drawn from feminist thought; the types are not merely interesting logical possibilities.[2] P-type feminists (Polarists) assume that women's liberation from sexist oppression can be achieved the Polarist way. Like the three other ideal types, Polarism is not the exclusive preserve of a special clique in feminism. All feminists at one time or another voice themes belonging to all four ideal types. As an ideal type, Polarism embodies a composite of themes against which the ideas of concrete feminists might be compared; this composite describes no particular women in the movement.

Second, Polarism is not the same old sexist line. It takes the position that the instrumentality and expressivity males and females act out in their present sex roles are distorted forms. True femaleness and true maleness are hidden beneath today's sex roles and must be rediscovered and allowed to flower without social interference. For Polarism, the instrumental-expressive dichotomy is identical with the male-female one only if we remember that the versions of the two pairs we see today are shams.

What complicates Polarism are its subthemes. Three major sets of subthemes are worthy of note.

1. The origin of male-female dualism. The dominant explanation for female-male differences has a physical-biological base. Such things as embryology, chromosomes, hormones, biochemistry, and anatomy are mentioned. But there exists another way of looking at sexual dualism. Some Polarists eschew biology and talk about ontology (the metaphysical study of the nature of being) as the source of the innate male-female difference. References to "yin and yang" forces in the universe might also further the argument feminists use in explaining the origin of the female and male principles.[3]

2. The power relationship between the sexes. Some Polarists see sexual dualism in

hierarchical terms with females superior to males; others use equalitarian premises—females and males are different but equal.
3. The question of male-female relationships. Some Polarists advocate the segregation of males and females so that members of each sex can lead separate and independent lives. Others favor integration of the sexes so that, as polar opposites, males and females will complement one another.

These subthemes—biological or ontological, hierarchical or equalitarian, and segregation or integration—are combined in a number of ways by Polarist feminists, making it difficult to describe this ideal type adequately. This chapter focuses on biological and hierarchical Polarism because these subthemes were dominant in the research on P-types.

THE POLARIST WORLD-VIEW

Polarism strongly disagrees with the other ideal types when they say that males and females are equivalent and interchangeable beings. Polarists also reject any attempt to create a unisexual world. P-type feminists enthusiastically cite statements such as:

... the assumption is debatable . . . that qualities of masculinity and femininity are lightly donned, attributable only to cultural reward and punishment. It will be my thesis that differences between the sexes have early genetic origins and that these constitutional dispositions are responded to differentially by a particular culture according to the values of that culture. . . .

It is clear that parents and the general culture reinforce behaviors appropriate to one sex or the other. But Erikson suggests that there is a body contribution to sexual identity which is normal and independent of pressure and reward. . . . In addition to societal reinforcement of sex-role behavior, physical states directly affect psychological states, and there are different physical states in the two sexes.[4]

The woman quoted above is Judith Bardwick, a contemporary feminist psychologist who has taken the position that traditional sex roles must be redefined, but that sex differences have biological roots that cannot be ignored. The idea that different bodies lead to different psychological development is a key theme in Polarism.

Polarist feminists insist that female biology is central in understanding women. Jane Alpert, probably the best known of the Polarist feminists, says:

> For centuries feminists have asserted that the essential difference between women and men does not lie in biology but rather in the roles that patriarchal societies (men) have required each sex to play. The motivation for this assertion is obvious: women's biology has always been used to justify women's oppression. . . . However, a flaw in this feminist analysis has persisted: *it contradicts our felt experience of the biological difference between the sexes as one of immense significance.* . . . The unique consciousness or sensibility of women, the particular attributes that set feminist art apart, and a compelling line of research now being pursued by feminist anthropologists, all point to the idea that *female biology is the basis of women's powers.* Biology is hence the source and not the enemy of feminist revolution.[5]

Alpert, at one time involved in New Left politics (she calls herself a former "New Left politico"[6]), converted to radical feminism while in the New Left underground. She jumped bail in 1970 after being convicted of conspiracy to bomb military and war-related corporate buildings. In spring 1973 Alpert sent her now famous "Letter from the Underground" and an article, "Mother-Right," to various aboveground feminist sources including *Ms., Off Our Backs,* and radio station WBAI's Nanette Rainone. In November 1974 Alpert surrendered to the FBI. Her attorney's statement that she had "fully cooperated" with the government [7] set off a controversy within the feminist movement that is still raging.[8] After her surrender, Alpert reaffirmed her belief that feminism rests ultimately on a biological basis:

> In the passage of these two years, I have become more sure of what I said in "Mother Right" in affirming the biological differences between men and women and affirming the biological basis of feminism. It reclaims ancient roots that we women have and projects them in a futuristic, not reactionary, way.[9]

For Alpert, as well as for many other Polarists, the capacity to bear children is the biological common denominator among women and at the heart of the "female principle":

> It seems to me that the power of the new feminist culture, the powers that were attributed to the ancient matriarchies (considered either as historical fact or as mythic archetypes), and the inner power with which many women are beginning to feel in touch and which is the soul of feminist art, may all arise from the same source. That source is none other than female biology: the *capacity* to bear and nurture children. It is conceivable that the intrinsic *biological* connection between mother and embryo or mother and infant gives rise to those *psychological* qualities which have always been linked with women, both in ancient lore and modern behavioral science. Motherhood must be understood here as a potential which is imprinted in the genes of every woman; as such it makes no difference to this analysis of femaleness whether a woman ever has borne, or ever will bear, a child.[10]

Potential for maternity and the qualities it gives rise to are the source of the female essence. Males and females are not interchangeable creatures. Another version of the idea that female nature is based in the mother-child bond uses "instincts" as the biological common denominator: *RAT* published the following excerpt:

Nor do I need to pray for courage to join a riot, throw stones, scratch faces, tear clothes, or anything else that comes along in the course of defending my ideals. When driven to despair of the use of milder methods—despair of argument with a wolf or moral suasion with a snake—we start in fighting, nerved and spurred to it by one of the *oldest instincts in the world: defense of our offspring of body and brain.* The instinct has never changed, and may Heaven defend us from the *woman who isn't womanly enough* to stand up and fight, regardless of self-interest, for the thing she loves! The woman who isn't willing to isn't a woman at all, she's only an apology in petticoats. Realizing this now, I frankly glory in being "*a creature of instinct.*" It makes me feel consciously allied, as I never did before, with the whole living world, one with its primal forces, partaker of its progress, assistant creator of its coming achievements.[11]

THE IDEAL POLARIST FEMALE

The female nature is beautiful in the Polarist view—rich, mysterious, aligned with primal forces, and flowing from the wellspring of existence. The Polarist resembles the Expressivist here: both see females as the personification of Expressivity. (Yet the two are different because Expressivism extends the scenario to males, which Polarism does not.)

Much of what Polarism uses to describe the female it considers ideal traces back to early theory on matriarchies. For example, Bachofen's *Mother Right*, published in 1861, depicted the matriarchal society as one that stressed love and compassion rather than the anxiety and submissiveness common to patriarchal society. Speaking of the mother-child relationship, he said it

> . . . stands at the origin of all culture, of every virtue, of every nobler aspect of existence . . . it operates in a world of violence as the divine principle of love, of union, of peace. Raising her young, the woman learns earlier than the man to extend her

loving care beyond the limits of the ego to another creature, and to direct whatever gift of invention she possesses to the preservation and improvement of this other's existence. Woman at this stage is the repository of all culture, of all benevolence, of all devotion, of all concern for the living and grief for the dead. Yet the love that arises from motherhood is not only more intense, but also more universal. . . . The idea of motherhood produces a sense of universal fraternity among all men, which dies with the development of paternity. . . . Every woman's womb, the mortal image of the earth mother Demeter, will give brothers and sisters to the children of every other woman. . . .[12]

In addition to universal love, motherhood gives women a pacifist outlook and enormous capacity for compassion:

. . . [the universal love of motherhood] is the basis of the universal freedom and equality so frequent among matriarchal peoples, of their hospitality, and of their aversion to restriction of all sort. . . . And in it is rooted the admirable sense of kinship and [fellow feeling] which knows no barriers or dividing lines and embraces all members of a nation alike. Matriarchal states were particularly famed for their freedom from intestine strife and conflict. . . . The matriarchal peoples—and this is no less characteristic—assigned special culpability to the physical injury of one's fellow men or even of animals. . . . An air of tender humanity, discernible even in the facial expression of Egyptian statuary, permeates the culture of the matriarchal world.[13]

All the qualities Bachofen tied in with motherhood—universal and intensive love, compassion, pacifism, tenderness, equalitarianism —can be found in Polarism's image of the authentic female. A contemporary version of how motherhood shapes female nature would go something like this:

. . . feminist culture is based on what is best and strongest in women, and as we begin to define ourselves as women, the qualities coming to the fore are the same ones a mother projects in the best kind of nurturing relationship to a child: empathy, intuitiveness, adaptability, awareness of growth as a process rather than as goal-ended, inventiveness, protective feelings toward others, and a capacity to respond emotionally as well as rationally.[14]

This ideal female image—tender, empathic, intuitive, compassionate, inventive, protective, nurturant—harks back to images of earth mothers, goddesses, and ancient matriarchs.

The ideal female is rarely seen today, say the Polarists. This is why women need liberation from the imprisonment of their false roles. Instead of having women who are in touch with their inborn natures, we have silly, fragile cartoon characters. Genuine feminine expressivity is reduced to Doris Day and Raquel Welch types; the mother is seen as possessive, overprotective, and masochistic. P-type feminists often quote Erich Fromm. Echoing Bachofen's characterization of matriarchal society, Fromm says:

The matricentric complex . . . is characterized by a feeling of optimistic trust in mother's unconditional love, far fewer guilt feelings, a far weaker superego, and a greater capacity for pleasure and happiness. Along with these traits there also develops the ideal of motherly compassion and love for the weak and others in need of help.[15]

In Fromm's view, this positive image of the mother is distorted in today's patricentric society:

Basically, this society only knows about courage and heroism on the part of the man (in whom these qualities are really tinged with a large dose of narcissism). The image of the mother, on the other hand, has been a distorted one of sentimentality and weakness. In place of unconditional motherly love, which embraces not only one's own children but all children and all human beings, we find the specifically bourgeois sentiment of possessiveness injected into mother image.[16]

Polarism considers today's mothers far from beautiful because of the roles imposed on them. Instead of being nurturant, they smother. Their passion is turned into sentimentality, and anger becomes crankiness. Mothers are transformed into martyrs, bitches, nags, or whiners. The biological connection to woman's true self is buried under layers of cultural trappings:

> Biology alone is in no way an adequate explanation of what it is to be female. Women have been exploited in our society for at least five thousand years and female powers have been correspondingly weakened and frustrated. The effects of powerlessness on us are nowhere more obvious than in contemporary motherhood. In the patriarchy, we do not rise to a position of special esteem and authority when we have children. On the contrary, we are denied even the few options for meaningful participation in society that are available to us as childless women. We react to this powerlessness in a myriad of negative ways, ranging from overpossessiveness of our children (as in the hypertense Jewish-mother stereotype) to utter self-abnegation (as in the Madonna image) to child-murder (as in the myth of Medea).[17]

Some Polarists see the trivialization of females and the contamination of their expressivity as stemming from males:

> Ever since man first abrogated to himself the role of god on earth and proclaimed himself the master of woman, he has sought to mold her to his desires; and, as Mill says, by clipping here and watering there, by first freezing and then burning off unwanted growth, "he has cultivated woman for the benefit and pleasure of her master; and now he indolently believes that the tree grows of itself in the way that he has made it grow." And so, like the majestic mountain pine, potted and pruned to grotesque dwarfism by a ruthless gardener, the stunted roots and branches of woman's essential being struggle to be free again, to know once more the boundless sky and unrestricting earth of her native peak.[18]

Other Polarists attribute the loss of true femaleness to a more abstract patriarchalism. But no matter the source, the effects on females are the same:

> Men insist that they don't mind women succeeding so long as they retain their "femininity." Yet the qualities that men consider "feminine"—timidity, submissiveness, obedience, silliness, and self-debasement—are the very qualities best guaranteed to assure the defeat of even the most gifted aspirant. And what is this vaunted "femininity"? To the masculinists of both sexes, "femininity" implies all that *men* have built into the female image in the past few centuries: weakness, imbecility, dependence, masochism, unrealiability, and a certain "babydoll" sexuality that is actually only a projection of male dreams. To the feminist of both sexes, femininity is synonymous with the eternal female principle, connoting strength, integrity, wisdom, justice, dependability, and a psychic power foreign and therefore dangerous to the plodding masculinists of both sexes.[19]

Today's woman is seen by Polarism as trivial, possessive, hypertense, self-abnegating, silly, weak, imbecilic, and masochistic—in short, the embodiment of corrupted expressivity. To some feminists, this position smacks of "group self-hatred," of putting down your own group as trivial and inferior, not worthy of time and attention. Polarists insist that their hatred is not directed against women, but against the roles that males and male society have foisted on women. After all, they say, all women are sisters in the most basic way possible: biologically. They also emphasize that the true women lurking underneath the caricatures are beautiful—strong, wise, just, and heroic. Polarism's fight is with the false forms that expressivity-femininity has taken. In the Polarist Utopia, females will no longer be overemotional, flighty, temperamental, childish, or sentimental. Gone too will be the kind of razzle-dazzle sexiness so often expected of today's women, a sexiness that taunts and teases but has little to do with genuine sexuality and female passion.

FEMALES ARE INFERIOR
BECAUSE THEY ARE SUPERIOR:
THE WOMB-ENVY THESIS

Why do some feminists find today's expressivity-femininity a smothering, marshmallowlike possessiveness, a lack of spine, a mushy-headed approach to the world? According to Polarism, the answer can be found in males' basic insecurity. The insecurity of men is explained in various ways by Polarists; one explanation is the womb-envy thesis.

Reversing the more conventional notion of penis envy, Karen Horney [20] proposed that it is actually males who are envious of the opposite sex. While her theory is less anatomically deterministic than orthodox Freudianism (she considered herself neo-Freudian), it is still a variation on the "anatomy is destiny" theme. But in her hands, the theme takes on feminist implications—Polarist ones.

For Horney, the ability of females to give birth is unsurpassed as a creative potential. Males are awestruck by this power; unable to compete with it, they begin to envy women. But men cannot tolerate this feeling of inferiority for long, so they compensate by taking and seizing social power. Because they have this power, they convince everyone that males are the superior sex. Thus, when penis envy occurs in women, it results from the self-fulfilling propaganda perpetrated by males as a coverup for their own inferiority. Women do not envy male genitalia, they envy males' social power. The penis merely represents a discernible physical difference between the sexes.

But Polarists hold that there are significant intrinsic differences between the sexes that entail much more than superficial anatomical differences. The womb-envy thesis appears over and over again in Polarism:

I think that the need men . . . felt, and feel, to invade the being of others (who are quite specifically women) rose from their deep jealousy of the fact that women and not men give birth. They may have seen us as conveniently disabled at times by motherhood, but they see our ability to give birth as just that—an amazing *ability*. Which they didn't have. I think this was the "initial insecurity" from which they suffered. Suffered so much that once they learned that they played some part in producing new life, they were moved to try to claim that they played the only part that mattered. To claim that women are simply their vessels, the receptacles of their "seed"—and so their private property.[21]

Even Margaret Mead, who is usually cited to support the position that sex roles are culturally and not biologically determined, reports the incidence of womb envy.[22] She says that every culture takes into account the universal male need for positive achievement that will surpass, or at least equal, the creative capacity of all women:

> . . . the life of the female starts and ends with sureness, first with the simple identification with her mother, last with the sureness that that identification is true, and that she has made another human being. The period of doubt, of envy of her brother, is brief, and comes early, followed by the long years of sureness. . . . While modern genetic theory has again dignified the paternal role to a genetic contribution equal to the maternal, it has not increased our ability to prove that a given man is, in fact, the father of a given child. . . .
>
> In every known human society, the male's need for achievement can be recognized. Men may cook, or weave or dress dolls or hunt hummingbirds, but if such activities are appropriate occupations of men, then the whole society, men and women alike, votes them as important. . . .
>
> The recurrent problem of civilization is to define the male role satisfactorily enough—whether it be to build gardens or raise cattle, kill game or kill enemies, build bridges or handle bank-shares—so that the male in the course of his life reaches a solid sense of irreversible achievement. If women are to be

restless and questing, even in the face of child-bearing, they must be made so through education. If men are ever to be at peace, ever certain that their lives have been lived as they were meant to be, they must have, in addition to paternity, culturally elaborated forms of expression that are lasting and sure.[23]

Some of Jessie Bernard's earlier work is cited by Polarist feminists in trying to explain why females and expressivity have succumbed to the male need for security. (Like Mead, Bernard is more frequently cited by those who believe sex differences are cultural inventions.) Drawing a parallel between cichlid fish and humans (a Polarist strategy, for sure), Bernard emphasizes the fragility of the male ego:

> The cichlid's masculinity depends on the female's awe; if she withholds it, his masculinity wilts, is extinguished. He must be dominant or, in effect, cease to be a male. She must defer to him or risk not conceiving. . . . It would be fanciful to suppose that human beings are just like cichlids. Yet it is hard to ignore the evidence of the widely ramifying cichlid-effect in human societies. Human male sexuality, like the cichlid's, is vulnerable to female aggression, or even to lack of subservience or awe. It is dependent on them. . . .
>
> Not only as the inhibition of aggression but also as the positive expression of subservience or awe, the cichlid-effect enters almost all relations between collectivities (i.e., males and females). It takes the form of "stroking" in some situations. It takes the form of "emotional-expressive" behavior in others. It takes the form of pseudonurturance in still others. We are going to find this cichlid-effect almost everywhere, in the family, at work, at play, in social life.[24]

Mead's and Bernard's arguments come more from ontological premises than from biological ones—they see an inherent difference between males and females that stems from essence and existence rather than from biological sources strictly conceived. Their arguments might be used to support the idea that male dominance is necessary for the survival of the human species. But they are also saying that males must be treated as superior because they are actually inferior to women—a secret too dangerous to let out. Bernard's argument that females must play the subservient role to protect males from their vulnerability to aggression can be turned around to support the idea that females are actually superior to males. This is the strategy taken by Polarists who would invert the present sexual hierarchy.

THE SUPERIORITY-INFERIORITY QUESTION: HIERARCHICAL POLARISM

All Polarists reject the idea that males are superior to females. On this point they are united. From here, the theme diverges into hierarchical and equalitarian Polarism. At present the hierarchical variation is the more popular: reverse the conventional hierarchy so that females hold the superior positions, or are at least considered the superior subspecies in the human race. This position is often a consequence of going to extremes in trying to repudiate male dominance—not only are males *not* superior to females, males are in fact inferior. Using such logic, one Polarist says:

> It is thus obvious that in Western society, at least, the cult of the inferiority of women is a product of our Judeo-Christian teaching and is neither natural nor innate in the human species. As a matter of fact, it is the very reverse of nature's usual arrangements. In nature, the female is the all-important pillar that supports life, the male merely the ornament, the "afterthought," the expendable sexual adjunct. Observe with what care the female of all species is protected and sheltered and preserved by nature. It is the female, according to naturalists, biologists, and human geneticists, who is given the protec-

tive covering, the camouflaged plumage, the reserve food sup-
ply, the more efficient metabolism, the more specialized organs,
the greater resistance to disease, the built-in immunity to
certain specific ailments, the extra X chromosome, the more
convoluted brain, the stronger heart, the longer life. In nature's
plan the male is but a "glorified gonad." The female is the
species.[25]

Here, females are superior because, in nature, primary consideration is given to the survival of the female of the species. Because
Polarism sees humanity in natural terms, female superiority must
hold true for the human species, too. The greater joy of parents
over the birth of a boy than over a female baby is a cultural dis-
tortion of the natural primacy of the female, say the Polarists. The
joy should be reserved for the birth of baby girls.

Polarists have launched a multipronged attack on the idea of
male superiority. They cite embryology and morphology, along with
chromosomal, hormonal, and biochemical evidence, to support their
argument that the present, culturally misshapen sexual hierarchy
needs to be turned on its head. Referring to recent findings in
embryology, Mary Jane Sherfey argues in Polarist fashion that the
female form is the primary one:

Strictly speaking, we can no longer refer to the "undifferentiated" or "bisexual" phase of initial embryonic existence. The
early embryo is not undifferentiated: "it" is a female. In the
beginning, we were all created females; and if this were not
so, we would not be here at all.[26]

Sherfey goes on to say that the cultural myth that Eve was created
from Adam does not square with the biological facts:

. . . the primacy of the embryonic female morphology forces
us to reverse long-held concepts on the nature of sexual differentiation. Embryologically speaking, it *is* correct to say that
the penis is an exaggerated clitoris, the scrotum is derived from

the labia majora, the original libido is feminine, etc. The reverse is true only for the birds and reptiles. For all mammals, modern embryology calls for an Adam-out-of-Eve myth! [27]

The attack against male superiority is grounded not only in the assumed morphological primacy of the female but also in the genital evolution of the sexes. Polarists say that the female genitals are more basic than those of males. This contention reverses conventional, Freudian-inspired thinking about female genitalia as vestiges of male sex organs. Elizabeth Gould Davis puts it this way:

Woman's reproductive organs are far older than man's and far more highly evolved. Even in the lowest mammals, as well as in woman, the ovaries, uterus, vagina, etc., are similar, indicating that the female reproductive system was one of the first things perfected by nature. On the other hand, the male reproductive organs, the testicles and the penis, vary as much among species and through the course of evolution as does the shape of the foot—from hoof to paw. Apparently, then, the male penis evolved to suit the vagina, not the vagina to suit the penis.[28]

Davis continues with her thesis that males are biological afterthoughts, in terms of their genitalia and their chromosomal formation:

Proof that the penis is a much later development than the female vulva is found in the evidence that the male himself was a late mutation from an original female creature. For man is but an imperfect female. Geneticists and physiologists tell us that the Y chromosome that produces males is a deformed and broken X chromosome—the female chromosome. All women have two X chromosomes, while the male has one X derived from his mother and one Y from his father. It seems very logical that this small and twisted Y chromosome is a genetic error —an accident of nature—and that originally there was only one sex—the female.[29]

The argument that males have inferior chromosomal development appears time and again in hierarchical Polarism:

> The first males were mutants, freaks produced by some damage to the genes caused perhaps by disease or a radiation bombardment from the sun. Maleness remains a recessive genetic trait like color-blindness and hemophilia with which it is linked. The suspicion that maleness is abnormal and that the Y chromosome is an accidental mutation boding no good for the race is strongly supported by the recent discovery by geneticists that congenital killers and criminals are possessed of not one but *two* Y chromosomes, bearing a double dose, as it were, of genetically undesirable maleness. If the Y chromosome is a degeneration and a deformity of the female X chromosome, then the male sex represents a degeneration and deformity of the female.[30]

An even more extreme version of this argument can be seen in the following statement by Valerie Solanas, widely associated with the hierarchical position:

> The male is a biological accident: the Y (male) gene is an incomplete X (female) gene, that is, has an incomplete set of chromosomes. In other words, the male is an incomplete female, a walking abortion, aborted at the gene stage. To be male is to be deficient, emotionally limited; maleness is a deficiency disease and males are emotional cripples.[31]

Males are glorified gonads, genetic accidents, biological afterthoughts, freaks, mutants, and deformities. Besides all these things, or perhaps because of them, males are also prone to emotional paralysis and criminality.

Further evils are said to be inherently tied to maleness and get unleashed when males hold social power:

> Man is the enemy of nature: to kill, to root up, to level off, to pollute, to destroy are his instinctive reactions to the un-

manufactured phenomena of nature, which he basically fears and distrusts. Woman, on the other hand, is the ally of nature, and her instinct is to tend, to nurture, to encourage healthy growth, and to preserve ecological balance. She is the natural leader of society and of civilization, and the usurption of her primeval authority by man has resulted in the uncoordinated chaos that is leading the human race inexorably back to barbarism.[32]

Solanas expresses the same theme even more colorfully:

> The male, because of his obsession to compensate for not being female combined with his inability to relate and to feel compassion, has made the world a shitpile.[33]

Elements of the womb-envy and male-insecurity explanations for male behavior can be seen in the last two quotes. Seizing social power was the males' way of compensating for their natural inferiority; it masked their fear and envy of women's superior creative capacities. In the hierarchical Polarist logic, males create havoc because they are basically inferior, and this fact sets up a chain of events that has produced all manner of social disasters. Women must stop pretending that males are superior and begin to take on social power, for only by so doing can the good society come about. For the survival of the species, women must stop protecting males from the knowledge of their own vulnerability and fragility.

Equalitarian Polarists disagree with the hierarchical assumptions. Equalitarians say that both males and females are victimized by sexual hierarchy. Such Polarists would agree with Mead's assessment that either male or female dominance is too costly:

> Externally at some given period of history and in some set of social arrangements it may look as if one sex gained and the other lost, but such gains and losses must in the end be temporary. To the extent that women are denied the right to use their minds, their sons suffer as well as their daughters. An over-

emphasis on the importance of virility will in the end make the lives of men as instrumental as an over-emphasis on their merely reproductive functions makes the lives of women. If our analysis is deep enough and our time-perspective long enough, if we hold in mind all the various possibilities that other cultures hint at or fully embody, it is possible to say that to the extent that either sex is disadvantaged, the whole culture is poorer, and the sex that, superficially, inherits the earth, inherits only a very partial legacy.[34]

For equalitarian Polarists, male dominance oppresses men as well as women, corrupting and contaminating true maleness and true instrumentality. One such Polarist, speaking about atrocities committed by American soldiers against Vietnamese women, disavows the idea that such acts have anything to do with real male nature:

Not all G.I.'s do these things. Many have refused, and many have been tortured for their refusal. The arch-enemy is those few men with power who directly profit from the war, who run the country, and who need hate among the people to keep us divided among ourselves so we can't work against them. They need to keep a bloodthirsty, "hate and conquer" male population at hand at all times to fight whatever war it is necessary to fight to make them richer. This terrible male-supremacist hate, this desire to rape and plunder and destroy at whim, as a show of the white male's power, is held up to men as what they should be, the "he-man," the "man of adventure." . . . The Army does its best to keep G.I.'s believing this phony idea of manhood.[35]

Equalitarian Polarism sees today's male sex roles as poor copies of authentic maleness. Genuine instrumentality has been turned into a caricature of itself, to be replaced by phony notions of manhood embodied in James Bond and John Wayne stereotypes. Males need to be liberated along with females and brought back to their true sexual selves.

THE POLARIST UTOPIA

The Polarist world would be vastly different from what it is now. Like the other ideal types, Polarism sees its program as solving all the major social ills and ushering in an era of happiness for everyone—but especially for women. Society would resemble the ancient matriarchies spoken of by Bachofen and Briffault. Mothers would be the most interesting people—closest to the birth process, in touch with the awesome physical and psychological development of their children. Yet all women would be so described, whether they had given birth or not. There would be no elites, certainly no maternal elite. An exception to this statement must be made if the new Polarist world is of the hierarchical sort, for in that case females would be considered superior to males. The restoration of females to what hierarchalists consider their rightful position would entail either of two possibilities. Either women would rule in a matriarchal society, or the Utopia would be modeled on Lesbos, where males were eliminated.

Polarists who find their inspiration in ancient gynocracies and goddess-worshipping religions foresee an era in which consciousness will undergo massive transformations and produce a major stage in evolutionary history. One feminist envisions a revolution in consciousness comparable to that of the Reformation:

> The changes which it [the uprising of women] will embody can perhaps be better imagined as primarily spiritual and religious, rather than economic and social, though they will include and embody the latter. Thus a more apt analogy than the Cuban or Chinese revolutions might be the Reformation or the Christian revolution, or perhaps the revolution made by the patriarchy itself when the ancient gynocracies were invaded. I use these analogies because in each of these cases the economic and political changes were enormous, but they followed rather than preceded sweeping changes in human consciousness. The ripples spread through the institutions from the masses of people, rather than the other way around. . . . Fem-

inism concerns more than political power, essential as *that* is.
It is closely tied to theories of awakening consciousness, of
creation and rebirth, and of the essential oneness of the Universe—teachings which lie at the heart of all Goddess-worshipping religions.[36]

Once women have assumed the superior position in society,
institutions under their control will be different from male-dominated ones. Polarists base this belief on the alternative institutions
women have already created:

Feminist newspapers, literary magazines, cooperative child-
care centers, anthropology collectives, legal clinics, poetry
workshops, self-help medical clinics, counseling services, music
groups and graphics collectives are a few of the newborn alternative institutions providing the access for women whose
values and vision are unacceptable to the patriarchy, or who
choose not to pay the artistic and emotional price exacted by
men in exchange for a share of male privilege.

Even more significantly, the products of these alternative
institutions (and of the individual women involved with them
or working on their own) are qualitatively different from the
products of men and male institutions. For instance, a feminist
all-women's rock band *sounds* different from a male rock band
or from an all-women's rock band trying to reproduce male
music; they are not only singing different lyrics but the melo-
dies and harmonies and rhythms are different. Feminist anthropologists are approaching their subject from a different perspective and with different assumptions than male anthropologists,
or women anthropologists in the past who had only male-defined
standards and methods at their disposal. Feminist teachers are
creating a different style of classroom situation with their
women students. Feminist lawyers are helping their clients to
use the law to help themselves. All of us are not engaged in
such activities but many of us share in the changing consciousness that these women are expressing publicly.[37]

In the meantime, Polarist feminists advocate specific institutional changes that relate directly to woman as childbearer and child rearer:

> The Women's Movement must, and will, begin to focus on those demands which relate concretely to women's role in childrearing. These more radical-feminist demands include: wages for all women engaged in child-rearing; paid holidays and vacations; collective child-care centers controlled by mothers with the participation of all members of the community, including fathers, older children, and childless adults; laboratories and research facilities to be turned over to *feminist* scientists so that research into contraception, fertility, pregnancy, and birth can be conducted in *women's interests;* hospital and outpatient facilities related to women's health to be run and staffed by women; self-help clinics, financed by the government but under community control, artificial insemination, sterilization procedures, facilities for extrauterine birth, and related technology to be made widely available. Technology is a powerful tool which will free us to bear and raise our children in our own way at our own time. It must be turned over to women *now*, in order to prevent its becoming an even more powerful weapon against us and indeed against all life.[38]

Polarist feminists who aim at a Utopia in which males and females will relate to one another in equalitarian, complementary ways often cite Mead's proposals for a more perfect society:

> If we once accept the premise that we can build a better world by using the different gifts of each sex, we shall have two kinds of freedom, freedom to use untapped gifts of each sex, and freedom to admit freely and cultivate in each sex their special superiorities. We may well find that there are certain fields, such as the physical sciences, mathematics, and instrumental music, in which men by virtue of their sex, as well as by virtue of their qualities as specially gifted human beings, will always

have that razor-edge of extra gift which makes all the difference, and that while women may easily follow where men lead,
men will always make the new discoveries. We may equally
well find that women, through the learning involved in maternity, which once experienced can be taught more easily to
all women, even childless women, than to men, have a special
superiority in those human sciences which involve that type of
understanding which until it is analyzed is called intuition. If
intuition is based, as it seems to be, upon an ability to recognize difference from the self rather than upon one to project
the self in building a construct or a hypothesis, it may well be
that the greatest intuitive gifts will be found among women.
Just as for endless ages men's mathematical gifts were ne-
glected and people counted one, two, two and one, and a
dog, or were limited to counting on the fingers of their hands,
so women's intuitive gifts have lain fallow, uncultivated, un-
civilized.[39]

Feminists who hold to this view say that equalitarian complemen-
tarity between males and females would take place across the whole
range of gender involvement. This type of male-female dualism
would be encouraged in sexual, procreative, family, and social relationships. These Polarists turn again to Mead for a warning on the
complexities that must be taken into account:

Each sex may be distorted by the presence of the other sex, or
it may be given a fuller sense of sex membership. Either solution is possible, neither is inevitable. . . . If society defines each
sex as having inalienable and valuable qualities of its own but
does not relate those qualities to the reproductive differences
between the sexes, then each sex may be proud and strong, but
some of the values that come from sex contrast will be lacking.
If women are defined without reference to their maternity,
men may find that their own masculinity seems inadequate,
because its continuance into paternity will also lose definition.
And if men are defined in terms of paternity rather than as

lovers, women will find that their own capacities of wifehood have been muted in favour of their capacities for mother-hood.[40]

PHILOSOPHICAL ASSUMPTIONS

The philosophical assumptions underlying Polarism are a strange mixture of modern and ancient ideas. Polarism reflects a new biologism that is sweeping the behavioral and social sciences. This neo-biologism follows many different paths. One thesis is that bio-grams—programmed structures in the human organism—predetermine the basic outlines of how we behave. Somewhat like instincts, biograms control such things as territoriality, aggression, passivity, sexual bonding, and parent-child behavior. At first glance, Polarism and neo-biologism appear to be saying the same things. Further inspection, however, shows that the two are different. Polarism takes biological premises, and even the latest biological knowledge, and transforms them into a view of the world that is far from modern. For the ethos of Polarism and that of modern science are not alike.

The female that Polarism talks about in ideal terms is awesome —a participant in nature's power, in the mystery of life, and in the whole animal kingdom (queendom, more aptly). When describing true femaleness and its idea of the future, Polarism never uses such terms as stimulus-response, reinforcement schedules, or input-output matrices; it speaks of nature, instincts, primal forces, and mysterious powers. Its underlying philosophy derives from an organicist, not a mechanistic, view of the world. It harks back to a romantic naturalism, not forward to a futuristic technocracy. Even though Polarism does not see itself as conservative (in the sense that it supports some status quo ante), it goes against the modern grain abrasively by saying that people are not the same because they have different bodies (or different essences). Feminists who consistently espouse Polarism are more likely to do so at a primal level than coolly and scientifically. Their confidence comes from a sense of being right in their bodies and having a body-politics connection.

In proposing an inverted sexual hierarchy, as some Polarists do, this feminist type rejects the modern rationalist idea that all humans are equivalent and interchangeable and that, all things being equal, each person can construct a unique personality if it is shaped by the proper social structures. Polarism posits a biological (or ontological) core to being, which must not be tampered with. And that core of being has everything to do with gender. Human nature is not malleable plastic (a modern idea), but given and fixed. This human nature does not go away even though attempts are made to push it this way or that. It lies buried, but struggling for expression. Because females have lost touch with their authentic natures, they are doomed to misery. The only hope for them, say the Polarists, is to push society this way and that, so it allows the unfolding of all our core beings. In this Polarism may strike a modern chord, but its social engineering will culminate in a natural Utopia.

NOTES

1. The most notable sociologist-feminist to take this position is Alice Rossi. See especially her "A Biosocial Perspective on Parenting," *Daedalus* 106 (Spring 1977): 1–32; and "The Missing Body in Sociology: An Essay on Closing the Gap Between Physiology and Sociology" (Presidential Address at the 44th Annual Eastern Sociological Society Meeting, Philadelphia, Pennsylvania, 6 April 1974).

2. My interpretation enters in giving shape to these four types and not to some others. The names of the types are my invention, but they are selected for their appropriateness in depicting the contents of the themes I found in researching the feminist movement.

3. The analogy was used in a consciousness-raising group in which I participated in March 1971. Another argument that is similar to this is put forward by "Aesthetic Realism." It sounds at first like Synthesism, but its position in favor of sexual dualism and heterosexuality puts it squarely in the Polarist camp.

4. Judith M. Bardwick, *Psychology of Women* (New York: Harper & Row, 1971), pp. 12–15.

5. Jane Alpert, "Mother Right: A New Feminist Theory," *Ms.* 2 (August 1973): 90–91.

6. Ibid.

7. Cf. *New York Post,* 31 March 1975.

8. Cf. especially *Off Our Backs* 5 (May–June 1975) and *Plexus* 2 (August 1975).

9. Kirsten Grimstead and Susan Rennie, Interview of Jane Alpert, *Off Our Backs* 5 (May–June 1975): 20.

10. Alpert, "Mother Right," p. 92.

11. Anonymous excerpt from "The Evolution of a Suffragette, 1912," *RAT,* no. 18 (12–29 January 1971): 14. Emphases added.

12.   J. J. Bachofen, *Myth, Religion, and Mother Right* (Princeton, N.J.: Princeton University Press, 1967), pp. 79–81, quoted in Erich Fromm, "The Theory of Mother Right and Social Psychology," in his *Crisis of Psychoanalysis* (Greenwich, Conn.: Fawcett, 1970), pp. 124–25.

13.   Fromm, "Theory of Mother Right," p. 125.

14.   Alpert, "Mother Right," p. 92.

15.   Fromm, "Theory of Mother Right," p. 131. It must be noted that Fromm's overall view is more closely allied with Synthesism.

16.   Ibid.

17.   Alpert, "Mother Right," p. 92.

18.   Elizabeth Gould Davis, *The First Sex* (Baltimore: Penguin, 1971), pp. 334–35.

19.   Ibid., pp. 333–34.

20.   Cf. Karen Horney, "On the Genesis of the Castration Complex in Women," *International Journal of Psychoanalysis,* part 1 (1924), 5:50–65; and "The Flight From Womanhood," *International Journal of Psycho-analysis* (1926), pp. 324–39.

21.   Barbara Deming, "To Fear Jane Alpert Is to Fear Ourselves: Letter to Susan Sherman," *Off Our Backs* 5 (May–June 1975): 25.

22.   Margaret Mead, *Male and Female* (New York: Dell, 1968).

23.   Ibid., pp. 166–68.

24.   Jessie Bernard, *The Sex Game* (New York: Atheneum, 1972), p. 60.

25.   Davis, *The First Sex,* p. 329.

26.   Mary Jane Sherfey, *The Nature and Evolution of Female Sexuality* (New York: Vintage, 1973), p. 38.

27.   Ibid., p. 46.

28.   Davis, *The First Sex,* p. 34.

29.   Ibid.

30.   Ibid., p. 35.

31.   Valerie Solanas, *S.C.U.M. (Society For Cutting Up Men) Manifesto* (New York: Olympia Press, 1968), pp. 31–32.

32. Davis, *The First Sex,* pp. 335–36.

33. Solanas, *S.C.U.M.,* p. 35.

34. Mead, *Male and Female,* pp. 345–46.

35. Anonymous, "Vietnam Women," *RAT,* no. 12 (9–23 August 1970): 6.

36. Alpert, "Mother Right," p. 94.

37. Ibid., p. 90.

38. Ibid., p. 94.

39. Mead, *Male and Female,* pp. 358–59.

40. Ibid., p. 345.

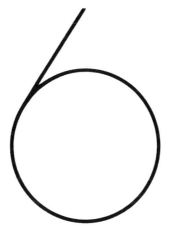

SOCIAL LOCATION OF THE WOMEN'S LIBERATION MOVEMENT

A number of factors must be taken into account if we are to understand the social and personal upheavals that prompted the emergence of the women's liberation movement in the late 1960s. Peter Berger's dialectical model of the social construction of reality (discussed in the Appendix: Theoretical Background) can be used to interpret a given social phenomenon in terms of the interplay of "objectivation," "externalization," and "internalization." [1] The model addresses social reality at macro and micro levels, both sociocultural "facts" and subjective consciousness. The assumptions of the model underlie this chapter's interpretation of the social location of the women's movement.

In order to generalize about the social context out of which today's feminism has arisen, this chapter examines briefly the feminist movement that appeared in America and England in the nineteenth and early twentieth centuries. The following parallels in social context surround both women's movements:

1. A widespread upheaval in general social consciousness as a result of war and its aftermath

2. The presence of human rights movements aimed at securing equal treatment for groups other than women

3. The public participation of women in wartime (or antiwar) activities and in human rights struggles, and the consequent change in their own expectations

4. A general social climate of liberal reformist activity

5. A trend toward group-based voluntarism

6. A diffused perception that woman's role was restrictive and demanding and that it was not based in any natural necessity

7. An increase in the differentiation and specialization that attends the expansion of technological production.[2]

The chapter approaches social reality at the micro level by examining the social location of movement members. It asks the question, What in the social character of these particular women prompted them to affiliate themselves with feminism? *Marginality* among upper-middle-class, college-educated women is posited as the most adequate explanation.

One clarification is in order. No attempt is made here to connect specific feminists with the four ideal types profiled in chapters 2–5. Ideal types, it must be reemphasized, are constructs that do not attach to any given individual or group. Some individuals may reflect all four types simultaneously or sequentially. Any attempt to sort out the social characteristics of movement members in order to find affinities for any ideal type would violate the methodological assumptions of ideal-typical analysis.

HISTORICAL LOCATION OF THE WOMEN'S LIBERATION MOVEMENT

The women's movement that took form in American society in the late 1960s was not the first organized expression of *feminism*,[3] which is here defined as the consciousness that perceives women as disadvantaged vis-à-vis men, out of which strategies are proposed to change those social conditions deemed responsible for the disparities between the sexes. Feminism may refer to organized and unorganized programs, to a state of consciousness, or to a social movement.

Most historians [4] identify the first expression of feminist consciousness in the late 1700s, marked by Mary Wollstonecraft's publication of *A Vindication of the Rights of Woman* in 1792. Organized feminism first appeared in the nineteenth century in America and England. It focused on the issue of women's right to vote and centered its strategies in pressures for a constitutional amendment which would give women that right. Once the amendment was passed in 1920, the organized groups dissolved.

Several interpretations have been advanced for the decline of the movement after the passage of woman's suffrage, for the feminist movement was not a single-issue one. On the contrary, several issues embodied in early feminism have reemerged in the current movement. For example, early feminists viewed marriage as institutionalizing the economic, social, and sexual disparities between men and women. The economic dependence of women on men was seen as an obstacle to women's opportunities to realize their full capabilities. Further, the dominance of male standards in defining women's self-images and expectations was deemed responsible for distorting the true nature of female humanity.[5]

SOCIAL CONDITIONS AND THE EMERGENCE OF FEMINISM

A number of hypotheses have been offered as to which social conditions are likely to give rise to feminism. One hypothesis is that feminism correlates with postwar social contexts. The social upheavals in the aftermath of war promote a general mood of introspection. During these times social consciousness highlights the relationship between self and society, and the applications of technology for destructive or constructive purposes. In this climate of reflectiveness several questions may be raised: Is the good of the society a just and reasonable motive for self-sacrifice? What is the relationship between individual interests and social necessity? Since weaponry is made possible through applied technology, must the role of technology be reexamined so as to align it with constructive rather than destructive uses?[6] It might be added that the more devastating the weapons, the more pressing the felt need for a reexamination of the role of technology.[7]

Postwar social reflectiveness may be extended to areas not directly impinging on the war. Women's rights and the female role in society are but two such issues.

The Second World War saw a tremendous increase in the participation of females in the labor force; at the same time, there was a sense of this participation as a temporary thing, for the duration of the emergency. Traditional definitions of woman's role persisted, though perhaps they lay dormant during the war years. Once the war was over, a campaign began to induce women to return to a home-and-family focus. In varying degrees of alarm, experts pronounced juvenile delinquency and all manner of social ills as traceable to women's having "gotten out of hand" during the war years. It seems, though, that many women were not enthusiastic about giving up their jobs.[8]

Although at first glance the Vietnam war and its aftermath seem to have ushered in a new era of feminism, some now think that World War II triggered significant transformations in social structure and in social consciousness that led to the current movement.[9] Women who had worked during the war in the instrumental public realm made sure that their daughters would not lack the skills and motivation necessary to succeed in the "outside world." (Most feminists of the present era were born during the baby-boom years after World War II, a time period that coincides with the massive push to have working women return to the home. Negative feelings experienced by these mothers, engendered by the role conflicts they were facing, "rubbed off" on their daughters.[10]) Even when domesticity was embraced enthusiastically, this activity was redefined in professional, instrumental ways, especially among middle-class suburban women, who stressed efficiency in the home and progressive child management.[11] Many women, of course, kept on working.[12] The mothers themselves did not coalesce into a feminist movement because other social conditions were not right. Moreover, the antifeminist campaign undoubtedly discouraged them.[13] Women who were unhappy in the traditional female role and turned to feminism were diagnosed as severely neurotic and suffering from penis envy and latent lechery (the Lundberg-Farnham thesis).[14] College officials were advocating curricular changes so that women could train for their future lives as wives and mothers. They could study the "theory and preparation of a Basque paella" rather than post-Kantian philosophy.[15]

Another hypothesis about the emergence of feminism is that a movement takes form if it addresses itself to changing the disadvantaged position of one social group relative to others. This can be seen in the civil rights or equal opportunity movements. Evelyne Sullerot,[16] for example, traces the struggle for female rights back to the French Revolution, which saw the dismantling of serfdom and the instituting of citizenship for men. For Sullerot, women began to demand enfranchisement once "the principle of universal male suffrage became current [and] parliamentary democracy became established." [17] She continues:

Throughout history there has been a constant interplay between a vanguard of women, aware of the growing lag between the condition of the two sexes in society, and the rearguard of men who wish, in practice if not in theory, to prevent male rights being applied also to women. This process still applies to modern society.[18]

Sullerot sees women's demands for closing the human rights gap between themselves and men as legitimated by the share women take in collective endeavors, particularly during times of war, political resistance, and revolution. This last point is a variation on the hypothesis that postwar conditions sharpen feminist consciousness, but with the addition that human rights questions emerge into movements following the upheaval of war and that feminism followed on the heels of other human rights movements.[19]

The abolition movement in the nineteenth century is one illustration of the hypothesis that feminism is likely to accompany or follow movements aimed at equalizing the position of one group relative to others. William O'Neill describes antislavery as the dominant issue arising out of the cries for reform that characterized American society in the 1830s and '40s. Interestingly, the part played by women in the abolition movement was crucial:

In the 1830's there were perhaps a hundred female anti-slavery societies, and women played some part in most other reforms. By this time women had been organizing long enough so that some precedent existed for this further expansion of their extra-domestic operations. They played a crucial role in the Abolition movement. More than half of the signatures on the great petitions that forced Congress to take up the slavery question were women's. Most of these were obtained by female circulators. Precedent and necessity alike, therefore, compelled males to swallow their qualms and allow women a part, however limited, in these activities.[20]

Women who participated in the abolition movement were also involved with the issue of women's rights. O'Neill suggests a number of possible reasons for this convergence of interest: (1) the tendency for involvement in one activity to lead to involvement in others; (2) female activists in causes aimed at relieving the sufferings of exploited or oppressed groups naturally affiliated with feminism to promote their own cause, winning the vote; and (3) female reformers became feminists because of discrimination on the part of males in the reform movement.[21]

With the Civil War over and the rights of the former slaves guaranteed (in theory) by constitutional amendment, women were even further committed to the feminist cause. Many women had assumed that the rights won by ex-slaves would be applied universally, but they were quickly disabused of that idea:

> Feminists were buoyed up by the libertarian spirit of the moment. Having helped to crush the great evil of slavery, they found it easy to think that the lesser evil of sex discrimination would be similarly dealt with. Moreover, as their heated debates on the question amply demonstrated, most of the radical feminists, for all their genuinely liberal sentiments, could not believe that men would humiliate them by enfranchising black males while leaving white women beyond the pale. . . . Feminists [were assured] that not only would Congress refuse to give women the vote, but that any attempt to secure such a Bill would jeopardize black suffrage. "This is the Negro's hour," they were told repeatedly; women would just have to wait their turn.[22]

Not every war or every human rights movement produces feminism. Other factors must be taken into account if feminism is to emerge. At least three additional social factors have been suggested: the family structure, a climate of liberal ideology and reformist activity, and an orientation to voluntary associational activity.[23]

Phillippe Ariès argues that the woman's place in the family changed from one of greater to lesser personal freedom with the coming of the Victorian era.[24] The feminism of the nineteenth and early twentieth centuries may in part have been a delayed reaction to the restrictions placed on women by Victorians. Further, the tightening of woman's role in the home came at a time when the male sphere was being expanded. Any notable gap in the position of men relative to women can set the stage for the emergence of feminist consciousness.

A climate of reform liberalism was part of the social context that surrounded feminist consciousness in the aftermath of the French Revolution and in American society during the 1830s and '40s. Again, although women shared in reform activity and took seriously the liberal-rational ethos of universal rights and justice, they were not included in the changes engineered for others.[25]

Voluntarism is also a key to understanding the rise of early feminism. For O'Neill, this factor was more decisive in feminist organizing than were either the effects of the industrialization process or the frontier experiences of American pioneer women:

> Probably of greater importance to American women was the tendency toward association that made such a deep impression upon Tocqueville, and that continues to be so distinctive a feature of American life. In church auxiliaries and missionary societies, and then in philanthropic and charitable bodies, thousands of women found outlets for their altruism and wider fields of enterprise beyond the domestic circle. Barred from the society of men they discovered among themselves talents and resources enough to advance many good causes and perform many good works. By the 1830's there were literally thousands of separate women's groups holding meetings, collecting funds, discussing public issues, and variously improving themselves. In this manner a revolution of rising expectations was launched. The more women did, the more they wished to do, the more they pressed against the barriers that prevented them from exercising their full powers, and the more eager they became to equip themselves for the tasks ahead.[26]

To summarize: Feminism can be located in a social context that features a wartime or postwar social reflectiveness; a generalized spirit of change, be it reform or revolution-oriented; a perception of inconsistencies in applying human rights, especially if women have actively participated in the struggle for equality; a feeling by women that their role is too constraining and too demanding in their relationships with men, the family, or the larger society; and an impetus toward voluntary group activity. Significant parallels can be seen between early and current feminism. The war in Vietnam, the participation of females in antiwar activity, the involvement of women in movements aimed at equalizing human rights, the disillusionment of women who were involved in male-dominated New Left and other revolutionary groups, the social ferment that gave rise to student rights movements and a youth or counterculture; and the delayed reaction of women to a tightening of their role in the late 1940s are all factors that have their counterparts in early feminism.

Before leaving this discussion, it might be useful to examine briefly the demise of the earlier feminist movement in the 1920s. A lack of ideology among feminists proved fatal to the organized movement; once suffrage was passed, no issue was strong enough to take its place and unify women. In addition, recently won opportunities for women in the public sphere proved to be largely negative. Without supporting social facilities (e.g., child care and paid maternity leaves), and with no change in the distribution of domestic responsibilities between husbands and wives, women were unable to perform fully either as public or private persons if they tried to combine work and family life.[27] According to O'Neill, women, "like racial minorities . . . were free in theory but not in practice."[28] A change in attitude toward women's sexual behavior, before and after marriage, and the influence of Freudian psychoanalytic thought helped increase the attractiveness of family life and the private sphere for women. Women were encouraged to find self-fulfillment both in their sexual lives and in motherhood. Conscious of disappointments in the public sphere and a more enlightened attitude in the private sphere, women lost the incentive to become feminists.

SOCIAL LOCATION OF
WOMEN'S MOVEMENT MEMBERS

Most of the women who identify with, or actively participate in, the women's liberation movement are white, upper-middle-class, college-educated, and urban. True, women from every social category can be found in the movement. Several active women's groups are dominated by working-class, or nonwhite, or non-college-educated women.[29] Nevertheless, the current movement originated in, and continues to draw most of its members from, middle-class backgrounds. Most groups affiliated with the movement continually raise the question of how to reach women from other social categories and incorporate them into the ranks. The outreach attempts are most obvious in politically radical feminist groups that strongly identify with theories of socialist revolution.[30] But efforts to include a more representative mix of women can be observed in such establishment-reform-oriented groups as NOW. Reasons for the outreach effort are both ideological and strategic. Whatever their political orientation, most groups assume that women can affect a change in the overall society because they constitute 51 percent of the U.S. population. But they must be recruited into the movement.

Why does the current women's liberation movement remain predominantly middle class and white? What is it about the social location of these women that makes it plausible for them to participate in the movement? These questions are perhaps best approached through a hypothesis that centers on the marginality concept.

THE CONCEPT OF MARGINALITY

When the term was originally coined, marginality referred to the plight of the second-generation immigrant, who often had to tread a thin line between the culture of the parents and that of the new host country. Conflicts in expectations of the two cultures led to internal conflicts. By the third generation, barring patterns of severe discrimination and gross dissimilarity of the cultures in question, most problems were resolved. The grandchildren of the original immigrants, secure in their identities as "Americans," could safely and enthusiastically express interest in the customs, food habits, language, etc., of their grandparents, of their "roots." In this scenario, the marginality was more cultural than structural.

The marginality women experience today is more structural; that is, the expectations women are caught between are part of a thoroughgoing dualism that runs through the whole society. So, while modern assumptions about human nature lessen the strict reading of an inherent biological dualism, at the same time the society seems to be approaching an era of ever-increasing dualism. Thus it is not simply a matter of having the next generation of women learn a new culture, although that is never simple; it is a matter of coming to terms with the whole duality puzzle.

From a strictly structural view, middle-class, college-educated women experience a marginality that produces discrepant (antithetical) expectations about the role of women; these discrepancies promote an awareness of the unequal treatment of men and women; and such awareness sets the stage for the emergence of feminist consciousness. The more bases for structural marginality in any particular woman's social history, the more likely it is that she will be recruited into a feminist movement group.

Inspection of the sociological literature on marginality reveals differences in interpretation about the consequences of marginal social location for personality development. On the one hand, marginality has been interpreted as inducing demoralization, a tendency toward deviance, a lack of incentive, feelings of resentment, alienation, and anomie. On the other hand, marginality has been viewed as resulting in a "debunking" orientation toward social reality, a sharper critical ability, a detached and rational world-view, a wider horizon, keener intelligence, the cosmopolitan role, and higher creative capacity.

Without taking the long route into the issue of value assumptions and sociological interpretation, how do we come to grips with a variable that is said to produce such opposite outcomes? We might begin by asking whether the outcomes mentioned are mutually exclusive after all. For it is possible for a highly intelligent, creative individual to be at the same time deviant and alienated. The either-or approach, reflected in a good portion of the sociological literature on marginality, has limited the concept unnecessarily.

Perhaps marginality in social location—the experience of being caught between two different sociocultural orientations and at the same time participating by inclination or necessity in both—enables individuals to have a lesser hold on an unshakable, taken-for-granted reality so that, from this vantage point of relative distance from a single embracing world-view, they have more opportunity to see-by-contrast the world that others take as a given, as *the world*. This distance prompts the individual to develop awareness of the precariousness of social reality; this awareness may lead to a habit of critical insight, cynicism, or both. A few qualifications on this assumption are necessary.

Marginality implies the potential for dual internalizations, that is, dualized values, interests, life styles, identities, relevance structures, and the like—a potential that has consequences for personality articulation. The personality may remain dualized or become a synthesis of the twofold internalizations, depending on the nature of the discrepancies between the two structures involved. If the personality remains dualized, either ambivalence or conflict may result unless the discrepant reality is "kept in place." Of course, the two sources of internalizations may diverge to a greater or lesser degree; the greater the clash between the two, the greater the degree of conflict or "sociological ambivalence" (Merton and Barber).

Another qualification concerning marginality has to do with the social organization of the society in question. The chances for duality, if not fragmentation in general, in a modern technological culture are far greater than in a traditional society. Marginality may even be said to be alien to traditional societies except in the light of the role of the stranger-who-stays (Schutz; Simmel). Marginality is rooted in larger social realities. This rootage must be kept in mind in approaching the possibilities for personality articulation. Two conflicting spheres of relevance, located in divergent structures, may be subsumed or even neutralized by a larger, overarching world-taken-for-granted (i.e., a world in which one operates without critical detachment, one that provides guidelines for "business-as-usual").

It can be further posited that not all groups have equal power in getting their externalizations to "stick" as objective social reality (social facts), and that not all "externalized" productions have equal impact on the preexisting body of social facts (see the Appendix). A group (or structure) may not have sufficient power or salience to induce the state of marginality in individuals who must "do business" with them in everyday experience. To illustrate: Rural and urban structures have been described as encompassing different worlds-taken-for-granted. If an individual is raised in a rural environment and later takes up residence in a large city, the marginality induced may be relatively insignificant if the individual derives meaning from a larger structure carried with him or her from countryside to city—for example white, Anglo-Saxon, Protestant middle-class social location. In other words, rural childhood realities posited on social facts different from those that constitute urban life may not present that individual with a severe identity crisis if he or she has internalized a world predicated on WASP middle-class premises (and, if, of course, WASP middle-class realities have a strong impact on the reservoir of social facts describing American social life).

Pluralism, or increasing structural differentiation, which characterizes modern urban technocratic societies, is the macro social fact that sets the stage for increasing numbers of marginal personalities. In a pluralistic society, objectivated social reality is internalized as a variety of plausibility structures and, as a consequence, induces the development of marginal personalities. Because this model is a dialectical one, increasingly pluralization is, at the same time, a consequence of growing numbers of marginal personalities. In other words, pluralism is both a cause and an effect of marginalized personality articulation. Moreover, as society becomes increasingly differentiated, there is an increase in the possibilities for marginality, because marginality implies being caught between at least one set of two discrepant, salient structures. The greater the number of structures within societal organization, the more structural interstices for individuals to find themselves caught between. With progressive pluralization, more individuals may find themselves "spun-off," unable to fit comfortably in any one embracing structure. In sociology of knowledge terms, the situation can be described as one of "multi-relationality" and multiple-relevance structures, along with an increase of "finite provinces of meaning." Conventional sociological approaches have described the resulting situation as "role conflict," "role confusion," or "lack of status crystallization."

MARGINALITY OF FEMINISM

The concept of marginailty best comes to grips with why the college-educated woman has an affinity for feminist activity. The college-educated woman is marginal in that she typically finds herself caught between two major salient structures of modern society: the public sphere and the private sphere.

The educational experience of college women presents them with a world premised on pattern variables best summarized by the term *instrumentalism,* that is, affective neutrality, self-orientation, universalism, performance, and specificity. Males and females are to be treated alike, according to the ideal definitions and expectations of the educational institution. Despite this universalistic, instrumental ideology, many females experience treatment different from that accorded males, because the taken-for-granted definitions of women as expressive beings carry over into this instrumental context.

On the one hand, women are expected to develop their intellectual life and become competent economic and political beings; they are encouraged to develop their "talents" and participate in civic and social projects. On the other hand, women are reminded in myriad ways that they are women first; they must look to their future lives as wives and mothers. The expanding sociological literature on sex roles documents the dimensions of this dilemma for women. Probably the earliest identification of the dilemma was provided by Mirra Komarovsky when she identified the "feminine" role and the "modern" role as two roles in conflict within the social environment of the college woman:

> One of these roles may be termed the "feminine" role. While there are a number of permissive variants of the feminine role for women of college age (the "good sport," the "glamour girl," the "young lady," the domestic "home girl," etc.), they have a common core of attributes defining the proper attitudes toward men, family, work, love, etc., and a set of personality traits often described with reference to the male sex role as "not as dominant, or aggressive as men" or "more emotional, sympathetic."
>
> The other and more recent role is, in a sense, no *sex* role at all, because it partly obliterates the differentiation in sex. It demands of the woman much the same virtues, patterns of behavior, and attitude that it does of the men of a corresponding age. We shall refer to this as the "modern" role.[31]

The "feminine" role and the "modern" role resemble what the present book has referred to as the "expressive" orientation and the "instrumental" orientation. Komarovsky's data can be reinterpreted using "marginality" in place of "contradictions":

> . . . [there exist] serious contradictions between [the] two roles present in the social environment of the college woman. The goals set by each role are *mutually exclusive,* and the fundamental personality traits each evokes are at points *diametrically opposed,* so that what are assets for one become liabilities for the other, and the full realization of one role threatens defeat in the other.[32]

As reinterpreted, the above description of the situation faced by college women points to their being caught between public (instrumental) and private (expressive) relevance structures. At the time of her report (1946) Komarovsky concluded that the resolution of the contradiction (marginality) usually prompted the woman to play both roles halfheartedly:

> Generally speaking, it would seem that it is the girl with a "middle-of-the-road personality" who is most happily adjusted to the present historical moment. She is not a perfect incarnation of either role but is flexible enough to play both. She is a girl who is intelligent enough to do well in school *but not so brilliant as to "get all A's";* informed and alert *but not consumed by an intellectual passion;* capable *but not talented in areas relatively new to women;* able to stand on her own feet and to earn a living *but not so good a living as to compete with men;* capable of doing some job well (in case she does not marry or, otherwise, has to work) *but not so identified with a profession as to need it for her happiness.*[33]

Notice the thrust of the above remarks. Although the happily adjusted woman is flexible enough to play both roles (but is not the perfect incarnation of either), the description of this happily adjusted personality spells out a halfhearted attitude toward, and an actual shortchanging of, *only* the instrumental orientation. Komrovsky does not say that the well-adjusted woman who plays the two roles shortchanges her roles as wife and mother by being "sympathetic," but not so sympathetic as to embody the valued characteristics of the ideal typical female. All the compromises are within the instrumental sphere. We might ask, if this was the "solution" to the dilemma in the mid-1940s, then why did it change by the mid-1960s? What induced significant numbers of women to reject this "middle-of-the-road" resolution and opt for social change?

As already suggested, several factors in the background of "social facts" set the stage for the rise of feminist consciousness, and a marginalized social existence turned women, particularly middle-class, college educated women, away from their prescribed roles. Also, the "baby boom" of the post–World War II years inflated the numbers of women who would not, or could not, tolerate such a "compromise" as the solution to the dilemma of marginality. This is not to say that in the 1940s (and, no doubt, long before then) many women did not resolve the dilemma happily and "adjust." Rather, in the 1940s, the women who were "unadjusted" were neither numerous nor powerful enough to impose these "externalizations" upon the social reality.[34]

In the 1960s, there was a larger pool of role dissidents among college-age females. They began to share with one another their perceptions about the oppressive nature of woman's role, and they were numerous enough to capture public attention. This attention, particularly in the mass media, served to "objectivate" dissatisfaction with the contradictions (marginality) of the female role and to have an influence on other women's perception of their situation (internalization process).

Besides the public-private sphere marginality that characterizes the role of women, other forms of marginal social existence come into play in interpreting the attractiveness of a feminist movement for women. Let us assume that middle-class, college-educated women archetypically exemplify the marginality of public and private spheres. But not all middle-class, college-educated females joined the ranks of the movement. This is in part explained by the "baby-boom" thesis; that is, a relatively small percentage of women publicly question their marginality, but the baby boom made even this small percentage a large enough number of women to make an impact on the body of social facts. Also, some women are "more marginal" than others. The more sources of marginality, the more likelihood of becoming detached from the available taken-for-granted sets of definitions that provide recipes for everyday life. In other words, those who are "caught in the middle" in several areas are more likely to observe and experience different plausibility structures, to experience the contradictions built into the structures in which they move.

Inspection of the social biographies of some intellectual and ideological spokeswomen for the movement—for example, Kate Millet, Germaine Greer, Jill Johnston, Gloria Steinem—usually uncovers marginality in their lives. Besides their public-private marginality, other marginality bases include a lack of "status crystallization," downward or upward social mobility, and cultural migration. In addition, one might speculate that women who are not ugly yet not beautiful, or who are not old yet not young, are more likely to experience alienation from the official versions of social reality and their place within this reality.

A final note to this discussion may tie in the notion of marginality with the four ideal typical dimensions of the women's movement. Many of the women in the movement were originally drawn into the ranks because of their refusal to tolerate the contradictions, the ambivalence, the marginality built into the female role. Four different solutions have been proposed as to how to remedy the situation: to instrumentalize both public and private spheres, to expressivize both spheres, to synthesize the two spheres, or to repolarize the instrumental-expressive dichotomy. None of these approaches accepts the present situation of role ambiguity. The first three would eliminate sexual differentiation so that males and females would have the same basic orientation; the fourth would reestablish some presocial essential male-female differentiation so as to strengthen the differences between the sexes and eliminate role marginality.

Marginality premises, however, must be considered within the context of modern technological society and the impact of one upon the other. The next chapter focuses on technological social organization and its part in the emergence of the women's liberation movement.

NOTES

1. Peter L. Berger and Thomas Luckmann, *The Social Construction of Reality* (Garden City, N.Y.: Doubleday, 1967).

2. The character of modernity will be examined in the next chapter.

3. Some scholars locate the origins of feminist consciousness at least as early as the fifteenth century. Cf. Simone de Beauvoir's remarks on Christine de Pisan in *The Second Sex*, trans. and ed. H. M. Parshley (New York: Bantam, 1961), p. 97.

4. Since I claim no expertise in history, nor an extensive knowledge of historical sources on the history of feminism, I rely heavily upon the accounts of William L. O'Neill, *The Woman Movement* (Chicago: Quadrangle, 1971); Aileen S. Kraditor, *The Ideas of the Woman Suffrage Movement: 1890–1920* (Garden City, N.Y.: Doubleday, 1971); and Eleanor Flexner, *Century of Struggle* (Cambridge, Mass.: Belknap Press of Harvard University Press, 1959).

5. O'Neill, *The Woman Movement*, pp. 15–32.

6. Technological considerations are discussed in the next chapter. It is assumed that both pro- and counter-technological stances are included in the current women's liberation movement.

7. This is especially important in understanding the massive reaction to the war in Vietnam, part of the social fabric out of which the current women's movement was formed.

8. William H. Chafe, *The American Woman* (New York: Oxford University Press, 1977).

9. Betty Friedan, *The Feminine Mystique* (New York: Norton, 1963).

10. I am indebted to Judy Balfe for the insight on mothers and daughters of World War II, and to Terri Glatz for her understanding of the experience of World War II on women's self-conceptions.

11. Chafe, *The American Woman*, pp. 217–220.

12. Ibid., chaps. 8 and 9.

13. Ibid., chap. 9.

14. Ibid.

15. Ibid., p. 208.

16. Evelyne Sullerot, *Women, Society and Change*, trans. Margaret Scotford Archer (New York: World University Press, 1971), pp. 201–202ff. Cf. Sheila Rowbotham, *Women, Resistance and Revolution* (New York: Vintage, 1974), chaps. 1 and 2, for a different interpretation of feminism and the French Revolution.

17. Ibid., p. 201.

18. Ibid.

19. This last point also has relevance for the beginnings of the current women's movement in that most observers locate its origin with the split of women from men in the New Left student campaigns against the war in Vietnam, most noticeably at Barnard-Columbia in the late 1960s.

20. O'Neill, *The Woman Movement*, pp. 19–20.

21. Ibid., p. 20.

22. Ibid., p. 24.

23. Ibid., pp. 16–19.

24. Phillippe Ariès, *Centuries of Childhood: A Social History of Family Life* (New York: Vintage, 1962).

25. The terms "culture lag" and "revolution of rising expectations" come to mind in the situation discussed here. Cf. Rowbotham's interpretation of woman's place in the aftermath of the French Revolution. Rowbotham, *Women, Resistance and Revolution*, pp. 37–58.

26. O'Neill, *The Woman Movement*, pp. 18–19. For a different view of women and voluntary associational activity, cf. Doris B. Gold, "Women and Voluntarism," in *Woman in Sexist Society*, ed. Vivian Gornick and Barbara K. Moran (New York: New American Library, 1971), pp. 533–34.

27. O'Neill, *The Woman Movement*, pp. 93–97.

28. Ibid., p. 94.

29. Cf. Juliet Mitchell, *Woman's Estate* (New York: Vintage, 1971);

and Linda Gordon, "Women's Labor," *Radical America* 7 (July–October 1973): 1–8. See also the literature on welfare mothers' and working-class women's liberation groups, e.g., Susan Jacoby, "What Do I Do for the Next Twenty Years?" *New York Times Magazine,* 17 June 1973, pp. 10 ff.

30. A minority of women's groups advocate organizing small cells fervently committed to feminist goals, rather than seeking to recruit a broadly based membership. This qualification also applies to the early feminist movement. Cf. O'Neill, *The Woman Movement;* and Aileen Kraditor, *The Ideas of the Woman Suffrage Movement.*

31. Mirra Komarovsky, "Cultural Contradictions and Sex Roles," in *Selected Studies in Marriage and the Family,* ed. Robert F. Winch, Robert McGinnis, and Herbert M. Barringer (New York: Holt, Rinehart & Winston, 1962), p. 127. Emphasis added.

32. Ibid. Emphases added.

33. Ibid., p. 132. Emphases added.

34. The part played by the "baby-boom" must be explained more fully. The notion of a normal curve is useful in explaining general characteristics of the population within certain contexts; for example, intelligence, culturally defined "beauty," "creativity," motor skills, and speculatively, conformity. The latter context is taken as a tentative explanation as to why more and more numbers were involved in the tails of the curve even though the proportions were still those specified by the definition of the curve. In other words, the adolescents of the 1960s had been born during the baby-boom years. This is one explanation of why the 1960s witnessed a surge in innovative forms in popular music, experimental lifestyles, generalized nonconformity, inability to tolerate as taken-for-granted social conditions they defined as dehumanizing. There were more youths in the "tails" of the curve describing creativity, nonconformity and, in the case being considered here, more women who could share with one another and together externalize their dissatisfactions with the woman's role as culturally transmitted. In other words, there was a large base for movement recruiting.

Also, while the traditional relationship between socioeconomic status and birthrate has been an inverse one—the higher the class, the lower the birthrate—the late 1940s pattern suggests a trend from the lower middle class through the higher socioeconomic strata to have about four children. This bears upon the case here in that middle-class females are those considered as marginal and therefore recruitable into the feminist movement.

While the size of the post–World War II cohort was greater relative to those that preceded it, the ratio of the extremes remained the same, by definition of the normal curve. What I am saying is that some women have always found their role to be oppressive, but that the 1960s had more of a pool of such women, numerous enough to capture the public attention, which served to objectify this definition and to have an influence upon other women's perceptions of their role. This thesis needs to be empirically investigated—the age, class, "conformity-orientation," etc., of women who were in at the start of the movement would have to be measured—but the thesis is consistent with the theoretical framework presented here.

7

THE FEMINIST STRUGGLE WITH MODERNITY

FEMINISM: CENTRAL TO, OR DISPLACEMENT OF, THE CRISIS OF MODERNITY?

The feminist struggle with modernity entails discontent at both the structural and subjective levels. This discontent revolves around questions of identity and meaning, the disjunctions between public and private existence and experience, and anomie and alienation. The discontent is traceable to the structure of modern society, the most relevant aspects of which include increasing rationalization, specialization, multiple relationality, and pluralization.

The discontent generated by the modern social structure is not uniquely experienced by feminists. On the contrary, much of the social criticism directed at present-day society focuses on the alienation and anomie, fragmentation and role conflict, identity crises and "divided selves" [1] experienced by all people in the modern world. In the light of this generalized discontent, one might interpret feminism as simply another illustration of widely experienced difficulties, as symptomatic of a general social problem. If feminism is considered as a symptom of the larger problem of modernity, a likely conclusion would be that feminism is a false focus, a displacement of the real issue, that it represents "false consciousness" in the Marxian sense.

A similar conclusion is arrived at by feminists who identify themselves with socialism first and feminism second. [2] For them, an exclusive focusing on feminism without a recognition of the class-based nature of the present order mystifies the real issue—the woman's struggle with the status quo must be directed against the capitalist structure of society. We have here, again, the debate over whether the present social structure is to be perceived as "modern" (i.e., technology is prior to profit and commodity exchange as the defining force and carries intrinsic patterns that dominate social reality) or as "capitalist" (capitalist modes of technological production depend on dualism, rationalization, alienation, and like patterns; technological production in the socialist era will not operate on the same principles because it will not be dominated by the profit motive). Whatever the theory as to the genesis of the current social structure, both "modern" and "capitalist" analyses describe the same outcomes: increasing rationalization, specialization, public-private dualism, and so on. Feminism must be understood as directed against these social structural outcomes, whatever their origins, because of their bearing on the position of women in the modern era.

Another version of viewing feminism as a false focus is derived from ontological rather than sociological premises. But feminism addresses the question of identity ambiguity in sociological terms. Its solution, whatever the ideal type, is a social one. In fact, one premise that unites the four ideal types is that social change can be brought about through movement efforts to eliminate the present conditions women find undesirable. Yet many critics define the issue in ontological terms and charge feminism with naively seeking an unalienated life when such a goal is not humanly possible.

For such critics, the crisis of contemporary life is but one manifestation of the universal, essential human dilemma. This leads them to interpret feminism as a "symptom," a "mask," a "scapegoat" for the real problem—life itself. Moreover, they posit that the relationship between individuals and society must be understood in dualistic, rather than dialectical, terms. They assume that dualism is inherent in the human condition—individual, subjective existence stands apart from, if not in opposition to, social structural realities.[3] That is, they assume that present reality is the only reality that does not, or cannot, change into an alternative reality. For these critics, feminism displaces the real problem—inability to come to grips with adult human ambiguity—onto the social structure. In effect, these critics have turned the feminist analysis upside down by arguing that the resolution to the identity crisis, and the source for meaning in social existence, must be sought at the subjective level.

Nevertheless, feminism represents something other than a displacement of the problems inherent in the modern social structure or universal human existence. A case can be made that feminism is at the center of the subjective and structural crises of modernity. While all people must confront, to a greater or lesser degree, the ambivalences and ambiguities engendered by modernity, the "woman question" combines these confrontations in multiple ways.

"Female" represents an ascribed categorization recognized (with few exceptions) as defining a being who is different and separate from, and in most societies subordinate to, "male." Modern presuppositions define humanity in nonascriptive terms, but females in modern society have conventionally been perceived as not-quite-belonging to the same species as males by virtue of their biological distinctiveness from males. Differences in anatomy, in the part played in the birth process, and in physical strength have been socially defined and taken for granted as significant in human as well as sexual identity (self-concept) and sexual identification (definition of self by others). Where power has been allocated to males in a hierarchical order, females have been typically apprehended as subordinate "others."

Such a perception of females is clearly at odds with modern, universalistic-achievement premises about humanity. To the extent that ascriptive premises about women are found in modern society, and to the degree that power is monopolized by males in that society, females typically find themselves caught between traditional and modern identities regarding their sexual and human natures. The questions What does it mean to be female? What does it mean to be human? and What is expected of me as a female and a human? cannot be answered unambiguously in present-day society because of women's special location between the public and private duality engendered by the modern social structure, and between the expressive and instrumental orientations dualistically allocated to these spheres. This is yet another way of saying that women are the archetypical marginals in modern society.

Another reason for considering feminism as central to the crisis of modern society, rather than a displacement of it, is that the category "female" bridges other ascriptive identifications—females can be found in all ascriptively identified groups that are struggling with questions of identity, meaning, and equity in modern society. Because recognizable sexual differences are used to divide the human species into two halves—male and female—"female" is a designation that transcends age, race, and class. This is not to say that all women give primary salience to the quest for female identity and equity. Women in many groups organized around the struggle for equity may define ascribed characteristics other than female as primary—for example, black women, welfare rights women, aged women. Nevertheless, as long as "female" remains a salient social designation given credence by the permanent anatomical distinctiveness of females, and as long as females find themselves apprehended as "expressive" in an increasingly instrumentalized world, the "woman question" will remain at the center of the modernity crisis.

FEMINISM AS A SINGLE MOVEMENT

The four ideal types contained in current feminism show that the women's movement, contrary to the belief of feminists, can be considered as a four-faceted rather than a single movement. The ideal types latent in the movement are very different one from another. The underlying philosophical assumptions, the depiction of the status quo, and the program proposed diverge radically with each type.

Underlying these latent differences, however, is the manifest perception shared by feminists that women are oppressed, unhappy, and unfulfilled in the lives made possible for them by the structure and consciousness of present-day society. Women in the movement are motivated by a dissatisfaction with present society that they share in common. In expressing this dissatisfaction and proposing solutions, the common motivation may be molded into different ideological types. Nevertheless, women in the movement perceive one another as "sisters in struggle." The manifest understanding of most feminists is that feminism is animated by a common definition of the situation—women are oppressed, women are sisters.

The four ideal types verify that this understanding does not carry over into a common ideology; rather, it becomes elaborated into four different ideologies. Should feminists become aware of these latent ideological contradictions, the bases for, and implications of, identification with the movement would have to be examined more closely and critically by individuals and groups in the movement. This latter observation may help explain why attempts to initiate and carry through practical projects so often fail, and the women's group in question returns to personal "consciousness raising" activities.[4]

Despite the four divergent ideal types, the women's movement may be viewed as a single movement, not for the reasons offered by feminists, but because it is a movement implicitly aimed at resolving the marginality crisis engendered by modern society.

The key issue in the struggle of feminists with modernity is the lack of "symmetry" between self and society.[5] Their social location of marginality—of being caught between public and private life—is what all feminists find most intolerable. The identity crisis, endemic in modern society because of pluralization at both institutional and subjective levels, is experienced more acutely by women and most acutely by college-educated women. Women represent the archetypical modern marginals because of their special location between *the major fragmentation* of modern social structure—public and private. This thesis rests on the assumption that expressivity—or "symbolic communication" (Habermas) or "natural will" (Tonnies) or comfortable "at-homeness" (Berger, see the Appendix)—is the dominant mode of relating in the private sphere, holding aside for the moment questions of carryovers of public, instrumental patterns into the private, expressive sphere, or of "erosion" of the private institutional framework into instrumentality. This thesis also rests on the assumption that because of their early and continuous socialization into expressive identities and identifications, and into giving primacy to their roles in the private sphere (lover, wife, and mother), women are at odds with the instrumental patterns and expectations they must confront in their first direct, immediate encounter with the public sphere—the education institution. The crisis of identity for women grows increasingly more acute the longer and the more intense their exposure to these instrumental patterns and expectations.

"Who Am I?" is a question that must be addressed in expressive and instrumental terms for women. All four ideal types provide ways of answering the question in such a way as to achieve a clear-cut identity, on the one hand, and resolve the contradictions between public (instrumental) and private (expressive) existence, on the other. Instrumentalism, Expressivism, and Synthesism propose that the identification "female" no longer be considered real; instead, the designation "human" is to be the only identification that has meaning for all people. It must be remembered, however, that these three ideal types use as an organizing device the notion that all women are sisters; the fact of being female carries with it a common bond that is not available to males, at least not until the social changes these feminists advocate come into being.

As far as resolving the present contradictions between public and private existence is concerned, each ideal type proposes a new variation on symmetry between self and society. Instrumentalism solves the problem by eliminating the private, expressive sphere altogether. Meaning, *nomos*, and demarginalization are to be achieved by changing the present dualistic society and socialization process into a monistic or "one-dimensional" [6] one built along instrumental lines. With this change from dualism to monism, the individual will no longer have to face being pulled in two opposite directions, being caught between two antithetical orientations. Thus, to the Instrumentalist, the question "Who Am I?" must be answered: "I am human; I am instrumental."

The monistic solution is also adopted by Expressivism, but here it is turned on its head: it is basically counter-modern. The "reality" of the public, instrumental sphere is to be removed; one's formerly "private" self is to be totalized to all areas of social experience. What was formerly defined as instrumental in the public sphere is to be "expressivized." This implies, of course, radical changes in the organization of macro-realities. Expressivism thus agrees in part with Instrumentalism's answer to the identity question —"I Am Human"—but it resolves the marginality crisis by restricting "human" to the expressive orientation: "I Am Expressive."

Synthesism provides yet another variation for dealing with the question of identity for women and for coming to grips with the marginality crisis. This ideal type also proposes a unisexual solution whereby men and women are viewed as essentially equivalent humans. "I Am Human" answers the identity question by defining sexual differentiation as irrelevant and eliminating the notion of different identifications for males and females. "Human" is conceived of dialectically as a synthesis of instrumental (public) and expressive (private) orientations and activities. Symmetry between self and society is achieved by constructing a dialectical whole out of both, formerly antithetical, spheres of activity and orientation. In contrast to the two monistic solutions to the lack of symmetry, Synthesism reconciles the opposing spheres at a higher level (rather than eliminate either sphere) in order to abolish the public-private, instrumental-expressive dualities. The Synthesist program advocates those social changes needed to bring about a reorientation of the public and private realms of social organization: the private sphere will be "instrumentalized," while the public sphere will be "expressivized." No specializations or "monopolizations" are to be tolerated either at the structural or subjective levels.

The fourth ideal type, Polarism, solves the identity-symmetry problem by retaining the dualism of instrumental and expressive orientations, but in reconstructed form. The public-private split is approached similarly. Instead of eliminating one or the other reality (as do Instrumentalism and Expressivism), instead of combining the two into a dialectical unity (as does Synthesism), Polarism eliminates marginality by eliminating the dilemma currently experienced by women caught between the two. Once recovered from their present distorted forms, expressivity and instrumentality are to be kept distinct and associated with females and males, respectively. Rediscovery of their genuine, intrinsic expressivity will provide women with a natural, unambiguous identity. Since males are assumed to be essentially instrumental and females essentially expressive, the crises, confusions, and ambiguities currently experienced in self-perception and roles will cease once these intrinsic differences are recognized as clear-cut and unambiguous. Polarism is the only ideal type that advocates dualized sexual differentiation and specialization.

FOUR MOVEMENTS IN STRUGGLE WITH MODERNITY

The foregoing discussion pointed out the common basis for participation in the women's movement—dissatisfaction with modern society because of the marginality crisis. This section views the movement as embodying four distinct, contradictory ideological variations addressed to a critique of modern society.

Instrumentalism

Instrumentally oriented feminists are critical of modern technoculture because they maintain that in it women have not received their fair share of the benefits assumed inherent in the society. The quarrel is not with the rationalized ethos of modernity but with modern society's failure to apply and implement the instrumental-rational credo universally and fully. Instrumentalism represents a legitimation of modern technocratic ideology; its program is aimed at the reordering of society along instrumental lines.

Instrumentalism totally embraces modern consciousness. Its presuppositions about human nature and society are clearly modern in orientation. Feminists who espouse this theme give priority to *zweckrational* action and "rational will," and to the specific behavioral correlates of purposive rational action. (See the Appendix for background for the following discussion.) Instrumentally oriented feminists aim for behavior that entails coolness and reserve ("affective neutrality" in Parsons's term, "emotional management" in Berger's) that is oriented to self-interest and ego fulfillment ("self-orientation" in Parsons's pattern variables). Instrumentalism legitimates relating to others through abstract, generalized rules ("universalism" for Parsons, "anonymous social relationships" for Berger), and perceiving one's worth as measured and judged by objective, certifiable achievements ("performance" in the pattern variables). Instrumentalism also entails relating to others in means-specific terms ("specificity" in the pattern variables, "componential social relationships" for Berger). Instrumentalism implies a totalization of the instrumental ethos. All persons (male and female, children and adults) in all areas of social life (public and private, institutional and personal) are to be actualized instrumentally. "Componentiality," a modern theme identified by Berger, figures predominantly in the view that human nature is basically nonascriptive. Women, men, or any other conventionally recognized ascribed identifications are false; humanity must be thought of as essentially equivalent and interchangeable. Berger's "makeability" is also reflected in the Instrumentalist's assumptions that the self can be produced by human effort, as can the good society, if the appropriate techniques are put into practice. The correspondences between Instrumentalism and modern consciousness become readily apparent. Feminist Instrumentalism, then, is closely parallel with Tonnies's *Gesellschaft* and "rational will," with Weber's descriptions of *zweckrational* action and bureaucratic authority, with Berger's depiction of modern consciousness, and with Habermas's interpretation of "work" and subsystems of purposive rational action.

It is important to mention the implications for the future of modern society embedded in Instrumentalism. This ideal type would institute a totally rationalized future where expressivity finds no place. All the features associated with modernity would be carried to their logical extremes. In the future scenario, all individuals would be completely equivalent, interchangeable beings, but their actions would be governed by extremized individualism and total self-interestedness.[7]

What implications for future institutional changes are built into Instrumentalism? This ideal type plans a future that necessitates a complete revamping of the institutional order so that it totally reflects the instrumental orientation. Insofar as the economy is concerned, Instrumentalism would lead to massive changes in the labor market because women would be integrated into the existing occupational hierarchy in direct proportion to their numbers in the population. Two variations on this goal are possible: (1) half the jobs available at all ranks might be filled by women; or (2) the work world might be restructured so that half of each available job would be filled by a woman, thus doubling the number of jobs and enabling husbands and wives to share one job between them. The logistics of (2), splitting jobs, might become quite complicated because few husbands and wives are matched exactly in terms of specific job aptitudes and capacities. But the halving of available jobs could be arranged so that men and women, as individuals if not as couples, could each work half-time. Instrumentalists would probably find the half-time, half-job solution incompatible with their emphasis on extremized individualism and total self-interestedness, however. Instrumentalists would be more inclined toward career mobility goals premised on personal ambition and full-time occupational participation. The shared-job solution seems more compatible with Synthesism because of this ideal type's orientation toward a socialist economic philosophy. Nevertheless, if the present labor trend continues into the future—increasingly fewer jobs available for all—the Instrumentalist project of having all individuals work half-time might become a reality.

Instrumentalist premises legitimate the notion of meritocracy. The Instrumentalists envisage a world in which universalistic achievement credentials will be the only relevant measures for judging an individual's worth and suitability for a job. The present situation is criticized for its failure to implement the merit system fully in the allocation of opportunities and rewards, a failure evidenced in the ascriptive-based discrimination against women, nonwhites, and the lower classes. This utopian vision, however, does not come to grips with the question of ascriptive carryovers to the future.[8] In the future envisioned by Instrumentalism, meritocratic ideology will in all likelihood ignore the problem of past ascriptive discriminations. Failure to achieve will be attributed to personal failure rather than to a heritage of noninstrumental socialization. The implications of the Instrumentalist meritocracy, then, are not clearly worked out for adults who are at the present time female, working-class, and nonwhite.

Other institutions will also be changed if the Instrumentalist future scenario is actualized. The family, currently one of the few remaining institutional counterpoints to the instrumental public sphere because it is oriented to *Gemeinschaft*-type relationships and harbors expressivity, must change.[9] The instrumentalization of the family advocated by this ideal type portends an elimination of all counter-instrumental institutions. "One-dimensionality" will become a reality. If the family deinstitutionalizes its expressive orientation, the rationalization process will spread to all areas.

A number of theorists have suggested that the deinstitutionalization of the family is the prelude to totalitarianism because without firm counter-institutional supports, family socialization can no longer provide children with a character structure that resists the encroachments of the institutional public sphere, which is dominated by the state. Children raised to be instrumentally rational, extremely individualistic, self-interested, affectively neutral, and contractual will fit comfortably into a rationalized totalitarian order. Moreover, the instrumental style can be instilled by rationalized state-sponsored child-care units that will increasingly take on the function of child rearing at younger and younger ages.

These observations rest on the assumption that the family is currently founded on *Gemeinschaft* principles and thus fosters patterns of expressivity: affectivity, collective-orientation, particularism, diffuseness, and equality. If this is the case, the family serves to protect individuals from state domination by giving them a source of identity, a rootedness, a "home." Many sociological observers, however, point to the family, at least the middle-class nuclear family, as the major agency of socialization into patterns that are compatible with the "needs" of macro-economic and political realities. These patterns include emphasis on individualism, self-interest, competitiveness, and acceptance of hierarchical relationships. In this view the family represents not a counter-institution but an institution highly complementary to public institutions.

Moreover, it is the atypical, relatively "deinstitutionalized" upper-middle-class family that is likely to socialize children into patterns counter to those found in the instrumentalized public sphere. Patterns found in these families include an emphasis on equalitarianism between parents and children, "enlightened" permissiveness in child rearing, and the rewarding of spontaneity rather than conformity, self-expression rather than obedience. Such families have been associated with young people who rebel against what they consider a dehumanizing government. This view is held by Habermas, Keniston, and Slater, among others.[10]

But this discussion is somewhat beside the point. Clearly, Instrumentalism, as ideal typically conceived, does not imply the type of family referred to in the preceding paragraph. True, some deinstitutionalized families manage to provide a counter-instrumental rootage for individuals in modern society, but the Instrumentalist future seems more in keeping with the growth of state power over individual existence. Whether evaluated in terms compatible with Habermas's or Parsons's perspective, the conclusion is that the political order steps in when rationalized specialization increases in order to integrate (Parsons) or dominate (Habermas) the general society.

Expressivism

Expressivism is founded on dualistic premises and is thus similar to Instrumentalism. Although the two ideal types select opposite value outcomes, both project monistic Utopias. The monistic outcomes depend on a prior dualistic premise—it is assumed that duality antecedes the ascendance of one of the two polarities and the eventual extinction of the other.

Expressivism is a counter-modern type in content, if not in form. It is critical of modern technoculture because of its failure to recognize and reward expressive behavior adequately. Defining expressivity as sex-irrelevant (both women and men are true to their humanity when expressive), Expressivism repudiates social definitions that assign superiority to instrumental behavior and reward those who are instrumental (men) with power, privilege, and prestige. In this repudiation of the instrumental style, Expressivism attacks the ethos of modernity. But, as noted previously, this rejection is not total. Recall (from chapter 3) that Expressivism is built on modern philosophical assumptions in its antibiologistic and anti-ascriptive premises about the nature of humanity. Further, Expressivism assumes that society is perfectable through human endeavor. Modern themes of "componentiality" and "makeability" figure in this ideal type as much as they do in Instrumentalism. (See the Appendix for background for the following discussion.)

While Expressivism is counter-modern, it is not identical with *Gemeinschaft*, if the latter is conceived in dialectical terms. There is in fact a growing tendency to interpret *Gemeinschaft* as a dialectical rather than a dualistic social organization. For Tonnies, both forms of will and social relationships exist in *Gemeinschaft* if for no other reason than that both males and females have always co-existed in society, and each of the two sexes embodies these two forms separately.[11] Habermas interprets the institutional framework (roughly similar to *Gemeinschaft*) as containing pockets or "subsystems of purpose rational action" (or *Gesellschaft*) prior to capitalist rationalization. That is, prior to the progressive expansion of instrumental rationality and the accompanying erosion of the institutional framework, societal organization contained both types of social orientation in a potential dialectical relationship. Habermas's view is premised on the notion that the institutional framework, founded on symbolic communication, contains the possibility for a true human dialectic, whereas subsystems of purposive rational action do not. If the latter predominate, one-dimensionality takes hold. If the institutional framework predominates, it can exist in either a dualistic or dialectical relationship with rational subsystems.[12]

Expressivism's counter-modernity is found in its repudiation of *zweckrational* action and its exclusive emphasis on nonrational elements of life. Expressivism is elaborated as affectivity, collective orientation, quality (or ascription), particularism, and diffuseness in Parsons's terminology. Individuals are naturally and exclusively expressive. The principles embodied in this type are similar to those that Mannheim associated with Romantic Conservatism.[13] For Mannheim, conservatism represented a political and ideological reaction to the increasing rationalization of the social world ushered in by capitalism. The Romantic Conservative movement called for a reinstitution of the older way of life and values of precapitalist *Gemeinschaft*:

> "Community" is set up against "society" . . . family against contract, intuitive certainty against reason, spiritual against material experience. All the partially hidden factors at the very basis of everyday life are suddenly laid bare by reflection and fought for.[14]

Although Mannheim maintains that conservatism, as an intellectual, political, and ideological reaction against capitalism, can take form only "through the medium of class conflict—in a class society," [15] it is useful to note the similarities between Romantic Conservatism and the Expressivist ideal type. The two share a repudiation of the rationalization process and capitalist (or technocratic) *Gesellschaft,* an emphasis on the qualitative and concrete as opposed to the quantitative and abstract, and a rejection of rational techniques for problem-solving. Important distinctions between Romantic Conservatism and feminist Expressivism must also be noted. Conservatism repudiates rationalism and replaces it with a Utopia derived from past traditions—it seeks a return to a natural and social hierarchy. Conservatism's repudiation of natural-law philosophy includes a rejection of rationalism's idea that every individual has a claim to an intrinsic human validity and dignity and a rejection of rationalism's atomistic and mechanistic premises. Expressivism's rejection of rationalism is not total, in that this ideal type legitimates "makeability" and "componentiality." Moreover, Expressivism looks to a future form of nonrationality, not a reinstitution of some past form.

Although Expressivism contains several rational, modern premises in its mixture of philosophical assumptions, it nevertheless resembles Romantic Conservatism in that both may be interpreted as developing as antitheses to rationalized technoculture. Mannheim's remarks on the social strata that participated in German conservatism are instructive.[16] He suggests that young "unattached intellectuals" provided the major source of recruitment into the Romantic Conservative movement. For him, these intellectuals have no self-interested, class-based ideology and can therefore adopt the ideology of any class or cause. Although Mannheim attributes their incisive view to their disinterested, unattached intellectualism, feminist marginality can be manifested in the Expressivist mode in a manner similar to that identified by Mannheim. Also, Mannheim's analysis of "unattached intellectuals" as classless and therefore totally relative in their choice of ideological affiliation might be revised to include the point that the marginality (i.e., between classes) of these intellectuals must be viewed as that which animates their critique of an existing order in which they find no place. Mannheim describes the intelligentsia as an "interstitial stratum . . . between, but not above, the classes." [17] From this unattached position they are able to bring to bear a variety of perspectives on any given social issues. However, Mannheim also describes the unattached intellectual as not being able to find suitable employment in the growing capitalist bureaucracy. It could be posited that lack of attachment, or marginality, prompts a critical stance against the status quo, whether the Utopia aimed at is located in the past or in the future.

Expressivism, counter-modern in content if not in form, implies a radical restructuring of private and public institutions. Instrumentalized technological production and bureaucracy would be eliminated and replaced by forms not built on rationalist foundations. Values to be fostered would include a point-by-point acceptance of those pattern variables that summarize expressivity—affectivity, collective orientation, and the like.

As to the future, Expressivism implies an "expressivization" of work, of the political order. Individualism, the ethos of achievement, rational planning, calculation of means and ends, and mechanical fragmentation would be replaced by their opposites. The world would be restructured to reflect totality, collectivity, simplification, emotionality, spontaneity, intuition, sensitivity, passion, passivity, and surrender to the organic processes of life. The short-term program would set up female collectives, or mini-societies, run according to expressivist principles and values. Males would be excluded, or at least avoided whenever possible, because they are at present conditioned to be instrumental. In the long-run, all humans, males as well as females, would be included in the Expressivist Utopia.

In the economic future projected by this ideal type, no one would "work" in the present sense of the term. Tasks would have to be done, of course, but they would be fitted into an expressive orientation. Probably the mode of production most acceptable to Expressivism is a "back-to-nature" subsistence farming, which most easily is incorporable into an organic, total, simple order of expressive living. The promise held out by Expressivism is one of checking the rationalization process, along with all its negative features: alienation from self, others, and nature; possessive, competitive individualism; an ethos of equivalence of exchange that informs social relationships; and contractualness applied to all of life. In throwing out instrumentality completely, however, Expressivism also throws out its positive contributions to social life.

Synthesism

Synthesism represents a rejection of the modern notion of the division of labor and its accompanying role specialization. The Synthesist ideal disallows dualism in any sphere of human activity. Synthesism is thus counter-modern; specialization built on differentiation is an intrinsic feature of the modern era. Nevertheless, Synthesism's rejection of modernity is not total; several of its themes are compatible with modern consciousness. For example, Synthesism presupposes that humanity is essentially context-free that is, biological and ascriptive particulars have no bearing on universal, essential human nature. This supposition hints at an affinity with modern consciousness, as does the Synthesist premise that social progress can be brought about through human effort. But, though Synthesism mixes modern and counter-modern premises, its basic thrust is counter-modern.

Synthesism wishes to preserve expressivity and instrumentality, but in reconstructed form. Its program for the future entails forging a synthesis out of what are now considered polar dualities. In the Synthesist view the institutional order needs radical restructuring in order to embody this synthesis. The seeds of expressivity inherent in the public sphere will be nurtured and integrated dialectically with its antithesis, instrumentality. So, too, with the private sphere. Personality formation will entail a dialectical synthesis for men and women so that each sex will embody a synthesis of instrumental and expressive capacities. The direct changes called for would include an elimination of the division of labor, role specialization, and hierarchy. As a counter-modern type, Synthesism effectively addresses the dualism manifested in the public-private split and in male and female sex roles. In the Synthesist future, private and public identities and "roles" will fuse into an unfragmented identity.

Current divisions between "work" and "play," between "business" and "pleasure," will cease to have meaning. As Habermas describes it, the institutional framework, in itself potentially a synthesis of expressive and instrumental orientations, will inform and direct the "subsystems of purposive rational action." This limitation to the increasing rationalization process will come into being through the development of "unrestricted communication" (in itself dialectical) so as to release the self-formative dialectical processes inherent in human subjectivity. Thus subjectivity and society will be revitalized from the present paralysis of one-dimensional instrumental rationality.[18]

In the political realm, Synthesism projects a future in which no vestige of hierarchy will be tolerated. Full and complete participation by everyone in planning and decision making will be actualized. The family will also change to reflect the instrumental-expressive synthesis. Sex roles will vanish; both parents will have an equal share in child rearing. All people will mother-father children. Children will not "belong to" any one couple. Since hierarchical relationships will be abolished, the power imbalances between old and young and between parents and children, will also vanish.

Polarism

Polarism sees a future based on a more extreme dualism than that of present-day society, especially in the tendency to monistic rationalization that is becoming more evident in modern technoculture. Polarism, which is least compatible with modernity because of its biologistic assumptions about human nature, nevertheless contains modern assumptions in its ideology. Polarism's dualistic worldview and legitimation of pluralism fit comfortably with the modern themes of specialization and pluralization. But because of its assumption that males and females are essentially different, Polarism is a counter-modern ideal type.

Polarism resolves the marginality crisis in modern society by drawing the line between public and private, instrumental and expressive, more firmly and absolutely than it is at present. In this way, Polarism seeks to limit the monistic rationalization process by reinstituting full-fledged dualism: expressive and instrumental orientations will be "separate but equal." Recall the discussion in chapter 5 wherein Polarism insisted on restoring essential expressive-instrumental distinctions between females and males. Only when the institutional structure is rearranged to foster uniquely female expressivity and uniquely male instrumentality can the modernity crisis be resolved.

Polarism is not a traditional harking back to some status quo ante, for it asserts that genuine expressivity and instrumentality have yet to be uncovered and fostered in the social order. We might say that Polarism represents a conservative counter-modern ideology with regard to form (dualism) but not content (a new order of expressivity and instrumentality).

The future institutional makeup projected by Polarism will be one in which expressive orientation ("female" principle) and instrumental orientation ("male" principle) are both given full play, but dualistically. In the economic realm men will continue to work —but only in jobs that are genuinely instrumental. Females may work—but only at expressive-oriented jobs, for example, teaching, nursing, and other supportive, "stroking" activities. The political realm will be directed by males insofar as decision making and goal directing is concerned. Females will be conciliators, diplomats, public relations specialists, and the like. A much clearer definition of expressive and instrumental orientations will lead to a more absolute classification of "female" and "male" occupations. In the realm of the family, mothers will be unambiguously expressive with their children. But again, expressivity in the genuine sense implies unconditional love, nurturance, trust, openness, compassion—not the distorted expressivity we witness today. Thus, in the Polarist scenario, mothers will not be possessive, overindulgent, sentimental, or weak.[19] Fathers will relate to their children as genuinely instrumental; love will be conditional on task fulfillment, and there will be emphasis on obedience to authority, abstract thought, and hierarchy.[20]

Under a Polarist future program, identity will no longer be problematical. Definitions of male and female, derived from their essential characteristics, will find expression in institutional activities. Thus the Polarist proposals address several levels of the crisis of modernity: identity crises, institutional disintegration, and the lack of symmetry between subjectivity and objectivity or between the internal and the external self. Polarism's emphasis on the celebration of difference (ascriptive pluralism) will provide additional sources for the resolution of the identity crises inherent in modern society. By legitimating ascribed characteristics as sources for genuine identity (e.g., black, old, young), the Polarist approach provides a variety of unambiguous identity "hooks." Assuming, of course, that the Polarist variation is that of nonhierarchical, equalitarian pluralism, the linkages between ascribed identities and institutional involvements (educational, economic, political) will make possible stable, secure identities, along with a stable, secure institutional order.

The Polarist scenario resembles the conservatist Utopia discussed above; but in its allegiance to natural hierarchies, Romantic Conservatism diverges from Polarism. One variation of Polarism keeps the hierarchical premise, but in inverted form. Those who are oriented toward the inverse hierarchical Polarist theme (females superior to males) would likely extend this hierarchical legitimation so that it applies to other groups. We then would have an embodiment of the conservative utopia. Subordinate ascribed identities (e.g., black, old, young, poor), as defined at present, will remain subordinate and take on their "preordained" positions at the bottom of the social hierarchy. One possible variation on this outcome: if the inverse hierarchical theme is universalized, there might be a society-wide inversion—"the first shall be last; the last shall be first"—so that groups at present enjoying social power and privilege (e.g,. the rich, middle-aged, WASPs) would, in the Polarist future, find themselves occupying the bottom rungs of the hierarchy.

CONCLUSION

The theories presented in the Appendix depict modernity as carrying with it a fragmentation of subjective and objective points of reference, or private and public experience, and of expressive and instrumental orientations. In this sense, modernity may be described as "dualistic." [21] That is, with the passing of traditional society, the fabric of social life loses its "wholeness"; the typical social personality reflects this dualism most dramatically in the separation between the public and private realms.

A further derivation from the theories presented is that objective, public, and instrumental polarities are becoming increasingly dominant over subjective, private, and expressive polarities. In terms belonging to the theorists (see the Appendix), the future is one of increasing alienation (Marx), rationalization (Weber), rational will, and *Gesellschaft* (Tonnies), a "one-dimensional" expansion of the subsystems of purposive rational action (Habermas) and "homelessness" (Berger).

The emergence of feminism must be understood as a response to the crises engendered by modernity. What are we to conclude about the possible impact that feminism will make on modern society?

While the feminist movement must be understood as embodying ideological inconsistencies and contradictions among the four ideal types as well as within each type, it is useful, nevertheless, to dichotomize the types as either "modern" or "counter-modern." Instrumentalism legitimates an unlimited rationalization process, totally embraces modern philosophical assumptions, and aims at a future in which no sphere of personal or institutional experience will be left untouched by the instrumental style. Instrumentalism is thus thoroughly modern in ethos. Expressivism, Synthesism, and Polarism, even though their philosophical presuppositions entail a mix of modern and counter-modern themes, represent a challenge to the structure and consciousness of modern society because, in their depiction of the present situation, each encompasses a rejection of the instrumental ethos (especially as personified by males) and because their programs point to futures that are markedly different from the increasingly instrumental present. Thus these three ideal types mentioned can be characterized as counter-modern in ethos.

If the future is to be one of greater and greater rationalization, as legitimated by the Instrumentalist feminists, what is to become of the private sphere, of *Gemeinschaft*, of expressivity and their associated realities? Posed differently, are there any limits to the progressive rationalization process? Can any counter-tendencies (including the feminist movement's influence) be identified?

Marx assumed that the medium through which this chain of events would come into being would be class conflict. Nevertheless, Marx included the emancipation of women in his revolutionary goals because he saw the fate of woman tied up with the fate of the new order.[22] For Marx, the socialist epoch would embody a synthesis of objective and subjective states of being. Private and public life no longer would be dualistic; and the self, dialectically formed by the social realities, would no longer be split into public and private. Socialism would usher in an era of flexibility and generality in one's choices of active social and personal involvements, in contrast to the specialization into role identities that a capitalist division of labor requires. Feminist Synthesism is most compatible with this view.

For Weber, the future is premised on the assumption that technological production and mass administration necessitate increasing rationalization and bureaucratization at both objective and subjective levels. Weber's closing remarks in *The Protestant Ethic and the Spirit of Capitalism* leave room for the possibility that "new prophets [may] arise . . . [and there may be] a great rebirth of old ideas and ideals. . . ."[23] But Weber concludes that the future holds little hope of counter-rationalization processes. Whether the three counter-modern feminist ideal types will serve as "new prophets" remains to be seen.

Tonnies, on the other hand, implies that the change from *Gemeinschaft* to *Gesellschaft* ushered in the modern era (rationalized, specialized, bureaucratized). Although Tonnies refers to

Marx's positive contributions for understanding the capitalist order, Tonnies's work has been interpreted as explaining the political and economic patterns found in modern society as *consequences* of *Gesellschaft*-type social organization.[24] If this interpretation is accurate, a change in social organization could bring about changes in economic and political patterns so as to forestall the progressivity of the rationalization process. In other words, the view that the patterns *intrinsic* to technological production come to dominate social organization would say that the only way to check the rationalization process is to abandon technological production, a goal that is not feasible given the nature of the modern world. Tonnies, on the contrary, maintains that changes that originate in quarters other than those of the economy or polity can take hold of the rationalization process. Tonnies asserts that the fate of women is tied up with the fate of the proletariat. As women enter the occupational sphere they are likely to develop rational will, thereby speeding the formation of *Gesellschaft*. But Tonnies adds,

> . . . the possibility of overcoming this individualism [which is the prerequisite of *Gesellschaft*] and arriving at a reconstruction of *Gemeinschaft* exists. The analogy of the fate of women with the fate of the proletariat has been recognized and outlined long ago. Their growing group consciousness, like that of the isolated thinker can develop and rise to a moral-humane consciousness.[25]

Here Tonnies suggests that women as a group may have the potentiality for limiting the rationalization process and reconstructing *Gemeinschaft*. On the other hand, it must be remembered that Tonnies proceeds from dialectical premises—the form of will and the type of social organization are dialectically related to each other. Thus rational will reinforces *Gesellschaft*. *Gesellschaft* in turn reinforces rational will, and on and on. The possibility of limiting the rationalization process must be understood in this light. Moreover, the impression Tonnies leaves is that the era of *Gemeinschaft* has passed, even though natural will and *Gemeinschaft*-type relationships are part of the human condition and will appear in one form or another even if they do not predominate. Thus Tonnies assumed that while rational will and *Gesellschaft* predominate in modern society, natural will and *Gemeinschaft* (including passion, emotion, and sentiment) will not vanish from human experience.

Nisbet interpreted Tonnies's work to imply that the existence of *Gesellschaft* depends upon the persistence of *Gemeinschaft*.[26] The values of trust and brotherhood[27] fostered in *Gemeinschaft* make possible commerce and trade; these would become chaotic if business could not rely on others' trustworthiness.

Marx and Marxian-inspired theorists would interpret the matter of trust found in *Gesellschaft* differently. For them, the persistence of trust derives not from *Gemeinschaft* or similar superstructural norms (such as reciprocity[28]) but from the capitalist dynamic of "equivalence of exchange." Habermas takes the position that capitalist ideology (equivalence of exchange) emerges from below (i.e., is substructural) rather than above (i.e., superstructural).[29] For these theorists, the rationale for concluding that *Gemeinschaft* persists in *Gesellschaft* does not hold.

Is it possible for the rationalization process to dominate society and character formation so completely that it effectively eradicates the expressive, *Gemeinschaft* aspects of life, as Instrumentalism would wish?

Habermas and Marcuse maintain that it is possible to disempower the institutional framework (i.e., expressivity, or *Gemeinschaft*) so as to render it meaingless. The forms of expressivity that remain become shams—powerless parodies of true expressivity. Theorizing from different perspectives, Merton[30] has suggested that in modern society "pseudo-*Gemeinschaft*" is likely to develop. Relationships with the facade or appearance of *Gemeinschaft* are actually *Gesellschaft*. "You have a friend at Chase Manhattan" and "The Friendly Airline" come to mind. Pseudo-*Gemeinschaft* compensates for a lost, but longed for, *Gemeinschaft*. Does this survival, even in pseudo form, indicate something in the human condition that resists total rationalization? This conclusion can be derived from Marx's prediction of the eventual self-destructiveness of an extremized rational (in his view, capitalist) social order. The breakup of capitalism would propel society into a new epoch of socialist community animated by a synthesis of the rational and the affective.

According to Berger,[31] the family, as long as it does not become further deinstitutionalized, forestalls the total anonymity, componentiality, and homelessness of people fostered by a rationalized public sphere. Because it is *structured,* because it represents an institutionalized counter-style to instrumental public life, the family serves as a bulwark against the expansion of instrumental rationality. This view would interpret feminism as bringing about a further deinstitutionalization of the family, and thereby of the private sphere. In other words, attempts by feminists (particularly I-type feminists) to instill individualism and self-interestedness lead to further "turning inward" to self and hasten the process of "subjectivization." [32] In the eventual confrontation between subjective self and rationalized institutional structures, the latter will predominate. This conclusion rests on the premise that *institutionalized,* not subjective, counter-structures are equipped to do battle with the institutionalized public sphere. Left to its own capacities, the subjective self will succumb to the rationalized dominant institutions, most probably led by the state.

One larger question must be addressed: How adequate are the various models for grasping the interrelationship between expressivity and instrumentality? Many theorists assume that expressivity and instrumentality, *Gemeinschaft* and *Gesellschaft,* are antithetical and that action involves a choice between these polar opposites. As a consequence, societal organization at the macro level must necessarily entail dominance by one of the polarities. Some variations on this theme are possible.

It has been well established in the dualistic tradition to qualify the notion of a strict dichotomy with the notion that a continuum should be drawn between two extremes so as to locate concrete cases of relationships, groups or roles, and societies or cultures. That is, whereas the two polar types represent pure forms (ideal types or normal concepts), in actuality any concrete social phenomenon (action, role, or culture) must reside somewhere along the continuum between the two pure types. But this notion is still based on antithesis. To say that a society is oriented "more toward" instrumentality is premised on dualistic perceptions of the two types of social relationships: more of one implies less of the other.

Parsons, it may be recalled, posits that both instrumental and expressive axes must be present if a given system is to remain in equilibrium. For Parsons, "system" could be applied to social, cultural, or personality systems. By implication, societies, cultures, and persons would have to encompass both polarities. There is a problem inherent in this conception as his analysis moves from the personality to the social system level. If all persons embody both aspects, what of Parsons's other generalization that role specialization (into either expressive or instrumental orientation) is required for equilibrium in groups, especially in the family group? What becomes of the notion of dual-based personality equilibrium, especially for mothers and fathers? If both sexes are needed, what does it mean to characterize modern industrial society as oriented more toward the instrumental polarity? [33]

This leads us to ask whether the two polarized aspects are always present in action, roles, and societies. If one polarity predominates in any given system, is the other polarity always present? If we combined with this dualistic conceptualization the premise that human nature is socially based, conceived of as either a by-product of socialization or dialectically produced by (and in turn producing) the social order, and if we assume that either polarity predominates, the only conclusion possible is that human nature will eventually become one-sided (i.e., either expressive or instrumental). If we assume a dialectical process, then both social organization and consciousness must change so as to limit the rationalization process. If we assume a one-directional process of socialization (i.e., one in which social character is formed by absorbing macro-social realities), the only conclusion to be drawn is that change or limitation of the rationalization process must be instituted from above, at the structural level.

Habermas and Marcuse view the present social order as a dualistic one tending toward a monistic outcome.[34] They suggest that the ever-expanding patterns of instrumental rationality will "erode" their expressive, communal opposites (as now defined) to produce a one-dimensional outcome at both the social and subjective levels. The implication of this view is that there are no internal or external limitations to the process of rationalization short of radical change brought on by large-scale conflict. Further, the image of the human is a dialectical one—the social facts that make up social structure shape human nature, and vice versa. If the social structure becomes increasingly characterized by purposive rational action, then, through internalization, character formation will necessarily reflect the predominance of rational extremes and increasingly become rationalized to the extreme.

The only escape hatch in the above is that there is something more to human nature than social "programming." Some theories have suggested that something in human nature will not allow for the erosion of passion, emotion, collective involvement, and the like. Humans resist pressures toward total instrumentalism, either by active opposition or by passive resistance. Machines get junked, there is a resurgence of interest in the sacred (religion, mysticism, astrology), and love and emotion are hailed as the sources of genuine happiness. Some would also suggest that human nature will not long tolerate the separation of instrumentality and expressivity into specialized structures, whether at the personal, social, or cultural level. The structure of modern society—split between public and private, instrumental and expressive, *Gesellschaft* and *Gemeinschaft*—is contrary to natural human requirements. The natural condition is one of unity in all areas of being, the Synthesist ideal. Specialization distorts genuine human expression and experience on the personal and societal levels.

Feminism, then, is intimately tied to the future of modern society, each in turn acting on and being acted upon by the other. The most influential feminist type—Instrumentalism—may help accelerate the rush toward one-dimensionality. Yet some "natural" limits to the rationalization process must be assumed, whether these limits originate in human nature or in the social processes. The next chapter raises questions about what trends may counter the processes of one-dimensionality.

NOTES

1. R. D. Laing, *The Divided Self* (Baltimore: Penguin, 1965). Similar critiques of modern society include Philip Slater, *The Pursuit of Loneliness* (Boston: Beacon Press, 1970); Theodore Roszak, *The Making of a Counter-Culture* (Garden City, N.Y.: Anchor, 1969); and S. M. Jourard, *The Transparent Self* (Princeton, N.J.: Van Nostrand, 1964).

2. Cf., for example, Juliet Mitchell, *Woman's Estate* (New York: Vintage, 1971); Margaret Benston, "The Political Economy of Women's Liberation," in *From Feminism to Liberation*, ed. Edith Hoshino Altbach (Cambridge, Mass.: Schenkman, 1971); and Evelyn Reed, *Problems of Women's Liberation: A Marxist Approach* (New York: Pathfinder, 1970).

3. This dualistic view of individual and society is a prevalent one. It has taken the following forms: subjectivity against objectivity, feeling against form (Simmel), and *Homo internus* against *homo externus* (Luther). Cf. Anton Zijderveld, *The Abstract Society* (Garden City, N.Y.: Anchor Books, 1971), esp. chap. 2, for a discussion of the latter typology.

4. Peter Berger has suggested (private communication) that Pareto's distinction between "residues" and "derivations" may be useful in understanding how, in view of these different and sometimes contradictory ideal typical positions, their respective adherents can identify with each other as members of the same movement. Berger posits that in Paretian terms the "derivations" (ideal typical constructions) have little or nothing to do with the "residues" (psychological dynamic). In other words, the movement is animated by a psychological dynamic that is hidden by the ideological divergences. My interpretation differs from his insofar as I posit that the manifest understanding of feminists grants a common psychological motivation that is not warranted by virtue of the ideological contradictions that can be found in the movement. I nevertheless agree that, among feminists, a shared motivation is latent: female marginality in modern society.

5. Peter L. Berger, " 'Sincerity' and 'Authenticity' in Modern Society," *Public Interest*, Spring 1973, pp. 81–90; and idem, *The Homeless Mind* (New York: Random House, 1973).

6. Herbert Marcuse, *One-Dimensional Man* (Boston: Beacon Press, 1971).

7. Lewis Yablonsky, *Robopaths* (Baltimore: Penguin, 1972), discusses robopathic (from "robot") behavior along similar lines. Benjamin Barber describes in more colorful terms the kind of human implied by the Instrumentalist ideal type: "bleak," "bland," "banal," "neuter," "uniform," "automaton." "Man on Woman, Part 2," *Worldview* (May 1973), p. 52.

8. Cf. John Rawls, *A Theory of Justice* (Cambridge: Belknap Press of Harvard University Press, 1971) for a discussion of this issue. Cf. also Harry C. Bredemeier, "Review Essay: Justice, Virtue and Social Science," *Society* 10 (September–October, 1973), 76–83.

9. Peter L. Berger and Hansfried Kellner, "Marriage and the Construction of Reality," in *Recent Sociology Number Two*, ed. Hans Peter Dreitzel (New York: Macmillan, 1970), pp. 49–72. This thesis can also be found in works by Berger, cited in the Appendix.

10. Cf., Jurgen Habermas, *Toward a Rational Society* (Boston: Beacon Press, 1971); Richard W. Flacks, 'The Liberated Generation: An Exploration of the Roots of Student Protest," *Journal of Social Issues* 23, no. 3 (July 1967): 52–75; Kenneth Keniston, *The Young Radicals* (New York: Harcourt, Brace & World, 1965).

11. Ferdinand Tonnies, *Community and Society* (New York: Harper Torchbooks, 1963), passim.

12. Habermas, *Toward a Rational Society*.

13. Karl Mannheim, "Conservative Thought, in *From Karl Mannheim*, ed. Kurt Wolff (New York: Oxford University Press, 1971), pp. 132–222.

14. Ibid., p. 147.

15. Ibid., p. 159.

16. Ibid., pp. 183 ff.

17. Karl Mannheim, *Essays on the Sociology of Culture* (London: Routledge & Kegan Paul, 1956), pp. 104–5.

18. Habermas, *Toward a Rational Society*. Cf. his "Toward a Theory of Communicative Competence," in *Recent Sociology Number Two*, ed. Hans Peter Dreitzel (New York: Macmillan, 1970), pp. 115–48.

19. These characteristics are also suggested by Erich Fromm, "The Sig-

nificance of the Theory of Mother Right" and "The Theory of Mother Right and its Relevance for Social Psychology," in *The Crisis of Psychoanalysis* (Greenwich, Conn.: Fawcett, 1970).

20. Ibid., pp. 106, 130.

21. For an analysis of the origins and manifestations of dualistic rationalization in modern technocratic society, cf. Richard J. Butsch, "The Technological Ethos: Modern Life as Dualistic Rationalization" (Ph.D. qualifying paper submitted to the Department of Psychology, Rutgers University, New Brunswick, N.J., 1973).

22. See the citations of Marx in Friedrich Engels, *The Origins of the Family, Private Property and the State* (New York: International, 1942); and in V. I. Lenin, *On the Emancipation of Women* (Moscow: Progress, 1965).

23. Max Weber, *The Protestant Ethic and the Spirit of Capitalism*, trans. Talcott Parsons (New York: Scribner's, 1958), p. 182.

24. Robert A. Nisbet, *The Sociological Tradition* (New York: Basic, 1966), chap. 3.

25. Tonnies, *Community and Society*, p. 166.

26. Nisbet, *The Sociological Tradition*, chap. 3.

27. Cf. Benjamin Nelson, *The Idea of Usury* (Chicago: University of Chicago Press, 1969).

28. Alvin Gouldner, "The Norm of Reciprocity: A Preliminary Statement," *American Sociological Review* 25 (April 1960): 161–78.

29. Habermas, *Toward a Rational Society*, pp. 104–5.

30. Robert Merton, as cited in Fritz Pappenheim, *The Alienation of Modern Man* (New York: Modern Reader, 1968), p. 68.

31. Berger, " 'Sincerity' and 'Authenticity.' "

32. Ibid.

33. Talcott Parsons, *Societies: Evolutionary and Comparative Perspectives* (Englewood Cliffs, N.J.: Prentice-Hall, 1966).

34. Cf. Habermas, *Toward a Rational Society*; and Marcuse, *One-Dimensional Man*.

A CONCLUDING NOTE ON THE LIMITS OF ONE-DIMENSIONALITY

A new thesis that has emerged in critical theory repudiates the idea that one-dimensionality is a limitless process wherein more and more aspects of culture and personality can be instrumentalized in an ever expanding homogenization.[1] Piccone, for example, relegates one-dimensionality to that transitional period between entrepreneurial capitalism and its present advanced form—a period stretching roughly from the New Deal to the late 1960s.[2] One-dimensionality is no longer applicable because it is no longer necessary. In fact, it has become dysfunctional for the maintenance of the capitalist system it was instituted to protect. This is so because the spread of instrumental rationality, bureaucracy, and homogenization can achieve their maximum effect on areas that are not instrumentally rationalized, bureaucratized, and homogenized. In effect, these processes have been too successful for their own good; the system is in danger of feeding upon itself and falling into disarray from the excesses of one-dimensionality. It needs internal checks and balances to keep it on course.[3] These checks and balances take the form of Nader's Raiders and Common Causes, as well as movements toward ethnic identity and protest movements.

The civil rights movement, for example, was part of the homogenization process characterizing this transitional period. Its underlying assumptions considered all people equivalent, interchangeable units, thereby removing the focus from uniqueness, particularity, specificity, and otherness.[4]

The system now needs challenges to the homogenization process; hence, "artifical negativity" is fostered.[5] It is artificial rather than "organic" because it does not spring from a community base outside the system—such bases were eliminated in the homogenization and depersonalization processes of the transitional period. Thus, movements for black identity, ethnic celebration, and feminist consciousness provide sources of the lost particularity and otherness. Such movements challenge the system by challenging base assumptions upon which it rests—consumerism, technocracy, scientism, hierarchical relations in everyday life—and by addressing questions of meaning and value.[6]

In a sense, the feminist movement in its four ideal types represents a small scale version of the larger society. Instrumentalism would embody the push toward homogenization and depersonalization; Expressivism would entail one-dimensionality along sex-role lines, as well as challenging the supremacy of instrumental rationality and universalism; Polarism, by reintroducing biological duality, would also challenge homogenization processes; and Synthesism would involve artificial as well as potentially organic negativity in its opposition to technocracy and hierarchalism.

Although Instrumentalism seems to have the most influence of the four ideal types and is often taken to represent the whole of the women's movement, it, like other manifestations of the homogenization process, may be ready to be checked and limited. The Equal Rights Amendment represents a throwback to the homogenization process whose need has since passed.[7] If the amendment does not pass before time runs out on it, the defeat can serve either to keep feminism alive or to destroy it. The ERA draws upon Instrumentalist premises, but it has served to unite the many factions in the movement, as did the suffrage platform for the earlier feminism. But getting the vote all but destroyed feminism in the 1920s; it left the movement without a compelling platform.

If the ERA does not pass, the platform can remain active, holding together the many alliances now working for its passage. From that vantage point, feminism can act as artificial and possibly organic negativity, in the former case serving the needs of the system for an ongoing challenge to its excesses by women who feel locked out of the system, and in the latter case serving to challenge the system in its basic premises by women who question consumerism, technocracy, and hierarchalism. This is possible because the ERA's coalition is drawn from all four feminist ideal types.

If the forces opposed to passage of the ERA are able to strengthen their political coalition, they may serve as the embodiment of that artificial negativity required for system maintenance. In this sense, the traditional female role has become as much a challenge to one-dimensionality in the 1970s as it was a system support in the 1950s.[9] The next decade may witness a struggle between traditional and antitraditional female forms of negativity to check and challenge the homogenization processes. In other words, Expressivism, Polarism, and Synthesism represent blocks to the instrumentalization process, as does the conservative reaction to feminism. Conservative responses to feminism may also represent Instrumentalist homogenizing processes: the Total Woman group, for example, emphasizes "scientific," "expert" techniques of feminity presentation.

Strangely enough, the growing forces of the men's liberation movement seem also to offer a negation of some homogenization processes, insofar as groups within the movement do not involve male attempts to reassert dominance and superiority in areas lately defined as important: emotional expression, supportiveness, and so forth. Many male groups have members competing with one another in protestations of noncompetitive behavior. Here, too, we find many built-in contradictions.

Males are recruited into these groups to come to grips with what they perceive as shortcomings in expressivity: the inability freely and directly to show one's feelings, genuinely listen to another, shed tears, draw another out, be supportive, and so on. Usually, males are aware of problems in the instrumental style and can be genuine critics. But they have relatively little socialization in being expressive, so they are as awkward and unspontaneous in expressivity as females are in instrumental behavior in the dualized versions now characterizing sex roles. Many male liberation groups complain about injustices that have been done to them; they wallow in expressivist extremes. Some male groups even turn into variants of locker-room gatherings, where men can express resentment and hostility toward women and the expressive life.

In any event, the late 1970s are witnessing profound changes in the social fabric. The critical-theory reading of these changes has been noted. Other versions of where society is headed can be found in social analyses from left to right. Some decry the increasing trend toward "subjectivism" and "deinstitutionalization" as throwing the way open to totalitarianism. This interpretation is most commonly a variant of conservative social thought, but it is found in the writings of radical social critics as well. Others continue to decry trends toward homogenization along instrumentally rational lines, despite the latest theories that this process belongs to an earlier era. Still others indicate that those in the knowledge industries (e.g., education, welfare bureaucracies, science, technology), along with the multinational corporate elites, have the power and influence to direct the course of society, and their interests are in opposition to those of the old middle classes (small business owners) and the working class (ethnics, religionists, and traditionalists).[10]

In the realm of sex roles the instrumental-expressive interplay is especially germane. Feminism's four solutions to the present duality reflect larger social processes, but variations on these four are possible in theory as well as practice. For example, a growing tendency has been noted within and outside feminism for either instrumentality or expressivity to coopt the other. This has been discussed under Instrumentalism and Expressivism as monistic approaches to the duality. Instrumentalists of late expect a woman to use "being a woman" either in the Affirmative Action sense or, more traditionally, by using feminine charm and manipulative expressive skills to get ahead. There has also been an increase in the cooptation of instrumental activities for expressive needs so that one's public work life (particularly among the affluent) is engineered to suit one's inner needs and impulses.[11]

But the instrumental-expressive duality remains a key to understanding society—whether this is described as the separation of head and heart, rationality and arationality, work and interaction, object and subject, institutionalization and subjectivization, individuality and community, over and under classes, public and private life, work ethic and hedonism, or male and female roles.

NOTES

1. See, for example, Paul Piccone, "The Changing Function of Critical Theory," *New German Critique* 4, no. 12 (Fall 1977): 29–38; idem, "The Crisis of One-Dimensionality," *Telos* 11, no. 35 (Spring 1978): 43–54; idem, "From Tragedy to Farce: The Return of Critical Theory," *New German Critique* 3, no. 7 (Winter 1976): 91–104; and Tim Luke, "Culture and Politics in the Age of Artificial Negativity," *Telos* 11, no. 35 (Spring 1978): 55–72.

2. Piccone's argument can be found in the sources mentioned in note 1, but in its most succinct form in "The Crisis of One-Dimensionality."

3. "Checks and balances" would be referred to as "oppositions" and "negations" by critical theorists who follow an Hegelian model. I have used checks and balances for greater clarity, but these concepts may be misleading if one thinks in political terms.

4. The idea that people are interchangeable, equivalent units has been discussed throughout the chapters as a modern philosophical assumption. In this latest development in critical theory such an assumption would be considered not so much modern as belonging to that historical period that served as a transition from entrepreneurial to advanced capitalism.

5. "Artificial negativity" has been used here and there in critical-theory writings, but it seems to have been given its most systematic discussion in Piccone's works; see note 1.

6. Robert Bellah, hardly a critical theorist, would also see these as society's most pressing problems. See his "Religion and Legitimation in the American Republic," *Society* 15 (May/June 1978): 16–23.

7. Piccone, "The Crisis of One-Dimensionality," p. 49.

8. See, for example, William O'Neill, *The Woman Movement* (Chicago: Quadrangle, 1971); and William H. Chafe, *The American Woman* (New York, Oxford University Press, 1977).

9. "Identified with the forced bureaucratization of the last vestiges of individuality and specificity, the ERA is progressive neither from the

viewpoint of the new requirements of the system nor from the depersonalized perspective of the private woman who sees in her femininity the last protection against total anonymity and vulnerability." Piccone, "The Crisis of One-Dimensionality," p. 49.

10.   Caricatures of the New Class life style can be found in Cyra McFadden's *The Serial: A Year in the Life of Marin County* (New York: New American Library, 1978); and in Hans Magnus Enzensberger, "On the Irresistibility of the Petty Bourgeoise," *Telos* 9, no. 30 (Winter 1976–77): 161–66. Caricatures aside, commentators on the right and left have noted the ascendancy of this new grouping, the pervasiveness of its values and life style in American society, and its increasing invasion of Third World countries. Right commentary would refer to this as "modernization," left critics as "cultural imperialism," or "domination by cultural hegemony." For a more thorough analysis of New Class theories, see Alvin W. Gouldner, "The New Class Project, Part 1," *Theory and Society* 6 (September 1978): 153–203.

11.   See, for example, Richard Sennett, *The Fall of Public Man* (New York, Vintage, 1978); and McFadden, *The Serial*.

APPENDIX

THEORETICAL BACKGROUND

The women's liberation movement is in struggle with modern society. The movement implicitly addresses itself to basic problems that are intrinsic to modernity at both objective (structural) level and subjective (consciousness) levels. This appendix presents an overview of theoretical interpretations of the transition from traditional to modern society as background for understanding the four ideal types identified within the current feminist movement and for interpreting the relationship between feminism and modernity.

MARX

Marx's interpretation of capitalist society is a likely place to begin an examination of theories about modern society because his construction is referred to (approvingly or not) by the other theorists we will discuss. According to Marx, capitalist production, essentially the production and exchange of commodities with the profit motive predominating, ushered in an epoch of alienation: from nature, from other humans, and from the self. The seeds of alienation are not rooted in the human condition (as Hegel would maintain [1]), but flourish under capitalism.[2] Marx views alienation as tied to the social structure of societies based on capitalist economy because commodity exchange carries with it an ethos that pervades all areas of social life. Social structure is transformed by the dominance of commodity exchange patterns, social ties are more and more based on using oneself and others as means to specific ends. In other words, individuals perceive themselves and others as commodities that have exchange value. Traditional, communal bonds are shattered, and individuals find themselves isolated from one another. Atomization and alienation run rampant. The separation of life into public as opposed to private, personal existence owes its origins to capitalist production. The fragmentation of life and self and the split between public and private existence, which Marx characterizes as dehumanizing and alienation-inducing, become solidified through the legitimations of habit and capitalist ideology.[3]

Thus, for Marx, the modern era is equated with the capitalist era. The patterns attributed to capitalism are inseparable from this economic-historical base. Some subsequent theorists have adapted Marx's description of the modern era, but in so doing detached it from the base of capitalism per se. In other words, Marx's portrayal of capitalist society has been extended so that it includes any society primarily oriented to *technological* production, be it capitalist, socialist, or otherwise. The divergent conclusions that may be derived from these differing positions are obvious. For Marx, the overthrow of capitalism would usher in a new epoch of human relationships; technological production under the socialist mode would be characterized by patterns different from those found in the capitalist mode. Alienation, atomization, specialization, and the public-private gulf would be overcome with the passing of capitalism. On the other hand, some theorists who antedate Marx assume that technological production per se implies all the patterns that Marx relegated to capitalism, so that nothing short of a total abandonment of technological production will eliminate the specialization, alienation, etc., decried by Marx.

WEBER

Max Weber characterizes the modern era as one of increasing rationalization. Weber's *zweckrational* action and his descriptions of ideal typical bureaucratic administration are of particular relevance. *Zwekrational* action (i.e., expedient, purposive or instrumental rationality) implies separability and independence of both means and ends that an actor weighs in order to calculate the most efficient way to achieve his or her self-interested purposes. In Weber's words:

> Action is rationally oriented to a system of discrete individual ends (*zweckrational*) when the ends, the means, and the secondary results are all rationally taken into account and weighed. This involves rational consideration of alternative means to the end, of the relations of the end to other prospective results of employment of any given means, finally of the relative importance of different possible ends.
>
> Determination of action, either in affectual or in traditional terms, is thus incompatible with this type. Choice between alternative and conflicting ends and results may well be determined by considerations of absolute value. In that case, action is rationally oriented to a system of discreet individual ends only in respect to the choice of means.[4]

Weber terms the last type of rational action *wertrational*, that is, the realization of some absolute value dominates the actor's orientation so that even though alternative means to an end may be calculated, the action involved is less than purely "rational" and may even be construed as "irrational."[5] The other two ideal types of social action—affectually oriented action and traditionally oriented action—may be considered along with *wertrational* action as nonrational action types—in counter-distinction to *zweckrational* action.[6] For Weber, the expansion of scientific, technological, and bureaucratic processes implies an expansion of *zweckrational* action because the former processes are premised on it. Weber interpreted rationalized capitalist production as springing from, but later detaching itself from, the social consciousness shaped by Calvinist ideology.

The important point is that Weber foresaw the massive changes in social structure that would be wrought by the predicted expansion of technological (rationalized) production processes and bureaucratic administration. The *zweckrational* action orientation that permeates capitalist production has become the coordinating principle of economic, political and cultural life.

In a now famous passage, Weber describes the modern dilemma thus:

> The Puritan wanted to work in a calling; we are forced to do so. For when asceticism was carried out of monastic cells into everyday life, and began to dominate worldly morality, it did its part in building the tremendous cosmos of the modern economic conditions of machine production which today determine the lives of all the individuals who are born into this mechanism, not only those directly concerned with economic acquisition, with irresistible force. Perhaps it will so determine them until the last ton of fossilized coal is burnt. In Baxter's view the care for external goods should only lie on the shoulders of the "saint like a light cloak, which can be thrown aside at any moment." But fate decreed that the cloak should become an iron cage.
>
> Since asceticism undertook to remodel the world and to work out its ideals in the world, material goods have gained an increasing and finally an inexorable power over the lives of men as at no previous period in history. Today the spirit of religious asceticism—whether finally, who knows?—has escaped from the cage. But victorious capitalism, since it rests on mechanical foundations, needs its support no longer.[7]

Weber speculates as to the future of these expanding processes and comes to a bleak conclusion about the likely outcome:

> No one knows who will live in this cage in the future, or whether at the end of this tremendous development entirely

new prophets will arise, or there will be a great rebirth of old ideas and ideals, or, if neither, mechanized petrification, embellished with a sort of convulsive self-importance. For of the last stage of this cultural development, it might well truly be said: "Specialists without spirit, sensualists without heart; this nullity imagines that it has attained a level of civilization never before achieved." [8]

Weber refrains from extending this indictment any further in this context, in keeping with his stance of value-neutrality. ("But this brings us to the world of judgments of value and faith, with which this purely historical discussion need not be burdened." [9]) His characterizations of ideal typical bureaucratic administration reflect the theme of "specialists without spirit." Bureaucratic administration represents for Weber the most efficient, and therefore the most rational, type of mass administration, and as such it is a basic element in the modern Western state.[10] In his view it is irrelevant whether the mode of economic production is capitalist or socialist. Since bureaucracy is intrinsic to the large-scale corporate group administration needs that pervade modern society, the consequences of bureaucracy have an impact on the general character of social life.

The capitalist entrepreneur is, in our society, the only type who has been able to maintain at least relative immunity from subjection to the control of rational bureaucratic knowledge. All the rest of the population have tended to be organized in large-scale corporate groups which are inevitably subject to bureaucratic control. This is as inevitable as the dominance of precision machinery in the mass production of goods.[11]

According to Weber, ideal typical bureaucracy is animated by a style or "spirit" that increasingly permeates the fabric of society. Some aspects of this style include

the dominance of a spirit of formalistic impersonality. "*Sine ira et studio*," without hatred or passion, and hence without affection or enthusiasm. The dominant norms are concepts of straightforward duty without regard to personal considerations. Everyone is subject to formal equality of treatment; that is, everyone in the same empirical situation. This is the spirit in which the ideal official conducts his office.[12]

This description of the bureaucratic style is also reflected in other parts of *Economy and Society:*

When fully developed, bureaucracy also stands, in a specific sense, under the principle of *sine ira et studio*. Its specific nature, which is welcomed by capitalism, develops the more perfectly the more the bureaucracy is "dehumanized," the more completely it succeeds from eliminating from official business love, hatred, and all purely personal, irrational, and emotional elements which escape calculation. This is the specific nature of bureaucracy and it is appraised as its special virtue.[13]

Weber contrasts the bureaucratic style with the style that animated administration in traditional social structures: ". . . the master . . . was moved by personal sympathy and favor, by grace and gratitude." [14] In analyzing the transition from traditional to modern society, Weber posits that progressive specialization, bureaucratization, and rationalization are permanent features of modern society. What, then, does Weber have in mind as future fate of counterbalancing styles (e.g., emotionality, passion, expressivity, sympathy, grace, gratitude)? Weber does not directly address this issue; his conceptions of charisma come closest to the question. Charisma is defined as

a certain quality of an individual personality by virtue of which he is set apart from ordinary men and treated as endowed with supernatural, superhuman, or at least specifically exceptional powers or qualities. These as such are not accessible to the ordinary person, but are regarded as of divine origin or as exemplary, and on the basis of them the individual concerned is treated as a leader.[15]

For Weber, charisma implies the exact opposite of bureaucracy (and, for that matter, the opposite of traditional authority). In this formulation:

> Charismatic authority is thus specifically outside the realm of everyday routine and the profane sphere. In this respect, it is sharply opposed both to rational, and particularly bureaucratic, authority, and to traditional authority, whether in its patriarchal, patrimonial, or any other form. Both rational and traditional authority are specifically forms of everyday routine control of action; while the charismatic type is the direct antithesis of this. Bureaucratic authority is specifically rational in the sense of being bound to intellectually analysable rules, while charismatic authority is specifically irrational in the sense of being foreign to all rules. Traditional authority is bound to precedents handed down from the past and to this extent is also oriented to rules. Within the sphere of its claims, charismatic authority repudiates the past, and is in this sense a specifically revolutionary force.[16]

Charismatic authority is highly transitory and unstable, however, because it is located in persons, not in positions that transcend particular incumbents.[17] Because it is unstable, charismatic authority eventually disappears, either because the leader dies or because he or she is rejected.[18] Followers may attempt to perpetuate charismatic authority but, according to Weber, this is impossible, a contradiction of the nature of charisma, because once integrated into the institutional framework, charismatic authority becomes "routinized." For Weber, then, the needs of the followers for permanence and security oppose the nature of transitory, unstable charisma—charisma gives way either to traditional or rational authority, or to a combination of the two.[19]

Weber thus views charisma as a counter-force to rational bureaucratic processes in the short-run, but with no lasting impact on the trend toward progressive rationalization. Weber never discusses conditions under which charisma may emerge in the future. We may gather from his general sociology and his studies of religions that when charisma does emerge, it will be traced to an interplay between the needs of the followers and the qualities of a given leader (elective affinity).

TONNIES

Tonnies began a tradition of analyzing social organization in terms of a dichotomized typology.[20] Tonnies's ideal types (or "normal concepts")—*Gemeinschaft* and *Gesellschaft*—however, captured modes of psychological and societal organization in such a way as to influence subsequent theories about the transition from traditional to modern society. Tonnies's concepts have become commonplace in sociology. Typologies abound that have their roots in his seminal work:

> Notwithstanding the age of the tradition (typing social entities dichotomously), it still has a marked vitality, and appears to be one of the fundamental approaches to sociological phenomena. Examples of this tradition are such familiar conceptualizations as *Maine's* status society and contract society; *Spencer's* militant and industrial forms; *Ratzenhofer's* conquest state and culture state; *Wundt's* natural and cultural polarity; *Durkheim's* mechanical and organic solidarity; *Cooley's* primary and secondary (implicit) groups; *MacIver's* communal and associational relations; *Zimmerman's* localistic and cosmopolitan communities; *Odum's* folk-state pair; *Redfield's* folk-urban continuum; *Sorokin's* familistic vs. contractual relations; *Becker's* sacred and secular societies; as well as such nonpersonalized but common dichotomies as primitive-civilized; literate-nonliterate; and rural vs. urban.[21]

Additions to the list would include Weber's rational-traditional action types; Parsons's "left side" (i.e., affectivity, collectivity-orientation, particularism, quality, and diffuseness) v. "right side" (i.e., affective neutrality, self-orientation, universalism, performance, and specificity) pattern variables, or what the present book summarizes as the "expressive" v. the "instrumental" orientation. While question exists as to whether Parsons's pattern variables were intended to be applicable to whole societies, or to be comparable to Tonnies's usage of *Gemeinschaft* and *Gesellschaft,* sufficient grounds exist for considering them in this tradition. Parsons applies the pattern variables to all three levels of system analysis—personality, societal, and cultural. At each level, the pattern variables represent basic alternatives or choices of action, roles, and values. Parsons qualifies the interpretation of his pattern variables as representing a strict dichotomy by saying that any action, role, or value usually involves both choices; however, he does maintain that one of the two polarities can be "more present" than the other.[22] Thus, the pattern variables may be used in analyzing entire sociocultural entities, and in this sense may be considered as belonging in the tradition discussed here.[23]

For Tonnies, *Gemeinschaft* implies social relationships that involve the whole of the person and are conceived of as "real and organic life," [24] such as family and friendship relationships. *Gesellschaft* implies relationships that involve only those fragments of self that are relevant for joining with others in this type of relationship and may be conceived as "imaginary and mechanical structure," [25] such as business firms and professional associations. Tonnies further posits two typical forms of human will as foundations for all social relationships—*Wesenwille* ("natural will") and *Kurwille* ("rational will"). Natural will, the basis for *Gemeinschaft,* implies a will that spontaneously expresses the human's inner desires and necessities and prompts association with others as an end in itself. Rational will, the foundation of *Gesellschaft,* implies deliberation or calculation of both means and ends, and the perception of means and ends as separable; independent categories is at the heart of rational will and is similar to Weber's *zweckrational* action.[26]

The following passage from *Community and Society* describes some of the basic differences between the polar types of social association:

All intimate, *private,* and exclusive living together, so we dis-

cover, is understood as life in Gemeinschaft (community). Gesellschaft (society) is *public* life—it is the world itself. In Gemeinschaft with one's family, one lives from birth on, bound to
it in weal and woe. One goes into Gesellschaft as one goes into
a strange country. . . . There exists a Gemeinschaft of language, of folkways or mores, or of beliefs; but, by way of contrast, Gesellschaft exists in the realm of business, travel, or
sciences.[27]

The contrast between private (*Gemeinschaft*) and public
(*Gesellschaft*) life reflects the Marxian construction mentioned
earlier. Intimacy, emotionality, and like features of *Gemeinschaft*
are presumed to be found in the private sphere. It follows, then,
that Tonnies characterizes women as representatives or "carriers"
of *Gemeinschaft* ("expressivity" in the terminology of the present
book) because of their social location as child rearers. Let us look
more closely at Tonnies's thoughts on the contrast between the sexes.
Tonnies aligns women with natural will and *Gemeinschaft* and men
with rational will and *Gesellschaft*.[28]

In the first place we distinguish in general features the psychological contrast between the sexes. It is an old truth—but just
for that reason important as the outcome of general experience
—that women are usually led by feelings, men more by intellect. Men are more clever. They alone are more capable of calculation, of calm (abstract) thinking, of consideration, combination, and logic. As a rule, women follow these pursuits in-
effectively. They lack the necessary requirement of rational
will.[29]

Tonnies's rationale for dichotomizing sexual identities is the premise
that men are geared to a more active life; male roles require activity—breadwinner, hunter, robber, and the like. Women are less
active because their access to activity in the public world is curtailed by their having to spend most of their time and energy with
offspring. Moreover, rational will depends on activity for its formation, and activity is in turn increased by the facilities of rational

will. Thus men are likely to surpass women in the development of both rational will and activity.

In other words, rational will and activity are dialectically related—the more activity one person engages in, the more the likelihood of developing rational will; the more the facilities of rational will become developed, the more activity one will engage in. Women, curtailed in their activity because of social and species necessities, are prevented from developing rational will and, as a consequence, are doubly "passive" with respect to men.[30] The following passage illustrates further linkages between females with *Gemeinschaft* and males with *Gesellschaft*:

> If the privilege of cleverness is attributed to the man, it must be kept in mind that cleverness is by no means the same as general intellectual power. On the contrary, to the extent that intellectual power is productive or synthetic, the female mind excels. In the constitution of the male the muscular system prevails; in the female constitution, the nervous system. In accordance with their more passive, constant, limited activity, women are generally more receptive and sensitive to the impressions which come accidentally and unexpectedly from the outside; they rather enjoy present, constant happiness instead of striving for remote, future, rare happiness. . . . Moreover, all activity which expresses itself in a direct manner, either originally or from habit or memory, as consequence and expression of life itself, belongs to the realm of the woman. Thus, all expressions and outbursts of emotions and sentiments, conscience, and inspired thoughts are the specific truthfulness, naivete, directness, and passionateness of the woman, who is in every respect the more natural being.[31]

In characterizing female nature, Tonnies emphasizes what we have termed the "expressive orientation." Women are "receptive," "sensitive," present-oriented, and passionate—in short, the "more natural being." Once women enter the public realm, their impact (as "carriers" of *Gemeinschaft* and natural will) on the *Gesell-*

schaft will be less than the impact of the *Gessellschaft* on them. He does speculate that it is possible for the consciousness of women as a group to develop in such a way that it will be able to forestall the erosion of *Gemeinschaft.*

> As woman enters into the struggle of earning a living, it is evident that trading and the freedom and independence of the female factory worker as contracting party and possessor of money will develop her rational will, enabling her to think in a calculating way, even though, in the case of factory work, the tasks themselves may not lead in this direction. *The woman becomes enlightened, cold-hearted, conscious. Nothing is more foreign and terrible to her original inborn nature,* in spite of all later modifications. Possibly nothing is more characteristic and important in the process of formation of the Gesellschaft and destruction of Gemeinschaft. Through this development the "individualism" which is the prerequisite of Gesellschaft comes to its own. However, the possibility of overcoming this individualism and arriving at a reconstruction of Gemeinschaft exists. *The analogy of the fate of woman with the fate of the proletariat* has been recognized and outlined long ago. *Their growing group consciousness, like that of the isolated thinker, can develop and rise to a moral-humane consciousness.*[32]

BERGER

Using a sociology of knowledge perspective, Peter L. Berger views modern society as characterized by those cognitive styles and organizations of knowledge intrinsic to technological production and bureaucracy.[33] For Berger, the cognitive style (the "how" or habit of consciousness) emerging out of, and supporting, technological production entails twelve elements or themes. In his view, these elements cannot be "thought away" (in the sense of Weber's "thought experiment") if the production process, as we know it, is to continue.[34] Berger maintains that the twelve elements that inhere in technological production are archetypically modern because technological production is archetypically modern.[35]

We need not here detail all twelve elements, but several of them are directly relevant to the four ideal types within the women's movement. The following six themes are particularly useful:

1. "Componentiality," the style of viewing reality as composed of standardized, self-contained units.[36]

2. "Segregation of segments of paramount reality," the separation at institutional and consciousness levels of action and identity into public-work spheres as against private-socioemotional spheres.[37]

3. But, at the same time, carryovers of the technological cognitive style into "action" and "fantasy" not directly related to the production process. In other words, although public and private spheres are segregated in consciousness and activity, there is a tendency for the public-work (i.e., technological) style to carry over into one's private-socioemotional action and identity.[38]

4. "Anonymous social relationships," the interrelating of human beings entailing the perception of oneself and others in anonymous terms, as representatives of one or other socially defined category, as, for example, telephone operator, foreman, woman, husband.[39]

5. "Componential social relationships," the partialization or fragmentation of self and others so that interrelationships are restricted to limited pieces of one's and the other's total self.[40]

6. "Emotional management," the presentation of a cool emotionally controlled self.[41]

Berger suggests that the symbolic universe (roughly, "worldview" that provides an enveloping reservoir of meanings necessary to get on with the business at hand in the everyday world) characterizing the modern world is built on themes that have been transferred from technological production and bureaucracy.[42] He identifies six elements that figure in both technological production and the modern symbolic universe:

1. "Functional rationality," what the present book calls "instrumental rationality" or, is in Weber's terminology, *zweckrational* action.[43]
2. "Componentiality" (described above).[44]
3. "Multirelationality," a world-view characterized by a large variety of complex interrelationships which involve other individuals, concrete objects, and "abstract entities" that must be juggled together in subjective consciousness.[45]
4. "Makeability," a problem-solving approach to life, self, and society. "Life (including social experience and identity) is seen as an ongoing problem-solving enterprise." [46]
5. "Plurality," many reality levels such that there develops in modern society an ever increasing number and variety of "finite provinces of meaning" (Schutz-ian term implying pockets or "enclaves" of meaning and styles of experience separate from the predominant or "paramount reality" that bestows coherence and meaningfulness on experience in the everyday world); these finite provinces of meaning pose a problem for the construction of an "overarching" symbolic universe because of "the sheer number of items that must be included in such a construct." [47]
6. "Progressivity," an onward and upward view of the future of self and society which assumes that things can and will become better, happier, and more satisfying. (Berger suggests that this element is derived from the themes of "makeability" and "maximalization" that inhere in processes of technological production.) [48]

Berger's position, then, is that the patterns intrinsic to technological production processes have come to comprise an identifiable cognitive style and have also been objectivated as the symbolic universe for modern society. At the macro social level, this implies that the technological ethos is carried over into social spheres not directly related to technological production, as, for example, family, religion, or leisure activities—the private sphere.

To digress for a moment: Look closely at Berger's model of the relationship between objective and subjective realities that underlies his analysis of the relationship between technological production processes and modern consciousness.[49] Berger posits that reality is socially constructed by means of a dialectical interplay between subjective human consciousness and objectified social facts. The statements "Society is produced by consciousness" and "Consciousness is a social product" are then true simultaneously and incorporable into one theoretical (dialectical) scheme. Berger conceives of this objective-subjective dialectic as analyzable into three simultaneous moments: externalization, objectivation, and internalization.

Externalization refers to the outpourings of human consciousness, whether these are (1) material or immaterial; (2) social, structural, or cultural; or social or psychical products. *Objectivation* implies the process whereby products arising out of subjective consciousness take on an objective reality ("facticity") and exist in their own right, apart from specific human producers. These resulting objectivations are characterized by the features Durkheim attributed to social facts: externality, historicity, coerciveness, moral authority, and opaqueness.[50] *Internalization* (similar to "socialization") implies the process of introjecting objectified social facts into subjective consciousness so as socially to "preset" an individual's repertoire of expectations, definitions of the situation, values, norms, roles, or identity. Objective social reality, which has its origins in human consciousness, thus acts back upon human consciousness.[51] Internalized social reality, in turn, conditions or shapes the products of consciousness externalized. Thus the relationship between the moments—externalization, objectivation and internalization—entails a continual dialectical process whereby each moment "acts back" on, or informs, the other two. Social reality is thus a construction that results from the dialectical interplay of objectified social facts (e.g., such features intrinsic to technological production as componentiality and emotional management) and subjective consciousness (e.g., cognitive style and organization of knowledge).

Following from this model, then, it may be concluded that the dominance of the technological ethos at the macro social (objectified) social level and its seepage into the private sphere has implications for personality formation. The social facts derived from technological production are internalized by individuals in public and private spheres of their experience; individuals are thereby "produced" whose roles, identities, thoughts, emotions, modes of experiencing the world and themselves and others are shaped by the social facts of technological production (e.g., componentiality, anonymous social relationships, emotional management, functional rationality, multirationality).[52] Berger's model of the relationship between individuals and society is, however, a dialectical one—the moment of "externalization" must be kept in focus. To say that individuals are "produced" whose consciousness is shaped by the technocratic ethos must be counterbalanced by the perspective that persistence of, or innovation in, social facts is attributable to the externalizations of subjective consciousness.

One further feature of Berger's analysis of modern society is useful for interpreting the struggle of the women's movement with modernity. Berger posits a distinction between that view of the self which is contained *in* and *through* one's social roles, and that view of the self as manifested *behind* and *beneath* "official" social roles.[53] The former view of the self, where identity is bestowed on the individual in and through social roles, and where a "symmetry" exists between self and society, corresponds with an emphasis on the virtues of sincerity and honor. This view of the self, together with the corresponding virtues of sincerity and honor, is characteristic of traditional or premodern societies. The latter view, where one's true self is assumed to be located apart from social placements and roles, and where a tension is felt between one's true self and the demands of official society, corresponds with an emphasis on the virtues of authenticity and dignity. Berger posits that this latter view of the self, separate from and at times antagonistic to society, is eminently modern. The notion that "I am not really me" when playing institutional roles is grounded in everyday, taken-for-granted assumptions about the relationship between individuals and society and about the differences experienced between private and public spheres of involvement.

On the other hand, in premodern societies, according to Berger, the self is experienced as "most real" when carrying out socially based "roles" (the latter term is in quotation marks because the notion of role is at odds with the experience described—one did not then think in terms of roles). In pre-modern societies, the conception of a self located apart from socially grounded statuses is alien. I would thus be "most myself" when carrying out the duties and enjoying the rights of "mother" or "carpenter" or "knight" or "serf." According to Berger, the shift from concern with sincerity-honor and the experience of a symmetry of self and society to that of concern with authenticity-dignity and the experience of asymmetry of self and society must be understood as a result of the modernization of social institutions. In the modern era, social facts (objectivations) are highly pluralized; this pluralization is reflected in the internalization (or socialization) process so that there is little possibility of stable, coherent (symmetrical) personality formation and resulting self-concept.

One major effect of the modernization of institutions has been the pluralization of the worlds of social experience. More and more, and earlier and earlier biographically, individuals are thrown back and forth between grossly discrepant social contexts. Consequently, what experiences of symmetry there are, are unclear and unreliable: The mirrors are constantly shifting. As a result, both image and reflection take on an aspect of vertigo, that is, of unreality. As the individual becomes uncertain about the world, he necessarily becomes uncertain about his own self, since that self can be subjectively real only as it is continually confirmed by others. Put differently, as the social identification processes become increasingly fragmented, the subjective experience of identity becomes increasingly precarious. If nothing else, the old question, "Who am I?" then attains a new measure of urgency. The contemporary German social theorist Arnold Gehlen has given the term "subjectivization" to this new interest in the self, and he has very persuasively linked it to what he calls "under-institutionalization," that is, to the increasing inability of modern society to provide a stable order for its members.[54]

Berger goes on to say that the problem of precarious identity in modern pluralized society has to date been solved by splitting social experience into public and private spheres. The private sphere has evolved as "the major plausibility structure" wherein the individual can construct and maintain his/her identity, feel "at home" and "be him/herself." But in his view the private sphere, having few if any direct, indispensable functions for the public sphere, is thereby highly arbitrary and unstable. Berger foresees a progressive invasion of the private sphere by public (technological) patterns because the central institution of the private sphere—the family—is moving in the direction of increasing deinstitutionaliza-tion, as evidenced by rising divorce rates, permissiveness in child rearing, sexual liberation, and, one might add, feminist ideology. Thus, for Berger, the weakening of an already precarious private sphere will result in an increased "turning inward" of individuals.

. . . the private sphere has become more and more affected by pluralization, and has more and more lost its capacity to pro-vide a stable social foundation for a "weighted" self. In conse-quence, the private sphere has been weakened in its function of interposition between the reality of the self and the unreal-ity of the institutional world. Inevitably, this has threatened the reality of the self and deepened the turning inward that Gehlen calls "subjectivization." If nothing "on the outside" can be relied upon to give weight to the individual's sense of reality, he is left no option but to burrow into himself in search of the real. Whatever this *ens realissimum* may then turn out to be, it must necessarily be in opposition to any external social formation. The opposition between self and society has now reached its maximum. The concept of authenticity is one way of articulat-ing this experience.[55]

HABERMAS

Jurgen Habermas provides another interpretation of technological society that has bearing on the women's movement. Habermas views technological society as increasingly dominated by "instrumental rationality." [56] Reinterpreting Weber's analysis and Marcuse's critique of Weber's analysis of "rationalization" in the transition from traditional to modern society, Habermas posits his version of the dichotomy needed to distinguish modes of relating in the modern era—"interaction" (symbolic, communicative interaction) and "work" (purposive rational action or, in Weber's term, *zweckrational* action).[57] Habermas defines "work" as follows:

> By "work" or *purposive-rational action* I understand either instrumental action or rational choice or their conjunction. Instrumental action is governed by *technical rules* based on empirical knowledge. In every case they imply conditional predictions about observable events, physical or social. These predictions can prove correct or incorrect. The conduct of rational choice is governed by *strategies* based on analytical knowledge. They imply deductions from preference rules (value systems) and decision procedures; these propositions are either correctly or incorrectly deduced. Purposive-rational action realizes defined goals under given conditions. But while instrumental action organizes means that are appropriate or inappropriate according to criteria of an effective control of reality, strategic action depends only on the correct evaluation of possible alternative choices, which results from calculation supplemented by values and maxims.[58]

"Interaction" is defined this way:

> By "interaction," on the other hand, I understand *communicative action,* symbolic interaction. It is governed by binding *consensual norms,* which define reciprocal expectations about behavior and which must be recognized and understood by

at least two acting subjects. Social norms are enforced through sanctions. Their meaning is objectified in ordinary language communication. While the validity of technical rules and strategies depends on that of empirically true or analytically correct propositions, the validity of social norms is grounded only in the intersubjectivity of the mutual understanding of intentions and secured by the general recognition of obligations.[59]

Habermas maintains that social systems can be differentiated according to the type of action that predominates in them; he distinguishes between the institutional framework of a society ("sociocultural life-world") made up of norms that guide symbolic interaction, on the one hand, and subsystems of purposive rational action ("work") "embedded" in the institutional framework, on the other (e.g., the economic system and bureaucracy).

For Habermas, modern societies are distinguished from traditional ones in that modern societies institutionalize the extension of subsystems of purposive rational action; in traditional societies, subsystems of purposive rational action can be developed only within the limits legitimated by the institutional framework. Habermas posits that the expansion of subsystems of purposive rational action is made permanent by the mode of capitalist production; the traditional form of the legitimation of power—the institutional framework—succumbs to the forces of production (i.e., subsystems of purposive-rational action). Further, early capitalism provides its own legitimation (equivalence of exchange), which is generated "from below" or from the base of social labor, to replace the older, traditional legitimations "from above" (i.e., from social norms comprising the institutional framework). In addition, science and technology have become the new major forces of production, as well as the new legitimation (or ideology) for political power:

> Since the end of the nineteenth century the other developmental tendency characteristic of advanced capitalism has become increasingly momentous: the scientization of technology. The institutional pressure to augment the productivity of labor through the introduction of new technology has always

existed under capitalism. But innovations depended on sporadic inventions, which, while economically motivated, were still fortuitous in character. This changed as technical development entered into a feedback relation with the progress of the modern sciences. With the advent of large-scale industrial research, *science, technology, and industrial utilization were fused into a system.* . . . Thus technology and science become a leading productive force, rendering inoperative the conditions for Marx's labor theory of value. . . .

As long as the productive forces were visibly linked to the rational decisions and instrumental action of men engaged in social production, they could be understood as the potential for a growing power of technical control and *not be confused with the institutional framework in which they are embedded.* However, with the institutionalization of scientific-technical progress, the potential of the productive forces has assumed a form owing to which men *lose consciousness of the dualism of work and interaction.*[60]

In Habermas's view, science and technology take on the appearance of independent, neutral legitimations for maintaining the social system and ensuring economic growth. In other words, as the institutional framework becomes more absorbed into subsystems of purposive rational action, technology and science become increasingly important in explaining and legitimating system maintenance "necessities." Moreover, science and technology are operative as ideology at the micro social level:

[Scientific-technical ideology] can also become a background ideology that penetrates into the consciousness of the depoliticized mass of the population, where it can take on legitimating power. It is a singular achievement of this ideology to detach society's self-understanding from the frame of reference of communicative action and from the concepts of symbolic interaction and replace it with a scientific model. Accordingly the culturally defined self-reification of men under categories of purposive rational action and adaptive behavior. . . . For the first time man can not only, as *homo faber,* completely objectify himself and confront the achievements that have been taken on independent life in his products; he can in addition, as *homo fabricatus,* be integrated into his technical apparatus if the structure of purposive-rational action can be successfully re-produced on the level of social systems. According to this idea the institutional framework of society—which previously was rooted in a different type of action—would now, in a funda-mental reversal, be absorbed by the subsystems of purposive-rational action, which were embedded in it.[61]

Habermas foresees the future of late capitalist society as one in which the institutional framework will be relegated to the status of "subsystem" with purposive rational action as the dominant system of social organization and as the dominant mode of relating to others. The symbolic interaction realm will become absorbed by the rational instrumental one in subjective consciousness as well as in the sciences of human behavior, thereby inducing a state similar to what Marcuse terms "one-dimensionality."[62] In Habermas's words:

[The "creeping erosion" of purposive-rational action into the institutional framework] . . . is paralleled subjectively by the disappearance of the difference between purposive-rational ac-tion and interaction from the consciousness not only of the sci-ences of man, but of men themselves.[63]

Habermas envisions an alternative future in which a new *atti-tude* toward technology, rather than a new technology per se, will transform the society and check the absorption of symbolic inter-action by expanding subsystems of purposive rational action.[64] A new mode of "rationalization" must be instituted in the sphere of symbolic interaction, as distinguished from the rationalization tak-ing place at the level of purposive-rational subsystems.[65]

. . . this process of the development of the productive forces can be a potential for liberation if and only if it does not replace rationalization at another level. *Rationalization at the level of the institutional framework* can occur only in the medium of symbolic interaction itself, that is, through *removing restrictions on communication.* Public, unrestricted discussion, free from domination, of the suitability and desirability of action-orienting principles and norms in the light of the socio-cultural repercussions of developing subsystems of purposive-rational action—such communication at all levels of political and repoliticized decision-making processes is the only medium in which anything like "rationalization" is possible.[66]

For Habermas, unrestricted communication will make possible a qualitative change in the character of modern society. In his words:

> In such a process of generalized reflection institutions would alter their specific composition, going beyond the limit of a mere change in legitimation. A rationalization of social norms would, in fact, be characterized by a decreasing degree of repressiveness (which at the level of personality structure should increase average *tolerance of ambivalence in the face of role conflicts*), a decreasing degree of rigidity (which should multiply the chances of an *individually stable self-presentation* in everyday interactions), and approximation to a type of behavioral control that would allow *role distance* and the flexible application of norms that, while *well-internalized,* would be accessible to *reflection.* Rationalization measured by changes in these three dimensions does not lead, as does the rationalization of purposive-rational subsystems, to an increase in technical control over objectified processes of nature and society. It does not lead per se to the better functioning of social systems, but would furnish the members of society with the opportunity for further *emancipation* and *progressive individuation.* The growth of productive forces is not the same as the intention of the "good life." It can at best serve it.[67]

How will this transformation come about? Habermas maintains that the potential for protest against the technocratic ideology exists in certain groups of students. Habermas assumes that new "zones of conflict," instead of the class conflict and the conflict of under-privileged, peripheral groups, must be activated. For Habermas, students can activate conflict because (1) they are privileged and therefore cannot be "bought off" by increasing systems rewards; (2) active students do not identify with the status and achievement orientation inherent in technocratic consciousness, and their affinity for the social sciences and humanities checks an uncritical acceptance of technocratic assumptions; and (3) student activists have for the most part grown up in families that provide more psychological understanding and liberalized approaches to education than is found among nonactive adolescents.[68]

NOTES

1. Hegel's thesis that alienation is ontological is developed most fully in his *The Phenomenology of Mind* (New York: Harper Torchbooks, 1967; original–1910).

2. Cf. Fritz Pappenheim, *The Alienation of Modern Man* (New York: Modern Reader, 1968), esp. chapter 4, for a lengthy discussion of these opposing views of alienation, and a comparison and synthesis of the theories of Marx and Tonnies.

3. This brief summary of Marx's interpretation of modern society is derived from several of his works, especially: *The Poverty of Philosophy*, trans. H. Quelch (London: Twentieth Century Press, 1960); *Economic and Philosophical Manuscripts of 1844*, trans. Martin Milligan (London: Lawrence & Wishart, 1959); and "On the Jewish Question," in *Writings of the Young Marx on Philosophy and Society*, trans. and ed. Loyd D. Easton and Kurt Guddat (Garden City, N.Y.: Doubleday, 1967), pp. 222–48.

4. Max Weber, *The Theory of Social and Economic Organization*, ed. Talcott Parsons (New York: Free Press, 1964), p. 117.

5. Ibid.

6. It may be feasible to reinterpret Weber's *wertrational* action as comprising the dialectical rationality implied in Marx's, and later Marcuse's and Habermas's characterizations of alternative modes of technological production.

7. Max Weber, *The Protestant Ethic and the Spirit of Capitalism*, trans. Talcott Parsons (New York: Scribner's, 1958), pp. 181–82.

8. Ibid., p. 182.

9. Ibid.

10. Weber, *Theory of Social and Economic Organization*, pp. 337 f.–40. Weber may not have understood that bureaucratic size and efficiency may be inversely related.

11. Ibid., pp. 339–40.

12. Ibid., p. 340.

13. Max Weber, *From Max Weber: Essays in Sociology,* ed. H. H. Gerth and C. Wright Mills (New York: Oxford University Press, 1958), pp. 215–16.

14. Ibid., p. 216.

15. Weber, *Theory of Social and Economic Organization,* pp. 358–59.

16. Ibid., pp. 361–62. Cf. also Gerth and Mills, *From Max Weber,* pp. 247–49.

17. Gerth and Mills, *From Max Weber,* pp. 248–50.

18. Charismatic authority depends essentially on the belief of followers in the leader's charisma. Weber, *Theory of Social and Economic Organization,* pp. 359 ff.

19. Ibid., pp. 363–86.

20. Tonnies was not the first to conceive of behavior and society dichotomously. This type of approach extends back in intellectual history at least as far as Confucius and can be found in the writings of Aristotle, Cicero, the Church Fathers, medieval philosophers, Ibn Khaldun (the Arabian philosopher), the Historical School in Germany, and Hegel. Cf. Pitirim A. Sorokin, "Foreword," in Ferdinand Tonnies, *Community and Society* (New York: Harper Torchbooks, 1963), pp. vii–viii.

21. Charles P. Loomis and John C. McKinney, "Introduction," in Tonnies, *Community and Society, p.* 12. Emphases added.

22. Talcott Parsons, *The Social System* (Glencoe: Free Press, 1951), pp. 58–67.

23. In their introduction to Tonnies's work, Loomis and McKinney suggest that if the following combinations were made, then the pattern variables could be considered as subtypes of *Gemeinschaft and Gesellschaft:* retain the pattern variables of Affectivity–Affective Neutrality, Particularism-Universalism, Quality-Performance, and Diffuseness-Specialty (eliminating the remaining variable of Collective–Self-Orientation) and add to these four Sorokin's familistic contractual dichotomy and Weber's traditional-rational action types. Loomis and McKinney, "Introduction," pp. 21–23.

24. Ibid., p. 33.

25. Ibid.

26. While Tonnies's approach may seem from the above remarks to be based on psychological dimensions (will as the basis for social association), his intent is otherwise. A dialectical relationship is involved between psychological and social levels of behavior: "Since this book starts from individual psychology, there is lacking the complementary but opposing view which describes how *Gemeinschaft* develops and fosters natural will, on the one hand, and, on the other, binds and hinders rational will. The approach does not describe how *Gesellschaft* not only frees rational will but also requires and furthers it, even makes its unscrupulous use in competition into a condition of the maintenance of the individual, thus destroying the flowers and fruits of natural will. Thus, adjusting to the conditions of *Gesellschaft* and imitating the actions of others as lead to gain and profits are not only the results of a natural drive, but such action becomes imperative and failure to conform is punishable under pain of destruction." Tonnies, *Community and Society*, pp. 169–70.

27. Ibid., pp. 33–34. Emphases added.

28. Tonnies similarly posits that children, the lower classes, and peasants are oriented toward *Gemeinschaft*; adults and the upper classes are parallel with *Gesellschaft*. One conclusion Tonnies derives from these assumptions is that the *younger woman* represents the purest form of natural will. Cf. these parallels in chapter 3 of the present book. Tonnies, *Community and Society*, pp. 156–59.

29. Ibid., p. 151.

30. Ibid., pp. 153–54.

31. Ibid.

32. Ibid., p. 166. Emphases added.

33. Peter L. Berger, Brigitte Berger, and Hansfried Kellner, *The Homeless Mind: Modernization and Consciousness* (New York: Random House, 1973). I will restrict my discussion to their analysis of the impact of technological production on the ethos of modernity because, for the most part, the impact of bureaucracy is related to the general influence of technology and its accompanying themes; also the foregoing discussion of Weber's analysis of bureaucracy is in keeping with Berger's overall interpretation.

34. Ibid., p. 39.

35. Berger's position is in agreement with Weber's that technological production per se, be it enmeshed in capitalist or (socialist) social organization, is the root factor in modernity, in contrast with Marx's position that such patterns are products of capitalism.

36. Ibid., p. 27.

37. Ibid., pp. 29–30.

38. Ibid., pp. 30–31.

39. Ibid., pp. 31–32.

40. Ibid., pp. 33–34.

41. Ibid., pp. 35–36. The remaining six themes identified by Berger as intrinsic to the process of technological production are (1) interdependence of components and sequences, (2) separability of means and ends, (3) implicit abstraction, (4) institutional representations, (5) assumption of maximalization, and (6) multirelationality. These six are important for understanding the feminist struggle with modernity, but they are reflected in the overall view of modernity.

42. Again, I restrict my discussion to the themes derived from technology.

43. Ibid., pp. 111–12.

44. Ibid., p. 112.

45. Ibid.

46. Ibid.

47. Ibid., pp. 112–13.

48. Ibid., p. 113.

49. Peter L. Berger and Thomas Luckmann, *The Social Construction of Reality* (Garden City, N.Y.: Doubleday, 1967).

50. Emile Durkheim, *The Rules of Sociological Method* (Chicago: Free Press, 1950). See also Berger and Luckmann, *Social Construction of Reality*.

51. This last point becomes more clear if it is understood that the consciousness that "produced" social reality need not coincide on *the indi-*

vidual level with the consciousness that is a product of objective reality; in addition, not all items have equal weight in their impact on the out-coming facticities. Cf. Berger and Luckmann, *Social Construction of Reality*, pp. 108–10.

52. Berger's position on the predominance of the technological ethos is compatible with that of Marx, Weber, Tonnies, and Habermas; however, the position Berger takes does not allow for the relegation of this pre-dominance to capitalist production modes. Further, Berger's model (which reflects the Marxian premise that "Men make history; history makes men") makes it possible to focus on the linkage between macro social (techno-logical social facts) and micro social (personality articulation) realities.

53. Cf. Peter L. Berger, " 'Sincerity' and 'Authenticity' in Modern So-ciety," *Public Interest*, Spring 1973, pp. 81–90; Berger et al., *The Home-less Mind*, pp. 83–96. Cf. also Anton C. Zijderveld, *The Abstract Society* (Garden City, N.Y.: Anchor, 1971), chap. 2, for his discussion of the theory of "homo duplex," i.e., of the double nature of humanity as lo-cated both within and apart from society.

54. Berger, " 'Sincerity' and 'Authenticity,' " p. 86.

55. Ibid., p. 88.

56. Jurgen Habermas, *Toward a Rational Society* (Boston: Beacon Press, 1971).

57. "Interaction" and "work" are to be understood as a variation of Marx's "relations of production" and "forces of production." In another sense, they are similar to Tonnies's concepts of *Gemeinschaft* and *Gesell-schaft*.

58. Ibid., pp. 91–92.

59. Ibid., p. 92.

60. Ibid., pp. 104–5. Emphases added.

61. Ibid., pp. 105–6.

62. Herbert Marcuse, *One-Dimensional Man* (Boston: Beacon Press, 1971).

63. Habermas, *Toward a Rational Society*, p. 107.

64. Ibid., p. 88.

65. Some have termed this "dialectical rationality" as opposed to "instrumental rationality"—cf., e.g., Marcuse, *One-Dimensional Man* and *Reason and Revolution* (Boston: Beacon Press, 1960).

66. Habermas, *Toward a Rational Society*, pp. 118–19.

67. Ibid., p. 119. Emphases added.

68. Ibid., pp. 120–21.

BIBLIOGRAPHY

Alpert, Jane. "Mother Right." *Ms.*, August 1972, pp. 90 ff.

Altbach, Edith Hoshino, ed. *From Feminism to Liberation*. Cambridge, Mass.: Schenkman, 1971.

Anonymous. "Alix at *Ms.*" *Ms.* 3 (March 1975): 55.

————. "The Evolution of a Suffragette, 1912." *RAT*, no. 18 (12–29 January 1971): 14.

————. *I am Furious (Female)*. Detroit: Radical Education Project, n.d.

————. "International Sisterhood." *RAT*, no. 18 (12–29 January 1971): 9.

———. "Introduction to C.L.I.T. Papers." *Off Our Backs* 4 (July 1971): 12.

———. "Jewish Consciousness Raising." *RAT*, no. 18 (12–29 January 1971): 6.

———. "Language." *Off Our Backs* 4 (July 1974).

———. "Letter to RAT." *RAT*, no. 17 (17 December–6 January 1970–71): 24.

———. "*Newsweek*, the Man's Media." *RAT*, no. 5 (4–18 April 1970): 4.

———. "Our Hands–Our Feet–Our Bodies–Our Minds Are Tools for Social Change." *RAT*, no. 24 (12–29 January 1971): 13.

———. "Starting to Think about Class." *RAT*, no. 24 (2 August 1971): 13.

———. "Vietnam Women." *RAT*, no. 12 (9–23 August 1970): 6.

———. "Why Are Women Arrested?" *RAT*, no. 17 (17 December–6 January 1970–71): 9.

Ariès, Philippe. *Centuries of Childhood: A Social History of Family Life*. New York: Vintage, 1962.

Arthur, Marilyn. "Early Greece: The Origins of the Western Attitude Towards Women." *Arethusa* 6 (Spring 1973): 7–59.

Bachofen, Johann Jacob. *Myth, Religion and Mother Right: His Selected Writings*. Translated by Ralph Manheim. Princeton: Princeton University Press, 1967.

Barber, Benjamin. "Man on Woman, Part 1." *Worldview*, April 1973, pp. 17–23.

———. "Man on Woman, Part 2." *Worldview*, May 1973, pp. 47–54.

Bardwick, Judith M. *Psychology of Women*. New York: Harper & Row, 1971

Barth, John. *End of the Road*. New York: Bantam, 1969.

Bar Yoseph, Rivkah. "The Role of Women in Israeli Society: Past and Present." Lecture delivered at Douglass College, New Brunswick, N.J., 4 April 1973.

Becker, Howard. *Man in Reciprocity*. New York: Praeger, 1956.

Bellah, Robert. "Religion and Legitimation in the American Republic." *Society* 15 (May/June 1978): 16–23.

Bengis, Ingrid. *Combat in the Erogenous Zone*. New York: Knopf, 1972.

Benjamin, Jessica. "The End of Internalization: Adorno's Social Psychology." *Telos* 32 (Summer 1977): 42–64.

Benston, Margaret. "The Political Economy of Women's Liberation." In *From Feminism to Liberation,* edited by Edith Hoshino Altbach. Cambridge, Mass.: Schenkman, 1971.

Berger, Peter L. *Invitation to Sociology.* Garden City, N.Y.: Doubleday, 1963.

———. " 'Sincerity' and 'Authenticity' in Modern Society." *Public Interest,* Spring 1973, pp. 81–90.

———; Berger, Brigitte; and Kellner, Hansfried. *The Homeless Mind: Modernization and Consciousness.* New York: Random House, 1973.

———, and Kellner, Hansfried. "Marriage and the Construction of Reality." In *Recent Sociology Number Two,* edited by Hans Peter Dreitzel. New York: Macmillan, 1970.

———, and Luckmann, Thomas. *The Social Construction of Reality.* Garden City, N.Y.: Doubleday, 1967.

Bernard, Jessie. *The Sex Game.* New York: Atheneum, 1972.

———. *Women and the Public Interest.* Chicago: Aldine, 1971.

Bernstein, Basil. *Class, Codes, and Control.* New York: Schocken, 1975.

Borgese, Elizabeth Mann. *The Ascent of Woman.* New York: George Braziller, 1963.

Bredemeier, Harry C. "Review Essay: Justice, Virtue and Social Science." *Society* 10 (September–October 1973): 76–88.

Brooks, Patricia. "Plugging Into the Old Girl Network." *Working Woman* 2 (July 1977): 26–29.

Brown, Arlene. "Grateful Dead." *RAT,* no. 5 (4–18 April 1970): 26.

Burris, Barbara. *Fourth World Manifesto.* New Haven: Advocate Press, 1971.

Butsch, Richard J. "The Technological Ethos: Modern Life as Dualistic Rationalization." Ph.D. qualifying paper submitted to the Department of Psychology, Rutgers University, New Brunswick, N.J., 1973. Mimeographed.

Camus, Albert. *The Stranger.* Translated by Gilbert Stuart. New York: Random House, 1954.

Chafe, William H. *The American Woman.* New York: Oxford University Press, 1977.

Daly, Mary. *Beyond God the Father.* Boston: Beacon Press, 1973.

Davidson, Bill. "Marriages That Work: Norman and Frances Lear." *Family Circle* 91 (1 March 1978): 134.

Davis, Elizabeth Gould. *The First Sex.* Baltimore: Penguin, 1971.

deBeauvoir, Simone. *The Second Sex.* New York: Bantam, 1961.

Decter, Midge. *The New Chastity and Other Arguments Against Women's Liberation.* New York: Coward, McCann Geoghegan, 1972.

dell'Olio, Anselma. "A Plea to the Women's Movement." *Liberated Guardian,* 11 March 1971, p. 10.

Deming, Barbara. "To Fear Jane Alpert Is to Fear Ourselves: Letter to Susan Sherman." *Off Our Backs* 5 (May–June 1975): 25.

Deutsch, Helene. *The Psychology of Women.* 2 vols. New York: Grune & Stratton, 1944–45.

Didion, Joan. "The Women's Movement." *New York Times Book Review,* 30 July 1972, pp. 1–2, 14.

Douglas, Mary. *Natural Symbols.* New York: Pantheon, 1970.

Dreitzel, Hans Peter, ed. *Recent Sociology Number Two.* New York: Macmillan, 1970.

Durkheim, Emile. *The Rules of Sociological Method.* Chicago: Free Press, 1950.

Easton, Loyd D., and Guddat, Kurt, eds. and trans. *Writings of the Young Marx on Philosophy and Society.* Garden City, N.Y.: Doubleday, 1967.

Engels, Friedrich. *The Origin of the Family, Private Property and the State.* New York: International, 1942.

Ehrlich, Carol. "The Male Sociologist's Burden: The Place of Women in Marriage and Family Texts." *Journal of Marriage and the Family* 33 (August 1971): 421–30.

Enzensberger, Hans Magnus. "On the Irresistibility of the Petty Bourgeoise." *Telos* 9, no. 30 (Winter 1976–77): 161–66.

Firestone, Shulamith. *The Dialectic of Sex.* New York: Bantam, 1970.

Flacks, Richard W. "The Liberated Generation: An Exploration of the Roots of Student Protest." *Journal of Social Issues* 23, no. 3 (July 1967): 52–75.

Flexner, Eleanor. *Century of Struggle*. Cambridge, Mass.: Belknap Press of Harvard University Press, 1959.

Freedman, Ronald; Whelpton, Pascal A.; and Campbell, Arthur A. *Family Planning, Sterility and Population Growth*. New York: McGraw-Hill, 1959.

Friedan, Betty. *The Feminine Mystique*. New York: Norton, 1963.

Fuller, Jan. *Space: The Scrapbook of My Divorce*. Greenwich, Conn.: Fawcett, 1973.

Fromm, Erich, ed. *The Crisis of Psychoanalysis*. Greenwich, Conn.: Fawcett, 1970.

––––––. *The Art of Loving*. New York: Harper & Row, 1956.

Gans, Herbert. *Urban Villagers*. New York: Free Press, 1965.

Geiger, H. Kent. *The Family in Soviet Russia*. Cambridge, Mass.: Harvard University Press. 1968.

Geiger, Theodor. *Arbeiten zur Sociologie*. Neuwied-Rhein: Luchterhand, 1962.

––––––. *Ideologie und Wehrheit. Stuttgart-Wein: Humboldt & Verlag*, 1953.

Gilligan, Carol. "In a Different Voice: Women's Conceptions of Self and Morality." *Harvard Education Review* 47 (November 1977): 481–517.

Glennon, Lynda M. "A Sociology of Knowledge Analysis of the Women's Liberation Movement." Ph.D. dissertation, Rutgers University, New Brunswick, N.J., 1974.

Godwin, Gail. "The Southern Belle." *Ms.* 4 (July 1975): 49–51.

Goffman, Erving W. "Status Consistency and Preference for Change in Power Distribution." *American Sociological Review* 22 (April 1957): 275–81.

Gold, Doris B. "Women and Voluntarism." In *Woman in Sexist Society*, edited Vivian Gornick and Barbara K. Moran. New York: New American Library, 1971.

Gordon, Linda. "Introduction." *Radical America* 7 (July–October 1973): 1–8.

Gornick, Vivian, and Moran, Barbara K., eds. *Women in Sexist Society*. New York: New American Library, 1971.

Gouldner, Alvin W. "The New Class Project, Part 1." *Theory and Society* 6 (September 1978): 153–203.

———. "The Norm of Reciprocity: A Preliminary Statement." *American Sociological Review* 25 (April 1960): 161–78.

———, and Gouldner, Helen P., eds. *Modern Society.* New York: Harcourt, Brace & World, 1963.

Grimstead, Kirsten, and Rennie, Susan. "Interview with Jane Alpert." *Off Our Backs* 5 (May–June 1975): 20.

Habermas, Jurgen. *Toward a Rational Society.* Boston: Beacon Press, 1971.

———. "Toward a Theory of Communicative Competence." In *Recent Sociology Number Two,* edited by Hans Peter Dreitzel. New York: Macmillan, 1970.

Hareven, Tamara K. "Modernization and Family History: Perspectives on Social Change." *Signs* 2 (Autumn 1976): 190–206.

Harrington, Stephanie. "Ms. versus Cosmo." *New York Times Magazine,* 11 August 1974.

Haskell, Molly. "The Woman in the 'All-Man' Legend." *Village Voice* 21 June 1973, p. 85.

Haughton, Rosemary. *Love.* Baltimore: Penguin, 1971.

Hechinger, Nancy. "Time and the Working Mother." *Working Woman* 3 (January 1978): 43–46.

Hegel, G. W. F. *The Phenomenology of Mind.* Translated by J. B. Baillie. New York: Harper Torchbooks, 1967.

Horney, Karen. "The Flight from Womanhood." *International Journal of Psychoanalysis* 7 (1926): 324–39.

———. "On the Genesis of the Castration Complex in Women." *International Journal of Psychoanalysis* 5 (1924): 50–65.

Jackson, Elton. "Status Consistency and Symptoms of Stress." *American Sociological Review* 27 (August 1962): 469–80.

Jacoby, Susan. "What Do I Do for the Next Twenty Years?" *New York Times Magazine,* 17 June 1973, pp. 10 ff.

Jaynes, Julian. *Origin of Consciousness in the Breakdown of the Bicameral Mind.* New York: Houghton Mifflin, 1977.

Johnson, Sheila K. "A Woman Anthropologist Offers a Solution to the Woman Problem." *New York Times Magazine,* 27 August 1972, pp. 7, 31–39.

Johnston, Jill. *Lesbian Nation.* New York: Simon & Schuster, 1973.

———. "Write About Face." *Village Voice,* 9 June 1975, p. 26.

Jong, Erica. "Visionary Anger: Review of Adrienne Rich's *Diving into The Wreck: Poems 1971–1972.*" *Ms.,* July 1973, p. 34.

Jourard, S. M. *The Transparent Self.* Princeton: Van Nostrand, 1964.

Keniston, Kenneth. *The Young Radicals.* New York: Harcourt, Brace & World, 1965.

Komarovsky, Mirra. "Cultural Contradictions and Sex Roles." In *Selected Studies in Marriage and the Family,* edited by Robert F. Winch, Robert McGinnis, and Herbert M. Barringer. New York: Holt, Rinehart & Winston, 1962.

Koslow, Sally. "Connections—How to Use Them to Pull Strings." *Working Woman* 3 (March 1978): 42–45.

Kraditor, Aileen S. *The Ideas of the Woman Suffrage Movement, 1890–1920.* Garden City, N.Y.: Doubleday, 1971.

Laing, R. D. *The Divided Self.* Baltimore: Penguin, 1965.

Landecker, Werner S. "Class Crystallization and Class Consciousness." *American Sociological Review* 28 (April 1963): 219–29.

Langer, Elinor. "Confessing: Forum." *Ms.* 3 (December 1974): 70.

Lenin, V. I. *On the Emancipation of Women.* Moscow: Progress, 1965.

Lenski, Gerhard. "Status Crystallization: A Non-Vertical Dimension of Social Status." *American Sociological Review* 19 (August 1954): 405–13.

Levine, Donald N. "Introduction to George Simmel." In *On Individuality and Social Forms,* edited by Donald N. Levine. Chicago: University of Chicago Press, 1971.

Levinger, George. "Task and Social Behavior in Marriage." In *The Family,* edited by Norman W. Bell and Ezra F. Vogel. 2nd ed. New York: Free Press, 1968.

Levi-Strauss, Claude. *Structural Anthropology.* Translated by Monique Layton. New York: Basic, 1976.

Lewin, Kurt. "Field Theory and Experiment in Social Psychology." *American Journal of Sociology* 44 (November 1939): 868–97.

Loomis, Charles P., and McKinney, John C. "Instroduction to Ferdinand Tonnies." In *Community and Society.* New York: Harper Torchbooks, 1963.

Luke, Tim. "Culture and Politics in the Age of Artificial Negativity." *Telos* 11, no. 35 (Spring 1978): 55–72.

Lundberg, Ferdinand, and Farnham, Marynis F. *Modern Woman: The Lost Sex*. New York: Harper & Brothers, 1947.

McFadden, Cyra. *The Serial: A Year in the Life of Marin County*. New York: New American Library, 1978.

Maccoby, Eleanor. "Women's Intellect." In *The Potential of Women*, edited by S. M. Farber and R. H. L. Wilson. New York: McGraw-Hill, 1963.

Mandel, William. "Soviet Women and their Self Image." *Science and Society*, Fall 1971, pp. 286–310.

Mannheim, Karl. "Conservative Thought." In *From Karl Mannheim*, edited by Kurt H. Wolff. New York: Oxford University Press, 1971.

————, ed. *Essays on the Sociology of Culture*. London: Routledge & Kegan Paul, 1956.

Marcuse, Herbert. *One-Dimensional Man*. Boston: Beacon Press, 1971.

————. *Reason and Revolution*. Boston: Beacon Press, 1960.

Marx, Karl. *Economic and Philosophical Manuscripts of 1844*. Translated by Martin Milligan. London: Lawrence & Wishart, 1959.

————. "On the Jewish Question." In *Writings of the Young Marx on Philosophy and Society*, edited and translated by Loyd D. Eaton and Kurt Guddat. Garden City, N.Y.: Doubleday, 1967.

————. *The Poverty of Philosophy*. Translated by H. Quelch. London: Twentieth Century Press, 1960.

————, and Engels, Friedrich. *Basic Writings on Politics and Philosophy*, edited by Lewis Feuer. Garden City, N.Y.: Doubleday, 1959.

May, Rollo. *Love and Will*. New York: Delta, 1969.

Mead, Margaret. *Male and Female*. New York: Dell, 1968.

————. *Sex and Temperament in Three Primitive Societies*. New York: Morrow, 1935.

Merton, Robert K., and Barber, Elinor. "Sociological Ambivalence." In *Sociological Theory, Values and Sociocultural Change*, edited by Edward A. Tiryakian. New York: Harper Torchbooks, 1967.

Miller, Nadine. "Shrunken Woman." *RAT*, no. 10 (26 June–10 July 1970): 20.

Millett, Kate. *Flying*. New York: Knopf, 1974.

———. *Sexual Politics*. New York: Avon Equinox, 1970.

———. "The Shame is Over: Forum." *Ms.* 3 (January 1975): 27.

Mitchell, Juliet. *Woman's Estate*. New York: Vintage, 1971.

Morgan, Robin, ed. *Sisterhood Is Powerful*. New York: Vintage, 1970.

———. "Goodbye to All That." *RAT*, no. 1 (6–23 February 1970): 7.

Ms. magazine 3 (March 1975).

Ms. magazine 6 (March 1978)

Musil, Robert. *Man Without Qualities*. New York: Putnam, 1965.

Nelson, Benjamin. "Conscience and the Making of Early Modern Cultures: The Protestant Ethic Beyond Max Weber." *Social Research* 36 (Spring 1969): 4–21.

———. *The Idea of Usury*. Chicago: University of Chicago Press, 1969.

Nisbet, Robert A. *The Sociological Tradition*. New York: Basic, 1966.

Off Our Backs 5 (May–June 1975).

O'Neill, William L. *The Woman Movement*. Chicago: Quadrangle, 1971.

Pappenheim, Fritz. *The Alienation of Modern Man*. New York: Modern Reader, 1968.

Park, Robert E. "Introduction." In Everett Stonequist. *The Marginal Man*. New York: Scribner's, 1937. Reprinted as "Cultural Conflict and the Marginal Man." In *Theories of Society*, vol 2, edited by Talcott Parsons, Edward A. Shils, Kaspar O. Naegele, and Jesse R. Pitts. Glencoe, Ill.: Free Press, 1961.

Parsons, Talcott. *The Social System*. Glencoe, Ill.: Free Press, 1951.

———. *Societies: Evolutionary and Comparative Perspectives*. Englewood Cliffs, N.J.: Prentice-Hall, 1966.

———. "Pattern Variables Revisited: A Response to Robert Dubin." *American Sociological Review*, August 1960, pp. 467–83.

———, and Bales, Robert F., eds. *Family, Socialization and Interaction Process*. Glencoe, Ill.: Free Press, 1955.

————; Bales, Robert F.; and Shils, Edward A. *Working Papers in the Theory of Action*. Glencoe, Ill.: Free Press, 1953.

————, and Shils, Edward A., eds. *Toward a General Theory of Action*. New York: Harper Torchbooks, 1964.

————; Shils, Edward A.; Naegele, Kaspar D.; and Pitts, Jesse R., eds. *Theories of Society*. 2 vols. Glencoe, Ill.: Free Press, 1961.

Piccone, Paul. "The Changing Function of Critical Theory." *New German Critique* 4, no 12 (Fall, 1977): 29–38.

————. "The Crisis of One-Dimensionality." *Telos* 11, no. 35 (Spring 1978): 43–54.

————. "From Tragedy to Farce: The Return of Critical Theory." *New German Critique* 3, no. 7 (Winter 1976): 91–104.

Plexus 2 (August 1975).

Rawls, John. *A Theory of Justice*. Cambridge, Mass.: Belknap Press of Harvard University Press, 1971.

Reed, Evelyn. *Problems of Women's Liberation: A Marxist Approach*. New York: Pathfinder Press, 1970.

Reich, Charles A. *The Greening of America*. New York: Random House, 1970.

Reville, Irene, and Blanchard, Margeret. "The Controversy over Androgyny." *Women, A Journal of Liberation* 4 (Winter 1974): 58.

Riessman, Frank. "Cultural Styles of the Disadvantaged." New York, 1964. Mimeographed.

————. "The Strategy of Styles." *Teachers College Record* 65 (1964): 484–89.

Roethlisberger, F. J. "The Foreman: Master and Victim of Double Talk," *Harvard Business Review* 23 (May 1945): 282–98.

Rossi, Alice. "A Biosocial Perspective on Parenting." *Daedalus* 106 (Spring 1977): 1–32.

————. "The Missing Body in Sociology: An Essay on Closing the Gap Between Physiology and Sociology." Presidential Address at the 44th Annual Eastern Sociological Society Meeting, Philadelphia, Pa., 6 April 1974.

Roszak, Betty. "The Human Continuum." In *Masculine/Feminine*, edited by Betty Roszak and Theodore Roszak. New York: Harper & Row, 1969.

————, and Roszak, Theodore, eds. *Masculine/Feminine*. New York: Harper & Row, 1969.

Roszak, Theodore. *The Making of a Counter-Culture*. Garden City, N.Y.: Anchor, 1969.

Rowbotham, Sheila. *Women, Resistance and Revolution*. New York: Vintage, 1974.

Rubin, Lillian Breslow. *Worlds of Pain*. New York: Basic, 1976.

Schroyer, Trent. *The Critique of Domination*. Boston: Beacon Press, 1975.

Schutz, Alfred. *Collected Papers*. 3 vols. The Hague: Nijhoff, 1962.

Scott, Joan, and Tilly, Louise. "Women's Work and the Family in Nineteenth Century Europe." *Comparative Studies in Society and History*, 17 (January 1975): 34–64.

Seeley, John; Sim, Alexander; and Loosley, Elizabeth W. *Crestwood Heights*. New York: Wiley, 1963.

Sennett, Richard. *The Fall of Public Man*. New York: Vintage, 1978.

————, and Cobb, Jonathan. *The Hidden Injuries of Class*. New York: Knopf, 1972.

"Sexism in Family Studies." *Journal of Marriage and the Family* 33 (August 1971). Special ed.

Sherfey, Mary Jane. *The Nature and Evolution of Female Sexuality*. New York: Vintage, 1973.

Slater, Philip E. *The Pursuit of Loneliness*. Boston: Beacon Press, 1970.

————. "Parental Role Differentiation." *American Journal of Sociology* 67 (November 1961): 296–308.

Solanas, Valerie. *S.C.U.M. (Society for Cutting Up Men) Manifesto*. New York: Olympia Press, 1968.

Sorokin, Pitirim A. "Foreword." Ferdinand Tonnies, *Community and Society*. New York: Harper Torchbooks, 1963.

Stonequist, Everett. *The Marginal Man*. New York: Scribner's, 1937.

Sullerot, Evelyne. *Women, Society and Change*. Translated by Margaret Scotford Archer. New York: World University Press, 1971.

Tiger, Lionel. *Men In Groups*. New York: Vintage, 1970.

Tiryakian, Edward A., ed. *Sociological Theory, Values and Socio-cultural Change*. New York: Harper Torchbooks, 1967.

Tonnies, Ferdinand. *Community and Society*. New York: Harper Torchbooks, 1963

Watts, Alan. *The Book*. New York: Vintage, 1972.

———. *Nature, Man and Woman*. New York: Vintage, 1970.

———. *The Two Hands of God: The Myths of Polarity*. New York: Collier, 1969.

A Weatherwoman. "Inside the Weather Machine." *RAT*, no. 1 (6–23 February 1970): 5.

Weber, Max. *From Max Weber: Essays in Sociology*, edited by H. H. Gerth and C. Wright Mills. New York: Oxford University Press. 1958.

———. *The Methodology of the Social Sciences*. Translated and edited by Edward A. Shils and Henry A. Finch. Glencoe, Ill.: Free Press, 1949.

———. *The Protestant Ethic and the Spirit of Capitalism*. Translated by Talcott Parsons. New York: Scribner's, 1958.

———. "Religion and Social Studies." In *Theories of Society*, vol. 2, edited by Talcott Parsons, Edward A. Shils, Kaspar D. Naegele, and Jesse R. Pitts. Glencoe, Ill.: Free Press, 1953.

———. *The Theory of Social and Economic Organization*, edited by Talcott Parsons. New York: Free Press, 1964.

Weller, Jack E. *Yesterday's People*. Lexington: University of Kentucky Press, 1965.

Winch, Robert F. *The Modern Family*. New York: Holt, Rinehart & Winston, 1963.

———; McGinnis, Robert; and Barringer, Herbert M., eds. *Selected Studies in Marriage and the Family*. New York: Holt, Rinehart & Winston, 1962.

Wolff, Kurt H., ed. *From Karl Mannheim*. New York: Oxford University Press, 1971.

Yablonsky, Lewis. *Robopaths*. Baltimore: Penguin, 1972.

Yorburg, Betty. *The Changing Family*. New York: Columbia University Press, 1973.

INDEX

Abolitionists, 152–153
Adam-Eve myth, 133–134
"All in the Family," 53–54
Alpert, Jane, 122
Androgyny, 107–110
Ariès, Phillippe, 153, 166

Bachofen, Johann Jacob, 86, 124–126, 138
Balzac, Honoré de, 25
Barber, Benjamin, 19, 20, 158
Bardwick, Judith, 122
Beauvoir, Simone de, 104–105
Berger, Peter L., 32, 147–148, 174, 177–179, 189, 193, 196, 217–223, 233, 234
Bernard, Jessie, 131–132
Bernstein, Basil, 12, 84, 85
Biology, as personality determinant, 121–127, 129–136, 142–143, 171–172. See also Polarism
Black women. See Women, black
Borgese, Elizabeth Mann, 86–87
Brando, Marlon, 108–109

Calvinism, 21
Capitalism, 21, 22, 47, 116, 170, 191, 192, 200, 204, 206–207
Chaplin, Charles, 109
Charisma, 211–212
   And Synthesism, 101–102
China, revolution in, 138
CLIT. See Collective Lesbian International Terrors
Collective Lesbian International Terrors (organization), 75–76, 94
Common Cause (organization), 200

Communism, 21
Conservatism, romantic, 92, 93, 182–183, 188
"Cosmo Girl," 48
Cuba, revolution in, 138
Curie, Marie, 48

Daly, Mary, 110
Davis, Bette, 48
Davis, Elizabeth Gould, 134
Decter, Midge, 20
Didion, Joan, 20
Douglas, Mary, 12
Durkheim, Emile, 220

Emotionality. See Expressivism
Enlightenment philosophy, 92
Equal Rights Amendment, 21, 61, 201–205
ERA. See Equal Rights Amendment
Erikson, Erik H., 121–122
Expressivism, 5, 12, 17, 18, 23, 43
   Defined, 7–8
   Society, views on, 181–185
   Tenets, 69–93, 174–175, 189
   Utopia, view of, 181, 183, 184–185
   Versus Instrumentalism, 2, 3, 17, 23–24, 26–40, 54–56, 65, 69, 77, 102, 183
   Versus Synthesism, 100, 116, 176
   Working-class life style and, 10, 83–86

Family, Peter L. Berger's views on, 193
   Instrumentalist views on, 61–63, 179–180

Parsons, Talcott, views on, 29–34
Sociology of, 2
Femininity, 5–6, 26, 37–39, 77, 105–106, 108–110, 128
Feminism,
Defined, 149. *See also* Women's liberation movement
Divergent ideas about, 9, 40, 122
Goals, 1, 77
Reasons for, 7, 18–21
Social structure as cause of, 169–176
Firestone, Shulamith, 83, 88
Franklin, Benjamin, 7
French Revolution, 151, 154, 166
Freud, Sigmund, 129, 134, 155
Fromm, Erich, 1, 126
Functionality. *See* Instrumentalism

Gans, Herbert, 84
Garbo, Greta, 108–109
Gehlen, Arnold, 223
Gemeinschaft. See Expressivism
Greer, Germaine, 163

Habermas, Jurgen, 174, 178, 180, 181, 182, 186, 189, 192, 194–195, 224–229
Hegel, Georg Wilhelm Friedrich, 204, 207
Homosexuals. *See* Lesbians
Horney, Karen, 129

Instrumentalism, 5, 12, 13, 15, 17, 18, 23, 65–66, 160
Defined, 7
Society, views on, 177–181
Tenents, 46–66, 174–175, 189, 195, 200, 201, 203
Utopia, view of, 178–179
Versus Expressivism, 2, 3, 17, 23–24, 26–40, 54, 56, 65, 69, 77, 100, 176, 181, 203
Versus Synthesism, 100, 116, 176
It Ain't Me Babe (newspaper), 75

Jagger, Mick, 109
Joan of Arc, 48
Johnson, Sheila K., 6
Johnston, Jill, 71, 73, 75, 163
Jong, Erica, 16–17

Kellner, Hansfried, 32

Keniston, Kenneth, 180
Komarovsky, Mirra, 161–162

Langer, Elinor, 72–73
Lazarre, Jane, 17
Lesbians, 73–74, 75–76, 91
Levinger, George, 30–31
Levi-Strauss, Claude, 42

Ms., 113, 122
Mannheim, Karl, 92, 182, 183–184
Marcuse, Herbert, 192, 194–195, 224
Marx, Karl, 113, 170, 189, 190–191, 192, 206–207, 215, 226
Masculinity, 5–6, 26, 37–39, 105–106, 108–110, 128
Mead, Margaret, 130–132, 136–137, 140–142
Men, characteristics of, 24–25, 26
Expressionist view of, 91, 92
Liberation of, 2, 21, 78, 202
Merton, Robert K., 99, 158, 192
Middle class, 4, 31, 47, 58, 59–60, 86, 156, 157, 158
Millett, Kate, 71–73, 75, 163
Morgan, Robin, 74–75

Nader's Raiders, 200
National Organization for Women, 2, 10, 48, 60, 156
Nelson, Benjamin, 22, 35, 84
New Left, 60, 122, 155, 166
Newsweek, 51
Nisbet, Robert A., 192
NOW. *See* National Organization for Women

Off Our Backs (newspaper), 75
O'Neill, William L., 152–153, 154, 155

Parents, single, and Synthesism, 103–104
Parsons, Talcott, 2, 4, 27–34, 36, 38, 177, 181, 182, 194, 213–214
Penis envy, 129–130, 151
Personality, development of, 31–32
Piccone, Paul, 199
Polarism, 5, 6, 200
Defined, 8
Society, view of, 186–188
Tenets, 119–143, 176, 189
Utopia, view of, 138–142, 186–188
Versus other ideal types, 121, 124, 176

Protestant ethic, 7

Rand, Ayn, 47
RAT (newspaper), 5, 74, 75, 122–123
Rationality. *See* Instrumentalism
Reformation, 22, 138. *See also* Calvinism
Reik, Theodor, 25
Rich, Adrienne, 108
Riessman, Frank, 85–86
Romance, 54
Russell, Rosalind, 48

Schopenhaur, Arthur, 25
Schutz, Alfred, 158
Sex roles, 9, 11, 12, 23–24, 27, 29–31, 34–35, 37–40, 60, 61, 62, 77, 90, 98, 109, 120, 122, 130, 136, 160, 172, 174, 202, 203
Sexism, defined by Instrumentalism, 56–59, 61, 63–64
Sexuality, Instrumentalist views on, 63
Sherfey, Mary Jane, 133
Slater, Philip E., 30, 180
Socialism, 21, 170, 190
Society, change in, 22, 116. *See also* Technocracy
 Expressivistic view of, 181–185
 Homogenation of, 199–203
 Instrumentalist view of, 177–181
 Instrumentation effects on, 24
 Polarist view of, 186–188
 Synthesist view of, 185–186
Society, structure of, 189–195
 Reason for feminism, 169–173
Society, technological. *See* Technocracy
Sociologists for Women in Society (organization), 10
Sociology, 3, 11–12, 37–38, 158
Solanas, Valerie, 135, 136
Spock, Benjamin, 25
"Star Trek," 48
Steinem, Gloria, 54, 163
Sullerot, Evelyne, 151–152
SWS. *See* Sociologists for Women in Society
Synthesism, 5, 13, 200
 Androgyny and, 107–110
 Charisma and, 101–102
 Defined, 8
 Single parents and, 103–104
 Society, view of, 185–186
 Tenets, 97–116, 174–175, 176, 189, 190

Utopia, view of, 112–175, 185–186
 Versus Expressivism, 100, 116
 Versus Instrumentalism, 100, 116, 176

Technocracy, 21, 22–23, 47, 116. *See also* Society
Tennyson, Alfred, Lord, 25
Tocqueville, Alexis de, 154
Tonnies, Ferdinand, 87–88, 174, 178, 181–182, 189, 190–192, 213–217, 232
Types, ideal, 171, 173, 174. *See also* Expressivism; Instrumentalism; Polarism; Synthesism
 Defined, 6–7, 9–11, 12

Up From Under (newspaper), 75
Utopia, Expressivist view of, 70, 88–90, 181, 183, 184–185
 Instrumentalist view of, 178–179
 Polarist view of, 138–142, 186–188
 Synthesist view of, 112–115, 185–186

Victorian period, 153–154
Village Voice, 71

Watts, Alan, 12
Wayne, John, 137
Weatherwomen (organization), 2
Weber, Max, 6, 22, 178, 189, 190, 208–213, 224
West, Mae, 109
Winch, Robert F., 2
Wolfe, Tom, 71
Wollstonecraft, Mary, 148
Womb-envy thesis, 129–132, 136
Women, black, 117, 172
 Synthesism and, 103
Women, characterization of, 24, 25, 26
Women's liberation movement, 2, 40. *See also* Feminism
 England, nineteenth and twentieth centuries, 148–149
 History, U.S., 148–149, 152–155, 162–163
 Social context of, 147–149, 150–166, 167–168
Working class, 4, 10, 40, 59–60
 Expressivist characteristics in, 83–86
Working Woman (magazine), 49–50, 62

Zelditch, Morris, Jr., 29, 38